MW00774764

Re-Vitalizing Our Marriage

Applying the Teachings of the Bahá'í Faith to Strengthen Our Union

Susanne M. Alexander

Re-Vitalizing Our Marriage

ISBN: 978-1-940062-13-6

Publisher: Marriage Transformation LLC
Printer: Lightning Source (Ingram), United States of America
https://www.marriagetransformation.com
susanne@marriagetransformation.com; +1 423-599-0153

©2020 Marriage Transformation LLC; all international rights reserved. No part of this book may be electronically shared, scanned, uploaded, or reproduced by any means, without the written permission of the publisher. Violations are regarded as theft of the authors' and publisher's intellectual property. *Thank you for respecting this legal copyright. Your integrity with this law spreads a spirit of loving respect throughout the world and makes us very happy.* If you wish to share the book, please direct people to our website or an online bookstore where they can purchase a copy. Quoting small portions in study groups, newsletters, and media is permitted. The publisher welcomes inquiries about use.

This publication provides helpful and educational information about marriage. If expert assistance is required, the services of a competent professional counselor should be sought. Most of the stories included are anonymous sharing from individuals and couples.

Cover Design: Steiner Graphics
Photographer: J. Horrocks, istockphoto.com
Layout: Marriage Transformation, LLC

Note: Marriage Transformation® is a registered trademark in the United States. The logo of two wings of a bird symbolizing two partners in a relationship or marriage, both in color and in black and white, is copyrighted by Marriage Transformation.

Dedication

To my husband Phil Donihe, my partner, prayer warrior, loving companion, friend, encourager, and collaborator. You are a blessing in my life!

To the faculty team of the Relationships, Marriage, and Family Department of the Wilmette Institute. Creating online courses based on the Bahá'í Faith's teachings together requires excellence in consulting, teamwork, learning-in-action, and mentoring participants. Serving together with you is a privilege and a joy!

Table of Contents

Track 3: Empowering Our Marriage to Go Forward

Appendices

Re-Vitalizing Our Marriage

Important: About Using This Book

Hello and welcome!

Audience

This book is primarily for those in a challenged marriage where the couple is in some marriage difficulty and wants to re-vitalize their relationship. It's likely that one or both are members of the Bahá'í Faith or are interested in applying Bahá'í teachings to their marriage. No book can be an exact fit for every reader, so see what is useful now and apply it. Other parts may be a better fit at another time or simply be set aside.

If you are not in a marriage that is in difficulty, you may still benefit from studying this book and doing many of the activities as a preventative measure.

You may use this book on your own; however, please refer to Chapter 2: Building a Support System, and consider requesting others to accompany your learning, healing, and progress. The greater your difficulties, the more support is needed.

Contents and Tracks

If you are in a challenged marriage or headed that direction, here in *Revitalizing Our Marriage* there are:

- Quotations of spiritual guidance from the Bahá'í Faith
- Suggestions that science has discovered are useful
- Personal insights from married individuals and couples
- Recommendations for how to shift in positive directions

Throughout this book are prompts to do activities and both Individual Reflection as well as Couple Reflection and Consultation. How you navigate these depends on the state of your individual well-being and your marriage, as well as on your preferences for reading alone or together. Individuals and couples will make choices about what to do separately or together and what is useful and wise. For example, at times you may read a chapter together and discuss the questions together; or you may read separately but discuss the content together.

The book is set up so that there are two sections or "tracks" that can ideally happen simultaneously, one track for a couple and one track for the individuals in the marriage (although couple discussion may happen during them at times). Carrying these out at the same time may be very useful for you. Here are the sections:

- Parallel Track 1: Sharing with One Another
- Parallel Track 2: Growing Our Individual Capacity

The couple track provides context about marriage, knowledge-building, and skill-building for you as a couple. The individual work in Track 2 is vital as a contribution to the health of your marriage. It allows you to reflect on where you need healing as individuals, what you each may have done that has added to the challenges, and where you both need to grow.

Sometimes individuals also need to see the marriage progress as motivation for the individual effort, and therefore Track 1 happening in parallel as a couple is excellent if you can do so. Then together you can complete:

- Track 3: Empowering Our Marriage to Go Forward

You will notice that this book is focused on increasing your knowledge and building your skills to re-connect and unify you as a couple. It does not cover many specific marriage topics in depth. Please refer to other books and resources for topics like money, sex, in-laws, and so on.

Serious and Disruptive Issues

If your marriage instead of being challenged is facing major serious and disruptive issues such as abuse, infidelity, or active addiction, you may still find benefit here in this book, but it will be even more essential for you to be accompanied by a professional. If this is your situation, please refer to the following sections of the book before beginning your study of any other sections:

- Chapter 2: Building a Support System
- Appendix C: Grappling with Serious Issues
- Appendix D: For Counselors Who Are Not Bahá'ís...

Hope for Re-Vitalizing Your Marriage

Many concepts about how to sustain a marriage are evolving, so this book is my current understanding of what will assist you to re-vitalize your marriage based on the Bahá'í teachings and current science.

Your individual and couple reflections and consultations, as well as those you do with others, will build your capacity to have a marriage with greater unity, intimate friendship, and connection. Please persevere to achieve a healthy, happy, and re-vitalized marriage as best as you can, and know that you are not alone.

I hope you find this book useful, and I look forward to hearing from you.

With loving welcome to this learning journey and my ongoing prayers,

Susanne M. Alexander, Marriage Educator and Coach
Marriage Transformation
www.marriagetransformation.com
www.bahaimarriage.net

A Brief Bahá'í Context for Strengthening Marriages

The Bahá'í teachings promote the importance of marriage and family as building blocks for a healthy, unified society. Partners wed in a Bahá'í marriage ceremony have pledged to each other, "We will all, verily, abide by the Will of God."[1] (Bahá'u'lláh) They agree that they are entering the divine institution of marriage and establishing a union and family, as shown in the quotation below.

> "And when He [God] desired to manifest grace and beneficence to men, and to set the world in order, He revealed observances and created laws; among them He established the law of marriage, made it as a fortress for well-being and salvation.... He saith, great is His glory: 'Enter into wedlock, O people, that ye may bring forth one who will make mention of Me amid My servants. This is My bidding unto you; hold fast to it as an assistance to yourselves.'"[2] Bahá'u'lláh

Then life together goes forward, and typically challenges present themselves from outside or inside the marriage. Sometimes couples have the knowledge and skills to respond well, and sometimes they struggle. When a couple feels like marriage is very difficult, their commitment to their sacred marriage promises can be part of what keeps them going. As they address their problems, their sincere effort will draw Bahá'u'lláh's and God's blessings. This may then sustain the energy needed to transform individual and couple behaviors to create the marriage the couple really wants.

Bahá'u'lláh talks about the dangers of "dissension and strife, contention, estrangement and apathy".[3] (Bahá'u'lláh) When a marriage is challenged, the couple may see their marriage "fortress" begin to deteriorate. As individuals and couples take steps to re-connect with God and spiritual guidance, their lives can become closer to a state of integrity, of wholeness. They more closely align their words and actions with Bahá'u'lláh's teachings:

> "The Bahá'í Writings contain many references to the importance of maintaining loving and unified family relationships. The friends are not only called upon to 'do everything in their power to preserve the marriages they have contracted', but they must also 'make of them exemplary unions, governed by the noblest motives'."[4]
> Research Department of the Universal House of Justice; on behalf of Shoghi Effendi

It's not easy or quick to create an "exemplary" union, and sometimes that can feel like a far-away goal. However, the Bahá'í teachings encourage harmonizing religion and science to obtain answers and develop solutions. Gaining knowledge and skills from both sources is a powerful act that can benefit a couple's marriage.

When a couple faces difficulties and makes strong efforts toward having their marriage survive and thrive, one perspective in the Bahá'í teachings indicates they are salvaging "their marriage for the sake of God, rather than for their own sake".[5] (On behalf of Shoghi Effendi)

Couples might think, why bother? Why not just get divorced? While this is often a common response in society, couples may not realize that many issues remain unresolved, and then they re-appear in further relationships. When the couple has children, divorce also has a strong effect on them. Members of the Bahá'í Faith are asked to approach marriage and divorce in a different way: "Bahá'u'lláh came to bring unity to the world, and a fundamental unity is that of the bond between the marriage partners."[6] (Research Department of the Universal House of Justice)

The Bahá'í teachings speak of marriage as a divine institution and that marriage and family have the vital social function of "the perpetuation of the human race and the preservation of social order."[7] (Research Department of the Universal House of Justice)

Divorce is strongly discouraged in the teachings, and here is this encouragement: "Bahá'u'lláh has laid great emphasis on the sanctity of marriage, and the believers should exert their utmost to create harmony in their homes...."[8] (On behalf of Shoghi Effendi)

Beginning any process of improvement and growth requires courage and commitment, and sustaining it requires qualities such as perseverance, forbearance, sacrifice, and faith, as well as assistance from others. For Bahá'ís, this outreach includes turning to the institutions, meeting with professionals, and consulting with trusted and experienced friends. Details about these efforts, as well as useful tools and practices, are in the chapters ahead.

For more information about the Bahá'í Faith and the sources for the Bahá'í quotations included in this book, please see Appendix A.

Parallel Track 1: Sharing with One Another

Note: This section is generally for couples, and the pronoun used is "we". Please ensure that as individuals you are also studying "Parallel Track 2: Growing Our Individual Capacity".

Chapter 1: Hope for a New Beginning

Few situations are too difficult to be improved. We can take what is here and use it to create a new beginning for our marriage and family. There is hope.

Living in a challenged marriage is difficult and often painful. When it happens to us, we can feel disconnected from our partner, experience grief and heartache, struggle with our communications, and have difficulty resolving issues. We often have critical and blaming words flying between us. We are so unhappy that we attempt to fix each other, setting up walls of resistance and frequent disunity between us. The following pattern may be familiar:

> "When we're unhappy in our marriages, we do something to try to fix the situation. If we're successful, life goes on. If we're not successful, instead of telling ourselves, *'That didn't work, better try something new,'* we simply keep doing more of the same. Often, because we assume that we weren't emphatic enough, we even step up our efforts, and try it 'one more time with feeling'. That's when real trouble begins."[9] Michele Weiner-Davis

When we become resigned to these unhappy dynamics in our marriage, we can withdraw and begin functioning independently more than working in partnership. At times, we can struggle with feeling embarrassed or ashamed about the state of our marriage and family, and we try to appear fine in public but struggle privately. Where we have cultural beliefs about the importance of not looking poorly in front of others, or we have strong beliefs that everything related to our marriage should be private, it reinforces this public-private duality. We find it difficult to seek help for our problems, and we make it clear to our children, if we have them, that they should also keep quiet.

Often, instead, we can benefit from turning to sources outside of our marriage. There are books, videos, online courses, websites, articles, classes, study groups, professionals, religious support services, and trusted friends that can assist us to remedy difficulties and prevent further ones. When you turn to someone for help, *Revitalizing Our Marriage* may be a companion resource for them to assist you. Someone shares:

*"When we recognized our marriage was in trouble, we knew we needed professional help. What we didn't initially realize was that we would need to do work as individuals as well. We also discovered that many of the principles of the Bahá'í Faith helped us to sustain this work so we could rebuild our marriage."**

In addition to offering principles you can apply to your situation, the teachings of the Bahá'í Faith also include a very vital tool: consultation. When carried out skillfully, consultation builds understanding and creates unified decisions. The subject of consultation is mentioned throughout the book, and there is also a chapter specifically about it. [See Chapter 10.] It's common in society to hear that conflict is an inevitable part of marriage (and human society!). However, when we become very good at consultation, we can increase peace and reduce the likelihood of conflict being an automatic part of our marriage culture.

As we re-commit to creating unity rather than disunity, it prompts us to make strong efforts to preserve our marriage. *Revitalizing Our Marriage* can guide us through many of the actions we can do both immediately and consistently over an extended period. Carrying these actions out and persevering will require our attention, effort, and sacrifice. For example, it may mean adjusting our schedules to allow for more time together. Remember this:

> "A companionship marriage is a construction project. Couples who accept the challenge of consciously designing and building their relationship reap rewards.... Couples who don't invest time and energy in building a rewarding marriage run a serious risk of failure. Or their marriage may endure—without ever reaching its highest potential of shared intimacy and joy."[10] A.C.M.E/Better Marriages

It's best not to tackle all our issues at once, because we will likely be more successful by beginning small and building our capacity. Staying in a learning mode aids this—we can study what's here, consult together and with others as we can, take action as individuals and as a couple (without expecting perfection), and reflect to identify what to do next.

As we engage as individuals in personal transformation efforts, and as we make efforts as individuals and as a couple, we can make progress with re-building connection. It becomes possible for understanding, acceptance, love, trust, and unity to grow between us again. An improved marriage is a goal that's achievable. Someone shares:

*"Marriage can be a service that betters the world if spiritual principles are implemented through deeds. Where the couple, with pure-hearted devotion and prayer, takes account of themselves and their impact on the marriage each day, improvement can happen."**

At times, when we feel discouraged about ourselves and our marriage, reading some of the lofty quotations in the Bahá'í teachings about how marriage is *supposed to be* can be difficult. If our marriage seems quite different than the ideal, we may feel demoralized rather than uplifted. It's important we keep in mind the "ideal" as a goal and context for what to strive for and take practical steps that move us closer to this goal. However, we need to notice our internal responses and moderate our reading of these types of quotations at times. As the marriage improves, it can become easier to read more. This is a spiritual journey toward a happier marriage. Someone shares:

*"I think that the spiritual goals we are given in the Bahá'í Faith need to be understood in terms of process, rather than as a finished product. The ideal marriage is a goal to be worked toward, as it gives direction to our striving. When we look at the ideal marriage as something that we 'should' have, the result is likely to be discouragement, guilt, a sense of futility, and so on. When we understand it to be the goal of a process, which we can move toward regardless of our current situation, and start working toward, we can feel hope, experience encouragement, and make progress. I believe the Bahá'í Faith teaches us that spirituality is a dynamic process, not a static condition. This process applies to marriage as well."**

Sometimes revitalizing our marriage prompts us to spend intense time together. However, at times we may feel restless with reading and reflection, and so it's useful to inject some physical activity as needed beyond the activities already suggested. Perhaps we reflect individually on the topics while riding a bicycle or chopping wood (safely!). Together, we can have discussions while walking, taking a car ride, or going out for coffee or a meal in a quiet location. Sometimes we also just need to take a break and lighten up with a social activity, with or without our children along. We can appreciate each other's efforts and celebrate each step of our progress!

One of God's greatest gifts is encouragement. As we encourage each other as marriage partners, and as we turn to others that we trust to encourage us and pray for us, the strength in our hearts increases, and it becomes easier to persevere. It becomes possible to thrive.

Revitalizing Our Marriage is a message of encouragement. A healthy, happy marriage full of vitality is a blessing to us as a couple, our children, and others.

* Throughout the book are *quotes in italics* from people with their personal perspectives and experiences.

Chapter 2: Building a Support System

The Bahá'í teachings encourage various responses for individuals, couples, and families who are struggling with some aspect of life. As individuals, we are to engage in ongoing transformation of ourselves, so our words and behaviors improve daily. This includes daily prayer, reading and sharing the teachings, meditation, improving our characters, and service to others. More on individual transformation is in Parallel Track 2 of this book.

Couple and family outreach are encouraged to seek:

- Consultation with those we trust who are wise and mature
- Connection to a Spiritual Assembly or other institution for spiritual accompaniment and guidance
- Assistance from professional counseling, balanced with Bahá'í insights

For couples where we also have a connection to another faith, we may also wish to do outreach to their clergy.

Reaching Out to Others

In our highly mobile world, we may not be living near close relatives, and many long-term friends may also be far away. It's often possible to become isolated and feel unsupported. We may also think that our marriage should be completely private, with no one else knowing what we struggle with. While there are confidentiality and loyalty boundaries that logically protect a marriage relationship, never letting others in to help us can create significant marriage and family difficulties. For example, sometimes a parent, close friend, or another experienced couple can make practical suggestions and address some issues in prayer and consultation with us.

Building support for our marriage may not be a common practice among those we know. It will be a learning-in-action and courageous effort to see what works for our marriage and family and what doesn't. Wherever possible and safe, it will be wise to work together as marriage partners and agree on what steps to take. Some of our efforts will be successful and some won't, but these will be opportunities to learn. Prayer, reflection, and consultation will guide us where to go next without blaming or arguing over what didn't go well. Here is encouragement:

> "The cause of most arguments is disagreement over what we believe, prefer, or value. The basis of all these is conditioning. By contrast, when we transcend our conditioned thoughts and operate out of free-flowing thinking, we enter the world of common ground—wisdom, common sense, and deeper feelings of love, understanding, and compassion."[11] Richard Carlson and Joseph Bailey

We must be leaders and advocates for our own marriage. This means assessing what is best for maintaining it and striving to achieve this. Being committed to our marriage includes addressing issues proactively and not threatening or rushing to consider separation or divorce as an option except in extreme cases. Our marriage will grow and strengthen as we invest in it, including:

- Learning new knowledge and skills about what contributes to healthy and happy individuals, a successful marriage partnership, and a unified family
- Engaging in service to each other and together in the community
- Parenting harmoniously and effectively, drawing on known best practices

- Praying and consulting regularly
- Looking for what to appreciate and be grateful for

Managing Our Communications with Others

Dr. Doherty in *Take Back Your Marriage* makes these key points below. He suggests choosing people to support a marriage who:

- Know and like both of us
- Appreciate marital commitment
- Will give clear and useful feedback about our personal flaws that are contributing to the issues

He says it's wise to ensure that when we talk to others about our marriage and family that we share the positives and not just the negatives. We can let trusted others know what types of support we are looking for and ask them not to say things that are unhelpful or that undermine our marriage. He suggests being cautious about talking to divorced friends if they are not marriage-friendly.[12] William J. Doherty

As we look for helpful support from others, we will begin to identify and share our own strategies and successes. As we pray with others and be open in some ways about our marriage, we can invite group consultation about common challenges. We will find that many problems in marriage are shared, and we can learn from others and solve them together. Where we find that a problem cannot be easily solved, we may receive encouragement to learn to live with it gracefully or seek assistance from other sources. Of course, gossip about any of the issues that arise in consultation would be highly destructive.

Particularly when we are in the early stages of experiencing challenges, we may find it useful to turn to experienced married couples for mentoring and consultation to build understanding and generate solutions. Often these couples have experience with overcoming many types of challenges and have learned how to maintain unity. They have a balanced view of when problems are minor and easily solved and when they are more serious and need professional assistance. Mentor couples can often provide encouragement and understanding that all marriages have times of difficulty and growth.

Community-Based Marriages

Dr. Doherty calls us to begin creating "community-based" marriages. This concept can include:

- Being more open about our marriage and family and constructively engaging with others about theirs
- Paying people compliments about their marriages when we see things we like in what they are doing
- Asking a couple who are close friends to be partners with checking in with each other about our marriages in a constructive way
- Attending marriage education and enrichment activities [Also consider studying a book about marriage together]
- Working with a mentor couple[13]

Dr. Doherty calls on us to "build a world that is safe for marriage."[14] This includes effectively handling a situation when we run into difficulties and not ignoring it. Action can include consulting with others, as this quotation encourages:

> "Neither you nor your husband should hesitate to...take advantage of the supportive counseling which can come from wise and mature friends."[15] On behalf of the Universal House of Justice

If we turn to friends, we must make sure they are friends of our marriage and not advocates for its failure. If we turn to family, it's important to ensure they will work with both of us to grow or save our marriage, not take sides or undermine our efforts.

It can also be a healthy marital practice to have periodic reflection consultations to pray and share our thoughts and feelings about our marriage and family progress. This provides a time to assess our growth and movement toward our goals. We may choose to schedule these to happen in parallel with the same 3-month cycle of activity and reflection that many Bahá'í communities follow.

Role of Institutions

The Bahá'í teachings have provided for spiritually based administrative institutions to guide the community. The Assemblies are the local and national institutions that oversee the administration of marriage, divorce, and related matters. They can provide materials with authoritative guidance on specific topics—some of which are not available publicly—loving encouragement, and recommendations or decisions on specific situations as needed.

If an individual or a couple knows of an Assembly they would like to reach out to—their own or one nearby—they are free to do so, and they are encouraged to "seek refuge in the Assembly for advice and help, when needed."[16] (Universal House of Justice)

If we are in such serious difficulty that we are thinking of divorce, the guidance below may be helpful:

> "In the strict legal sense there are no 'grounds' for a Bahá'í divorce. No question of misbehavior of either party is involved and the only condition under which a Bahá'í divorce may be considered is the irreconcilable antipathy of the parties. Thus it is not sufficient that one or both of the parties has asked that the date for the beginning of the year of waiting be fixed; the Assembly must find the

condition of irreconcilable antipathy to exist before the date can be fixed."[17] Universal House of Justice

"Concerning the definition of the term 'aversion' in relation to Bahá'í divorce law, the Universal House of Justice points out that there are no specific 'grounds' for Bahá'í divorce such as there are in some codes of civil law. Bahá'í law permits divorce but, as both Bahá'u'lláh and 'Abdu'l-Bahá have made very clear, divorce is abhorred. Thus, from the point of view of the individual believer he should do all he can to refrain from divorce. Bahá'ís should be profoundly aware of the sanctity of marriage and should strive to make their marriages an eternal bond of unity and harmony. This requires effort and sacrifice and wisdom and self-abnegation. A Bahá'í should consider the possibility of divorce only if the situation is intolerable and he or she has a strong aversion to being married to the other partner. This is the standard held up to the individual. It is not a law, but an exhortation. It is a goal to which we should strive."[18] On behalf of the Universal House of Justice

"... [I]f the Assembly finds that it is unable to persuade the party concerned to withdraw the application for divorce, it must conclude that, from its point of view, there appears to be an irreconcilable antipathy, and it has no alternative to setting the date for the beginning of the year of waiting. During the year the couple have the responsibility of attempting to reconcile their differences, and the Assembly has the duty to help them and encourage them. But if the year of waiting comes to an end without reconciliation the Bahá'í divorce must be granted as at the date of the granting of the civil divorce if this has not already taken place."[19] On behalf of the Universal House of Justice

However, it's wise for us to seek counsel long before marriage issues become so serious that we are talking about divorce. When couples delay seeking assistance, the problems become entrenched, and the couple may be at the point of strong antipathy and separation when they finally contact the Assembly. [Assemblies could consider encouraging their community members on this topic through an occasional general reminder at Nineteen-Day Feasts, a notice in a newsletter, a letter to the community, inclusion in the consultation portion at Feast on the topic, and so on.]

Early intervention can prevent problems from becoming more serious. It takes prayerful courage for us to do this outreach. It can be a difficult, private, and embarrassing situation, and we may not want to feel like a burden to an Assembly. It may also be more comfortable for us to turn to an Assembly outside of our immediate area or to our National Spiritual Assembly. Sometimes, meeting with designated Assembly representatives instead of the whole institution can feel more comfortable. Many Assemblies have appointed committees to aid marriages as well. Communications and meetings with all of these entities are considered highly confidential, and you can ask them for that assurance. Here is some guidance:

> "... [T]he believers have not yet fully learned to draw on each other's love for strength and consolation in time of need. The Cause of God is endowed with tremendous powers, and the reason the believers do not gain more from it is because they have not learned to draw fully on these mighty forces of love and strength and harmony generated by the Faith."[20] On behalf of Shoghi Effendi

> "The friends must be patient with each other and must realize that the Cause is still in its infancy and its institutions are not yet functioning perfectly. The greater

the patience, the loving understanding and the forbearance the believers show towards each other and their shortcomings, the greater will be the progress of the whole Bahá'í community at large."[21] On behalf of Shoghi Effendi

"Consultation is...available for the individual in solving his own problems; he may consult with his Assembly, with his family and with his friends."[22] On behalf of the Universal House of Justice

"The House of Justice is distressed to learn that you and your husband are continuing to experience marital difficulties. It has frequently advised believers in such situations to turn to the Spiritual Assemblies for advice and counsel, and to follow this advice in their efforts to preserve the unity of their marital relationship. It has been found useful in many instances to also seek the assistance of competent professional marriage counsellors, who can provide useful insights and guidance in the use of constructive measures to bring about a greater degree of unity."[23] On behalf of the Universal House of Justice

"The House of Justice advises you to continue the strenuous efforts you are making to overcome the difficulties in your marriage. It is pleased to note that you and your husband have turned to the Local Spiritual Assembly for guidance and have sought help from a Bahá'í who is a marriage counselor. Such endeavors, when combined with a strong and determined effort, improve greatly the prospects that your marriage can be maintained."[24] On behalf of the Universal House of Justice

"... [T]he provision of guidance on administrative matters such as the laws of engagement, marriage, and divorce falls under the purview of Local and National Spiritual

Assemblies; while Bahá'ís who are professional counselors are free to share with the friends extracts from the Bahá'í Writings and to offer advice of a general nature, it is best that they refer the friends in the first instance to their Local Spiritual Assemblies when questions arise about the application of the laws and Teachings of the Faith."[25] On behalf of the Universal House of Justice

Institutions and their representatives are charged with spiritually guiding those who turn to them and ensuring that individuals and couples are aware of Bahá'í teachings and laws that apply to their circumstances. Assemblies can often contribute to saving marriages through providing prayer, official guidance, ways to apply the guidance, compassion, love, and common sense. Institutions are not trained in counseling, although part of their role can be to encourage people to also draw on science and counseling professionals in harmony with the Faith, and they can refer people to support groups. Bahá'í marriage is a spiritual entity, and so it's important to have it be supported by spiritual institutions. Someone shares:

"Stable, beautiful, and devoted families will attract friends to the Bahá'í Faith through their reflection of the teachings of the Faith. I'm discovering the important place the Spiritual Assemblies have in protecting marriages. I understand that families turning spontaneously to them, and the ability of a Local Spiritual Assembly to guide a family through trials and difficult times, are indicators of the Assembly's maturity and strength. That's a reflection of the trust that the believers have in their institutions. This will surely be another magnet that attracts people to the Faith."

If we do not have easy access to an Assembly, or if we are hesitant to approach an Assembly, perhaps due to our close association with its members, there are other options. Auxiliary Board members are available to consult with any believer in their care. Those who serve in the role of Protection are often experienced with accompanying friends through challenges. While Auxiliary Board members do not have administrative authority and are not professional counselors, they can either directly or through an assistant, consult with a person or a couple, prompt them to consider the application of spiritual principles in their circumstances, and assist them to navigate the administrative processes with an Assembly, if necessary. Auxiliary Board members may also be familiar with the Local Assemblies in the wider area that can assist, should it be needed. We may also reach out to our National Spiritual Assembly, which can arrange for assistance.

Institutional representatives are available to help and will collaborate as needed to walk with the souls of those needing guidance. It's important for us to know that consulting with institutions about a problem is not backbiting. We may also request that individuals on the Assembly not offer personal opinions about our situation but that the Assembly consult after we leave the meeting and give their unified input later.

If we are not willing or ready to share specific information about our marriage, or the matters involved are ones where we are being helped by a professional, there is still spiritual benefit for us in turning to the institutions with a request for prayers. There is protection for our marriage and family by being under the umbrella of the institutions and the Covenant of Bahá'u'lláh. Here is encouragement and guidance:

> "The effort required to preserve and strengthen a Bahá'í marriage is prolonged and inescapable. It requires prayer, perseverance, self-sacrifice, mutual respect, a willingness to cooperate and to forgive, and frank and loving consultation. It can, at times, be very painful. However, the

Universal House of Justice provides the following assurance that the result of a 'consecrated and determined effort', even in seemingly impossible cases, is frequently blessed with a positive outcome:

> "There have been many instances in which a couple has, through a consecrated and determined effort, aided by the power of prayer and the advice of experts, succeeded in overcoming seemingly insuperable obstacles to their reconciliation and in reconstructing a strong foundation for their marriage. There are also innumerable examples of individuals who have been able to effect drastic and enduring changes in their behavior, through drawing on the spiritual powers available by the bounty of God."[26]

Research Department of the Universal House of Justice; on behalf of the Universal House of Justice

Drawing on the Power of Prayer

One foundational element in supporting our marriage is daily prayer, individually and as a couple. We can also pray as a family and hold devotionals where others are invited as well. We can ask Bahá'í institutions to pray for us. We can also request prayers from those we know going to Bahá'í Houses of Worship and the Holy Land for pilgrimage, without needing to share specifics about the situation. We may also choose to go to these places and pray directly for our marriage and family. In addition, some of the Bahá'í Houses of Worship take prayer requests for staff to fulfill, and we can use general wording without sharing specifics here as well. Here is assurance:

> "Shouldst thou recite any of the revealed prayers, and seek assistance from God with thy face turned towards Him, and implore Him with devotion and fervor, thy need will be answered."[27] 'Abdu'l-Bahá

Turning to Professionals and Others

There are professionals who are marriage and family therapists as well as those trained to educate individuals and couples in marriage, parenting, and family knowledge and skill-building. The Bahá'í Faith's teachings promote the harmony of religion and science, and there are now decades of research available in books and on the internet for everyone to draw on along with the teachings. Here is some guidance:

> "Your letter...to the Universal House of Justice makes clear that you are seeking to re-establish your marriage through study of the Writings and through various modes of consultation and assistance. We are asked to convey its advice on this vital subject of reconciliation of partners in marriage in the context of understanding of yourself and your relationship to others.
>
> "You are urged to persevere in your studies, in your prayers for resolution of your problems, and in your meditation which may provide guidance and confidence, inasmuch as the understanding of self and of relationships to others are contained in the Writings and in the example of the Master, 'Abdu'l-Bahá.
>
> "Neither you nor your husband should hesitate to continue consulting professional marriage counsellors, individually and together if possible, and also to take advantage of the supportive counseling which can come from wise and mature friends. Non-Bahá'í counseling can be useful but it is usually necessary to temper it with Bahá'í insight."[28] Universal House of Justice

"Bahá'í insight" could be achieved by our use of this book and by providing a counselor with a copy of *Revitalizing Our Marriage* as well as the information provided in Appendix D for non-Bahá'í counselors. If we seek marriage counseling, it will be wise to ensure that the professional is trained to work with couples and not just with individuals and that the person is an advocate for marriage. A couple shares:

"We resisted going to see a counselor for quite a while, certain we could solve our challenges by ourselves. When we finally went to one, we realized many of our notions of what it would be like were false. She helped us see our strengths and understand where we could make changes to align with current marriage research. She also accompanied us when we had difficulties in making consistent and positive changes. The structure of having regular sessions kept us on track, and our marriage is better now. I wish we had gone sooner."

Every counselor and professional has their own approach, so if we try one person and they are not a fit, we can try someone new. Some meet only in person with clients; others will meet by videoconference or phone. Some specialize in issues such as infidelity or addiction. Some counselors are Bahá'ís and some not. If someone is a Bahá'í, clear boundaries and confidentiality will keep counseling and community life separate.

It would be typical for a counselor to begin with deep listening to learn the dynamics and issues and raise questions like these:

- What has brought you to me?
- Has something happened that precipitated finding a counselor?
- How are you hoping this outreach action will help you? or What might be different after counseling?
- What are your highest aspirations and wishes if you decide to commit to this course of action?

Working with a professional tends to be most successful when couples are:

- Open and truthful about their issues (pretending to be perfect Bahá'ís can be a barrier)
- Clear about what they want as an outcome
- Willing to take the materials and input from the counselor and put them to use

We may also benefit at times from individual therapy or other modalities of healing; however, it's still important that the professionals involved respect the institution of marriage and that we apply the Bahá'í teachings throughout the process. A man shares his experience:

"[At times, nothing is a] substitute for a good therapist. ... If your life is not going as well as you would like, then finding an objective, compassionate person to consult with about it will do you a lot of good. ... Having a real, live person look into your eyes and say, 'You have a right to feel that way' can break through more layers of denial and fear than a hundred books, so give it a try. Before I visited my first therapist, I was terrified. ... Consider therapy a kind of consultation on how to improve your life, the way you would bring a contractor in to help remodel your home. If you don't feel you are making progress after half a dozen sessions, change therapists. Don't give up.

"Here is a list of healthy beliefs that a good therapist will help you internalize:

- *I am safe—though my body may be frail and vulnerable, my soul is strong and eternal.*
- *I am valuable—I matter to God and to the world. I make a difference.*
- *I am lovable—I am created in the image of God and reflect spiritual virtues.*

- *I am loving—I am attracted to the signs of God reflected in the people around me.*
- *I have capacities—I am not a helpless pawn of the universe. I can make choices and accomplish goals.*
- *I can grow—I am not static. I can learn and develop new skills and virtues."*

"A good therapist will also support your efforts at developing honesty, forgiveness, compassion, and faith."[29]

While counseling must have some focus on understanding and addressing problems, it's also wise to choose a professional who helps you see your strengths, encourages your progress, celebrates your accomplishments, and assists you with healing and re-building unity. If sessions are focused solely on the negative, you may feel worse about your marriage rather than better and become discouraged.

Possible Resources:

Religious communities or their chosen representatives may keep a list of trustworthy, experienced, and competent counselors. See Appendix D for information to give to a counselor who is not familiar with the Bahá'í Faith. It's useful when you do not want to spend significant time during counseling sessions explaining these beliefs. A downloadable copy of the document is also at www.bahaimarriage.net.

There are online Bahá'í-based courses for relationships, marriage, parenting, and family available through The Wilmette Institute, www.wilmetteinstitute.org, an agency of the National Spiritual Assembly of the Bahá'ís of the United States.

A selection of available books that may be useful are ones by: John Gottman, Shaunti Feldhahn (Christian), and Gary Chapman (Christian); *The Relationship Handbook* by George S. Pransky; *Divorce Remedy* by Michele Weiner-Davis; *Fighting for Your Marriage* by Howard Markman, Scott Stanley, and Susan Blumberg; *Mindful Matrimony* by Furugh and Raymond Switzer; *Re-Marriage Blueprint* by Maggie Scarf; *Hold Me Tight* by Sue Johnson; *30 Secrets of Happily Married Couples* by Paul Coleman; and *Pure Gold: Encouraging Character Qualities in Marriage* by Susanne M. Alexander.

Couple Actions

1. Pray individually and together for our marriage and family at least three times per week. Identify others who could pray for us and do outreach to them with the request.

2. Identify a couple and have social time with them to assess our level of comfort with talking with them about marriage and family topics.

3. Identify an experienced married couple and approach them about being mentors to us.

4. Consult to determine whether outreach to an Assembly, Auxiliary Board member, other institution, and/or a professional counselor is timely and helpful. Once a decision is made, take the necessary actions to make the connections and appointments. If we feel resistant to carrying out these steps, identify the reasons why and whether we can address these and move forward in some way to obtain supportive assistance.

Couple Reflection and Consultation

1. Who and what currently supports the health and well-being of our marriage?
2. How can we support healthy, unified marriages for others and ourselves? What new actions do we commit to trying? How will we remember to do these new actions?
3. When and how will we communicate our response to these new actions?
4. What benefits could come from reaching out for help?
5. What would stop us from reaching out for help? How could we address the issues that stop us?
6. Who are we willing to approach for assistance?

Chapter 3: Declaring a Cease-Fire

Note: Even if you are not actively battling with each other, there are parts of this chapter that are likely useful for you.

A Loss of Vitality

A vital marriage is dynamically alive and thriving. However, we can struggle with our vitality at any stage of marriage when we are distracted and disconnected. Challenges and a pattern of conflict may cause us to behave like independent individuals trying to survive instead of being partners. Yet, in our hearts, we can yearn for connection, unity, and peace with each other.

Many factors can negatively affect marriage vitality and couple connection, such as:

- Not maintaining our couple relationship while meeting the needs of children
- Overly high number of activities outside of our home
- High-demand work responsibilities that include spending time working during family activities
- Device use and distractions; social media preoccupation (phones, tablets, computers...)
- Losing a connection to God and having fewer spiritual practices
- Dominating or controlling each other; not functioning as equal partners
- Experiencing regular conflict
- Destructive behaviors [Note: if these include such actions as infidelity or abuse, please see Appendix C.]

We may no longer be able to see each other's perspectives and the good qualities that we each have, and we focus on our own unhappiness and negative feelings about our partner. We may be resigned that the current state of our marriage and family are in difficulty and always will be. Sometimes our home feels like a battleground with words as weapons. Or at times it feels like there is a cold war happening, with both of us withdrawn and sending occasional hot words or sharp looks over the "wall" between us. There may be periods of good interactions that are interrupted by frustrated or angry misunderstandings. We may experience painful difficulty in accepting and trusting each other and believing what we say.

Sometimes, the initial signs of difficulty in a marriage are small but troubling—a sneer of disrespect, cutting sarcasm, forgetting an important anniversary, or regularly acting distracted instead of listening. Signs of escalating difficulties can include less interest in sex with each other or increasing use of pornography, frequent misunderstandings, resistance to forgiving, recurring disagreements, regular power struggles, disharmony about parenting and disciplining children, and little ability to enjoy social time together.

Marriages in serious trouble have couples attacking each other's character, being defensive, withdrawing from each other, little or no communication, inability to make joint decisions, and conflict among many family members.

One person shares:

"It feels like my brain is full of fog. The anxiety over our relationship is constant. I can't think. I can't function. Our children look at us in fear, because they don't want to see us divorce. I'm fighting with my mother-in-law. It's just all so difficult. Our kids are scared, upset, and so disappointed in our behavior, well, and so are we. How did we get from passionately loving each other to this state? How can we turn this around?"

It doesn't have to be this way. To begin healing our marriage and bring it back to life, we need to stop the battle. We need to declare a "cease-fire". To have the strength to do this, we may have to turn to some of the most powerful prayers we know. Then we can begin to increase peace and unity, within ourselves and between each other. There is hope.

Turning from Conflict Toward Unity

It's not easy to transform negative patterns, however doing so is vital for our individual well-being and that of our marriage and family. Bahá'u'lláh gives us this guidance:

> "A kindly tongue is the lodestone of the hearts of men. It is the bread of the spirit, it clotheth the words with meaning, it is the fountain of the light of wisdom and understanding."[30] Bahá'u'lláh

> "Hear no evil, and see no evil, abase not thyself, neither sigh and weep. Speak no evil, that thou mayest not hear it spoken unto thee, and magnify not the faults of others that thine own faults may not appear great; and wish not the abasement of anyone, that thine own abasement be not exposed."[31] Bahá'u'lláh

It's time for us to:

- Take a step back
- Assess our patterns
- Begin to think about a new, more positive direction for our marriage
- Accept each other the way we are now (acceptance frees us to make improvements; criticism often prompts resistance to change, instead)
- Assess the current reality of our marriage and family dynamics
- Commit to learning new approaches
- Set in motion new courses of action

These behavior shifts will open the opportunity for each of us to begin making the necessary improvements in ourselves and our interactions. The guidance below provides perspectives on some of what is happening in marriages and society:

> "Regarding your query about conflict between the parties to a marriage, the term 'conflict' encompasses a variety of conditions, ranging from contention to friendly disagreement. As you indicate, Bahá'u'lláh has forbidden His followers to engage in contention. He has also stressed the importance of consultation. Indeed, consultation within the family, employing full and frank discussion and animated by awareness of the need for moderation and balance, can be the panacea for domestic conflict. Besides assisting couples through their professional expertise, counselors can draw upon their insights into the Bahá'í Teachings to provide further assistance, such as by encouraging them to develop the skill of consultation and by helping them to distinguish concepts and practices current in society from those found in the Teachings. The views of professionals and of the wider society that are contrary to the Teachings will naturally have an impact on the friends in this age of transition. As the community grows in strength and as the Teachings become more fully understood and practiced by Bahá'ís, the distinctive characteristics of Bahá'í family life will become increasingly apparent."[32] On behalf of the Universal House of Justice

A person shares their view of unity in marriage, which is a vital goal beyond simply ceasing to have conflict:

"Where there is a culture of unity in our marriage, it ensures that each person's concerns are heard, and that each person is treated with respect. Unity supports the principles of

fairness and equity, so relationships are not based on power struggles but on loving support and encouragement.

"When unity feels like it's struggling between us, we can pray for our family and for each other. We can focus on people's good qualities and acknowledge people's successes. We can learn about relationship building, and we can invest some time and attention in our marriage. Because of the focus my husband and I are now putting on unity, we are more able to depend on each other as partners."

The Bahá'í teachings call us to unity in the family:

> "Note ye how easily, where unity existeth in a given family, the affairs of that family are conducted; what progress the members of that family make, how they prosper in the world. Their concerns are in order, they enjoy comfort and tranquility, they are secure, their position is assured, they come to be envied by all. Such a family but addeth to its stature and its lasting honor, as day succeedeth day."[33]
> 'Abdu'l-Bahá

High standards can be difficult to strive for or achieve. It's merciful when we set in place a pattern of doing better little by little each day. Consider this perspective:

> "We learn from science that adaptability is the basis of survival. Those who are unwilling to adapt and change their behavior or consider compromise a sign of weakness do not understand that there is a world of difference between giving way to another person because we are forced to do so, or because we are threatened, and giving way because we want to, or out of affection. Indeed, such flexibility, far from being a weakness, is a sign of great strength of mind. Between people who love each other, giving is very important. What we think we are losing in power, control

or self-affirmation, we are in fact recovering in maturity, wisdom and serenity."[34] Mehri Sefidvash

Navigating Touchy Subjects

Important or sensitive communications require some planning of what we are going to say, how, and when. It's beneficial when we pause and check our personal well-being and whether the timing or content of what we want to say could cause harm instead of benefit. For some people it may be useful to use the acronym H.A.L.T. to consider how to proceed. Avoid (halt) important or sensitive communications and actions if we are:

- **H:** Hungry
- **A:** Angry
- **L:** Lonely [extrovert battery re-charge time needed with time with a marriage partner or others]; or Over-stimulated [introvert battery re-charge time needed with time alone]
- **T:** Tired

Courtesy and wisdom can guide us to ensure whenever possible that eating, calming down, building emotional connection and unity, resting, or other actions are handled first before communicating. For example, if "loneliness" has one of us upset and the result is unhappy or angry words, some quality couple time together without serious communication may be calming. The recipient of the unhappy words could prompt this transition by simply taking a deep breath, not becoming defensive, and saying, "How can I help?". Then after some time together, communication can proceed.

It's also wise for us to assess whether there are issues to address before consulting about a problem. For example, we may need to set up a private place or arrange for children to be watched by a trusted person or occupied with an activity. It can also be best to ensure that we have recovery time after a busy activity or day before addressing a serious topic.

When we do begin to consult, the process may go smoothly, or we may start to escalate into difficulty. It's useful to recognize that we can pause and calm down for a few minutes (or hours) before resuming. [More on communication and consultation is included throughout the book and especially in Chapters 8, 9, and 10.]

Being Truthful with Care

Truthfulness is a vital element in maintaining or re-building trust between us. We need to be able to count on the accuracy of each other's words. Even small lies, or hiding important information, can result in suspicion and disunity arising between us.

However, we may be concerned about the effect of truthful words on each other. Pairing other qualities along with truthfulness addresses this issue. Tactfulness is a primary quality to pair with it. We can also consider such qualities as kindness and compassion. Here is guidance:

> "Truthfulness is the foundation of all human virtues.... When this holy attribute is established in man, all the divine qualities will also be acquired."[35] 'Abdu'l-Bahá

We may find that introducing humor into our interactions at times lightens up our communications. Timeliness also applies here, however. If our humor leaves the other person feeling their words or actions are not being taken seriously, or if there is a negative message delivered with sarcastic humor, the outcome could be problems instead of connection.

Do We Still Love Each Other?

When we experience conflict frequently, or we go through a period where there is little connection between us, we may begin questioning whether we still love each other or whether the other person loves us. When love feels minimal or absent, sometimes we can re-generate love through turning our hearts to God or Bahá'u'lláh and asking for help in feeling loving again. We can also do loving actions and acts of service, which can increase loving feelings. Consider these perspectives:

> "If we wish to love even in moments when we feel that another person does not love us, we must firmly grasp the reality of God's love for us and understand that He is the source of our security and significance in life. If we accept this truth, repeat prayers and *Hidden Words* that affirm it, cling to it when we feel alone and abandoned, and learn to experience its reality in communion with God, we will be able to love and minister to our partners and to be a source of life and potential growth to them and ourselves.... Once we truly understand this truth, we will know that the quality of our lives and happiness does not depend on our partner with all [their] human failings, but on ourselves—our thoughts, our actions, and our relationship with God."[36] Joan B. Hernández
>
> "Love is a gift from God. You cannot make yourself feel love or make another person love you, just as you cannot create your own heartbeat. Loving feelings grow and flourish naturally in the presence of certain conditions, in the presence of loving behavior. To behave in a way that nurtures love, you must feel worthy of giving and receiving love. ...
>
> "It is not unusual for loving feelings to be covered over by hurt, anger, resentment, or fear. At such times, love feels dead or absent. Conflicts are the result of natural differences between partners, but most people do not know how to handle conflicts well. Painful emotions or deadness to love is a sign of partners handling conflicts

poorly. Hurt, anger, resentment, or fear can last for years if not dealt with. When you feel other intense emotions, you will not feel love at the same time. The unpleasant emotion must be attended to properly so that healing occurs, which allows the flow of loving feelings again. Most often, love only feels dead, but is waiting, ready to come to life with the hope that conflicts can be resolved. ...

"A happy marriage needs a mixture of intimate feelings and loving commitment. Loving commitment is determination and resolve that the loved person should flourish."[37] Sandra Gray Bender

The goal in re-vitalizing our marriage is:

"... mutual attachment of mind and heart. ... Their purpose must be this: to become loving companions and comrades and at one with each other for time and eternity...."[38] 'Abdu'l-Bahá

We will not be perfect at improving ourselves or our marriage. Giving each other the grace and space to try out new words and actions and learn from the experiences is vital. It may take many tries before we feel comfortable with something new. Being skeptical or distrustful of each other's efforts or motives can discourage improvements happening. If we encourage and affirm each other's efforts instead, our progress is likely to accelerate.

Sincerely and truthfully declaring a cease-fire between us is a courageous first step, and one that will empower us to grow in new directions.

Couple Actions

1. Say out loud to each other: "I declare a cease-fire with you" and "I promise to focus on creating a peaceful atmosphere and unity between us".

2. Each of us go through the following visualization process:
    a. Close our eyes and put an image in our minds of our tongues.
    b. Now think of the words "kindly tongue" and envision our tongues softening and becoming smooth and gentle.
    c. Envision talking with kind, considerate, and gentle words, and assess the effect on us and on the receiver.
    d. Commit to ourselves that we will do our best to speak with a "kindly tongue" with each other and with our children and other family members.

3. Discuss and determine some positive ways we will greet each other when we have been apart, such as being away at work or even in different parts of our home. We can consider an action like a hug, or some positive words. Some couples may be comfortable greeting each other at times using the Greatest Name, "Allah'u'Abhá" (God the All-Glorious). This quotation may inspire us: "If any differences arise amongst you, behold Me standing before your face, and overlook the faults of one another for My name's sake and as a token of your love for My manifest and resplendent Cause. We love to see you at all times consorting in amity and concord within the paradise of My good-pleasure, and to inhale from your acts the fragrance of friendliness and unity, of loving-kindness and fellowship."[39] (Bahá'u'lláh)

4. Researcher Shaunti Feldhahn challenges people to a "30-Day Kindness Challenge" for them to see how kind words and actions transform a relationship (for more information please go to www.shaunti.com). The Challenge has these three aspects noted below.

a. "Say nothing negative about your person, either to them or about them to someone else."
b. "Every day, find one positive thing that you can sincerely praise or affirm about your person and tell them, and tell someone else."
c. "Every day, do a small act of kindness or generosity for your person."

Feldhahn says that when these three aspects come together, they react and build "something remarkable, beautiful, powerful, and, above all, transformative."[40]

Individual Reflection

1. How do I feel when conflict arises between us?
2. What do I observe happening in our family because of conflict between us?
3. What steps am I willing to take to participate in moving myself and us in a peaceful direction?
4. How might my well-being improve if our interactions become more peaceful?
5. What kind, thoughtful, or loving words could I increase? What would assist me to be consistent with these?
6. What kind, thoughtful, or loving actions could I do for my partner? What would assist me to be consistent with these?

Couple Reflection and Consultation

1. What do we believe "unity" is?
2. What behaviors seem to be unifying between people in general?
3. What ways do we interact that seem to cause disunity or conflict between us?
4. When would using H.A.L.T. improve our interactions?

5. What small positive shifts in our words could increase unity between us? What shifts in our actions could prompt greater unity?
6. What happens inside us when we greet each other in a positive way? How do our children respond when they see us greet each other in positive ways?
7. How could applying kindness to our words and actions affect our relationship?
8. How might greater unity positively affect our physical, mental, emotional, and spiritual well-being?

Chapter 4: Achieving Early Positive Results

In any multi-focused, long-term endeavor, we can benefit from feeling a sense of success early on. Below are a few ideas for us to choose from to benefit our marriage, and we may come up with more. The intention is to act in positive ways, so we feel more connected and hopeful. Here is encouragement:

> "Nearly all of us have had the experience of a situation in which there was a lot of tension or people's nerves were frayed and a shared laugh was enough to make the atmosphere warm and joyful again. All too often we underestimate the importance of a smile, an embrace, a kind word, a sincere compliment, or the giving of one's attention. It is precisely the small things that can change difficult moments into special ones."[41] Mehri Sefidvash

We will learn through practice what can work well for us to establish as an ongoing couple habit and what's not a fit—at least not right now. If it has been a while since we did an action, we can't expect it to feel instantly comfortable now. It will take patient repetition and then reflection and couple consultation about what to continue or stop. If conflict arises, pause and resume when it's timely.

It's good to begin with simple and cooperative actions before tackling complex ones. For example, perhaps we do the dishes as a team rather than re-organizing the whole house! Also be aware that insisting something be done "my way, which is the right way" will likely create disunity rather than the harmony we are striving for. Often our approaches are not wrong but simply different, and we can accept each other's view.

Couple Actions

What follows are some simple activity ideas. Seeing a list like this may make us feel a bit overwhelmed, especially if we are having difficulty making decisions as a couple. If we are uncertain what to choose, we could simply write down the numbers on slips of paper that match actions we are willing to attempt, put them in a container, and draw one out to try.

Whenever we can include an element of the arts, it may bring inspiration and new understandings.

Some Ideas to Consider:

1. Do something today to laugh together, at least once. Possibilities are a funny story from work, finding a comic or amusing video to share, making a child laugh, making a funny face—whatever is a fit for us.

2. Spend 5-15 minutes in couple prayer together, daily if possible. Pray together as a family regularly.

3. Reflect on and discuss a character quality or virtue and how we could increase in in our lives. (Resources: *Pure Gold—Encouraging Character Qualities in Marriage* or a deck of cards from The Virtues Project, www.virtuesproject.org).

4. Do physical exercise together as a couple or family such as a nature walk or bike ride.

5. Play a game as a couple or family.

6. Do some type of non-sexual physical touch between us. This could be a hand on the shoulder, holding hands, hug, kiss, or cuddle on the couch. If we have children, they could be included in a family hug.

7. Spend an hour re-connecting to positive memories from our courtship, honeymoon, and early marriage. Identify some of the positive actions that happened at that time and put at least one into action in the present.

8. Enjoy music and/or another arts-related activity together.

9. Study a short quotation or a letter from the Universal House of Justice together.

10. Together do a small service project or act of kindness for someone.

11. Go for a walk in a park and hold hands.

12. Find something new and positive to add to our home that we both appreciate and see as useful or beautiful.

13. Share three aspects of our day or our lives that we are grateful for.

14. Think back over the last two days and find something specific we each did and express appreciation to each other.

15. Plan and carry out a couple date. Keep it simple to begin with, such as eating a meal or drinking coffee out of the house together or taking a walk outdoors with just the two of us.

16. Adjust a child's bedtime to allow for increased couple time in the evening. Determine together one or two simple activities that could happen together during this time.

17. Share something from the day that made one of us feel joyful.

18. Make our bed cooperatively with clean sheets and pillowcases.

19. Say out loud to each other: "Thank You God for our marriage. Please help us increase our unity."

Couple Reflection and Consultation

1. What are we appreciating from our early successes?
2. What did we enjoy doing?
3. In what ways have our interactions improved?
4. What reminders will we put in place to encourage positive actions to continue?

Chapter 5: Envisioning a Re-Created Marriage

Now that we have had some new positive experiences, it's good for us to envision what we want our marriage to be. When we picture our married life—what do we really want? We may be tempted to focus on: "What do we *not* want?". However, it's wise for us to focus on the positive we want to create, instead. We also need to consider what is or has been changing in our lives, what needs may have shifted, and what is important for us to prioritize. Consider this:

> "Throughout the marriage husband and wife must make room—even if reluctantly—for change and for difference, for altering values, tastes, needs, and careers. Husband and wife continually confront the issue of how to reshape their shared identity so it continues to express what they want as a couple and what they need as individuals. Given the vast number of choices and trajectories, this challenge creates a never-ending tension in marriage.
>
> "Paradoxically, it is out of this push-pull of autonomy and togetherness that the couple acquires a sense of good emotional, moral, and cognitive fit. To reach the conclusion that the relationship is uniquely gratifying requires the meshing of both partners' conscious and unconscious wishes and needs and the acceptance of compromise as reasonably fair or at least temporarily necessary. To achieve this state, not only must each person feel free to make his or her wishes known but both must agree on what is fair. This agreement allows each one to accept disappointments without rage and take a fair portion in lieu of everything. It works only if the couple regards the well-being of the marriage as more important than the separate desires of either partner. The sense of

what is fair is heavily influenced by the family of origin and the social milieu, but the final definition and modifications have to be worked out repeatedly in each marriage. In today's world each couple negotiates its own code of justice."[42] Judith S. Wallerstein and Sandra Blakeslee

While God created the *institution* of marriage, it's up to us to create or re-create our own unique experience. [There is an activity to begin this process at the end of the chapter.] Even if we have been married for a while and experiencing difficulties, we can begin anew. Here is a reminder about creative power:

> "Every created thing in the contingent world is made up of many and varied atoms, and its existence is dependent on the composition of these. In other words, through the divine creative power a conjunction of simple elements taketh place so that from this composition a distinct organism is produced. The existence of all things is based upon this principle."[43] 'Abdu'l-Bahá

We can draw on rich and diverse sources for developing possibilities to consider for our marriage:

- Bahá'í teachings and other spiritual sources
- Prayer and inspiration; devotional gatherings about marriage and family
- Our own unique characters, personalities, needs, and wishes
- Marriage enrichment books and courses
- Other married couples
- Input from Spiritual Assemblies
- Consultation with professionals

We have tremendous power and latitude in doing this creative work within the framework of the larger spiritual institution of marriage. We are creating something new in the world that *has never existed before*. A marriage is greater than simply the sum of the two of us as individuals who comprise it.

Using words to state what we are committed to creating or re-creating is powerful. We can think specifically about what is important to both of us and consider the actions that will make our marriage more successful. The more specific we are in stating what we want in our marriage, and in clarifying the actions we commit to carry out, the more we will discover our shared vision and priorities. *It's important that this visioning not include blaming or criticizing each other for what has or has not happened in the past!*

For example, we might write down that we are committed to praying as a couple at least once a week, more often when possible. Fulfilling this commitment then releases positive energy into our relationship. It's generally harder to criticize or fight with someone we pray together with regularly.

As challenges come up throughout our life, it will empower us to look at our commitments. When we are tired, the car has mechanical problems, the bills are due, we disagree about who is going to clean the bathroom, the kids are annoying each other, and it all just seems too much, remembering our commitments can restore some of our balance. They remind us of what is most important to both of us, and when we look at them, it prompts us to resume some of the beneficial actions that we may have stopped doing.

Our statement of commitments can also be useful in making choices and decisions. For instance, if we have a commitment to spend time in service activities beyond the ones we do inside of our home, we may choose to forgo another activity and do service instead. In a letter on behalf of Shoghi Effendi, is the concept that the "true basis of unity is service".[44] If we're having a conflict between us, then we can look to see if there is a commitment or service we are not carrying out with each other or with others. Re-starting the activity may prevent annoyances and larger disagreements. Here is guidance:

> "Bahá'u'lláh has upheld marriage as a most sacred and praiseworthy institution, and surely there is no better or more beautiful bond that can unite the hearts of two people than a common love for God and His work."[45] On behalf of Shoghi Effendi

> "... [T]he House of Justice feels it most essential for your husband and you to understand that marriage can be a source of well-being, conveying a sense of security and spiritual happiness. However, it is not something that just happens. For marriage to become a haven of contentment it requires the cooperation of the marriage partners themselves, and the assistance of their families...."[46] On behalf of the Universal House of Justice

At this stage, we may know items that we want to go ahead and note, but we will be gentle and let the ideas flow over a period of a few weeks. As we then strive to carry out our commitments, it will assist us in affirming that our marriage is a strong and viable entity.

Couple Actions

1. Write a brief statement of what we want our marriage to be like in the future after we have invested time and effort into new words and actions with each other. This can be like a "mission statement" to strive toward.

2. Create a visual display of the areas of our marriage and family that we appreciate. Create another visual display of what new elements we might want to add to our marriage and family life that we used to do or that we want newly included. Display ideas could include making a collection of

photos, creating a video, gathering a few objects, or making a collage (cutting pictures and words from various sources and gluing them onto a sheet of paper or cardboard; written words can be added, too.). This could be expanded into a family activity with children if appropriate and useful.

3. Set up a written or electronically generated document that we can both use easily. Put this title at the top: "Creating Our Marriage Commitments". Pray together and then record a few current ideas of commitments we could make that will enliven our marriage. We are wise to avoid evaluating or doing much editing of them at this stage, but certainly we can consider beginning to carry them out. Throughout the rest of the book, we will continue to add to our list. We will complete it at the end of the book. Examples: "We will pray together three times a week"; "We will go on a monthly fun date"; or "We will host or attend a regular devotional gathering".

Couple Reflection and Consultation

1. Are we committed to regularly invest energy in improving the quality of our marriage? What re-generates that energy when it dips low?
2. What is beneficial for us in writing down our commitments?
3. What resistance to this activity is arising? Does it feel like there is a significant gap between what exists now and what we envision? How can we respond to the resistance and the gap and keep going?
4. What seem to be some challenges that might arise or are arising in carrying out commitments?
5. Who could assist us to navigate these challenges?

Chapter 6: Considering Aspects of Marriage and Family

Organic Growth and Union

Our marriage is growing organically, so it requires regular tending and care. Consider this quotation:

> "And above all other unions is that between human beings, especially when it cometh to pass in the love of God. Thus is the primal oneness made to appear; thus is laid the foundation of love in the spirit. It is certain that such a marriage as yours will cause the bestowals of God to be revealed."[47] 'Abdu'l-Bahá

Someone reflects on this concept:

> "When a marriage takes place, we, as 'Abdu'l-Bahá says, come together and create a condition of union, which means we create a new entity, a new organism. This new organism is marriage, and this organism, this marriage, has to mature and grow up like any other organism. At one level it is like a child. At another level it is like an adolescent. At another level it is like an adult. Therefore, of the three entities of the wife, the husband, and the marriage, the one that is in most need of protection in the beginning is the marriage itself. In essence, marriage is the first baby of the couple, and the second baby is the first child. The first baby we give birth to is the marriage, and at the beginning, this marriage is very fragile. It needs attention and nourishment and care. It needs to be helped to grow, to become strong. It then must go through the next phase, which is the phase of adolescence in which rebellion and arguments and power struggles often take

place, like any teenager with the parents. And finally, it reaches the next stage, which is the stage of maturity. ...

"Because marriage is a union, it therefore has to have a special quality, a special characteristic. ... The majority of people do not have a notion of what the fundamental characteristic of a marriage should be, and this is primarily because they think of marriage simply as two individuals who love each other. And by 'love each other', they mean that they are attracted to each other, that they smell good to one another, that there are 'good vibes' between them, that they satisfy each other's needs, cry on each other's shoulders, laugh together, etc. They think that is love. Consequently, the fundamental characteristic that makes a union possible is not present. And what is that? That, of course, is unity. Most marriages do not create conditions of unity. And most marriages will not create conditions of unity because people do not understand what unity is all about.

"'Abdu'l-Bahá says in one of His prayers about marriage, for example: 'Glory be unto Thee, oh my God! Verily, this Thy servant and this Thy maidservant have gathered under the shadow of Thy mercy and they are united through Thy favor and generosity.' The first matter of marriage is unity. But what does unity mean? Well, unity does not mean that the husband and wife agree all of the time. Unity does not mean that they always think the same way. They may think the same way; they may not. Unity does not mean that they have the same appetites, or the same orientation, or the same sex drive, or the same levels of comfort and discomfort. Those are all the icing on the cake, so to speak. But these are not elements of unity.

"The first and foremost, or the greatest, aspect of what creates unity is that the relationship is just. ... Justice means that the husband and the wife have the same opportunities for development, for growth, and for becoming.... [W]e have to create conditions in the home in which the woman and the man both feel that they are being treated with justice. We each need somebody to encourage us. When there are things we need to change, perhaps things that we do not like about ourselves, it makes such a difference for somebody to say, 'My beloved, you are magnificent because of this and that and that'. It gives us courage to act upon our process of transformation. The act of encouragement is an expression of justice in which you give *courage* to another human to change him or herself. ...

"Fostering the condition of justice is not all that easy; ...the prerequisite for unity is justice. Bahá'u'lláh says that the purpose of justice is appearance of unity. But, what is the prerequisite for justice? The prerequisite for justice is the condition of equality. We need to create a marriage of equals, for that marriage to be just."[48] H. B. Danesh

A wife reflects about the fair division of tasks in their home:

"Whoever is best at a task should do that and be supported fully by the other partner. One manages the bills, the other cooks the meals, or does the laundry. Sharing these household tasks makes things and routines easier, but if the other wishes to break out of the usual role, we also support this 100%! For example, my husband will cook a great spaghetti sauce or Chicken a la King meal on occasion, when I am tired of cooking. Generally, though, I love cooking and he does the clean-up.

"For family business, we also have a 'dead file', which contains detailed instructions of all assets, debts, wills, and so on, so that the other is not lost in a tangle of financial affairs if and when one of us dies unexpectedly. We like to support one another's preferences for music and the arts and other things that might be enjoyable to the other. This causes us to get out

of our comfort zones. Heavy yard work is shared, but the garden is my domain, while the lawn is my husband's."

Honoring Sacredness

Every marriage is the beginning of a new family, and in the Bahá'í teachings, the family is the most basic unit of society. Establishing and maintaining marriages and families that are united, healthy, and full of vitality are therefore essential elements for the advancement of society. In addition to having physical, emotional, and intellectual aspects, marriage is designed to be spiritual as a lasting bond between two souls for eternity. Here is some guidance:

> "Marriage is a very sacred institution. Bahá'u'lláh said its purpose is to promote unity. [We] are trying to create a high moral standard, and reinstate the sanctity of marriage."[49] On behalf of Shoghi Effendi

> "Bahá'ís should be profoundly aware of the sanctity of marriage and should strive to make their marriages an eternal bond of unity and harmony. This requires effort and sacrifice and wisdom and self-abnegation."[50] On behalf of the Universal House of Justice

As we think about how to maintain the sacredness of our union, praying and serving together are concepts that arise. The second quotation above lists other factors. One of these is sacrifice. We both sacrifice our time to work, serve, help family members, look after our physical well-being, shop, cook, and more. However, this sacrifice usually flows best when we each value the other's efforts and choices. We must be equal partners in our marriage.

Wisdom tells us that if one of us does all the sacrificing and the other does little or none, the result is disharmony, which can lead to disrespect and resentment. It's vital for us to agree on the priorities for how we spend our time. When we think about sacrifice, it must wisely lead to the greater good, a positive outcome for us and our family, and often beneficial for others as well. If we unwisely sacrifice to the point that our well-being is an issue, we have robbed our marriage and family of our full participation. It's vital that we encourage and strive for balance, moderation, and caring for each other's physical, mental, emotional, and spiritual condition.

As we assess the quality of our marriage, we see that there is the potential for a regular flow of selfless service to each other, as well as to our children. This mutual support can then lead to selfless service outward to others. This for us is the heart of "self-abnegation". We shift our heads away from our device screens and social media posts as well as our self-centered concerns. We notice that we need to support each other by cooking, making love, consulting about family and work challenges, and socializing with each other and others. We must pay attention to what is going on with each other, so we notice each other's needs and ensure those needs are met. Thoughtfulness, kindness, caring, love, and more are the companion qualities for carrying out "self-abnegation".

Both Physical and Spiritual

When we pass on to the next world, our marriage becomes solely a spiritual union. However, in this world, our marriage is a blend of physical and spiritual elements. There is no clear demarcation for what counts as physical and what counts as spiritual—they are integrated. Here is guidance:

> "... [T]he union must be a true relationship, a spiritual coming together as well as a physical one, so that throughout every phase of life, and in all the worlds of God, their union will endure; for this real oneness is a gleaming out of the love of God."[51] 'Abdu'l-Bahá

"... [H]usband and wife should be united both physically and spiritually, that they may ever improve the spiritual life of each other, and may enjoy everlasting unity throughout all the worlds of God."[52] 'Abdu'l-Bahá

Here are some examples:

- We could do dishes with one washing and one drying, which is a physical act. However, we are practicing the spiritual quality of cooperation. Our conversation during the process might also include spiritual themes.
- With managing our household, we keep physical things in order as needed, and at the same time, we also practice cleanliness, respect, responsibility, and many more spiritual character qualities.
- Money is a physical entity. However, there are spiritual principles connected to it, such as trustworthiness, generosity, moderation, compassion, and thriftiness.
- Sexual intimacy is yet another example. Clearly there are many physical components to it. However, ideally sex is more satisfying and life-enhancing when we practice spiritual qualities such as love, respect, patience, flexibility, enthusiasm, and equality. Sexual intercourse can be considered an act of unity, another spiritual concept foundational in the Bahá'í teachings.

Someone reflects:

"It seems to me that primary reasons to marry include having a spiritual relationship and to deeply embrace the development of virtues necessary for marriage and family life. Marriage is a spiritual companionship that continues to evolve, reinforced by each partner and both of us together abiding by the will of God. Our souls' progress throughout eternity is contingent on our acquisition of virtues, expressed through 'pure and goodly deeds.' Marriage is a fortress where prayer, encouragement,

love of each other, and the love of God, help us acquire and cultivate virtues necessary for the development of our eternal soul and for the betterment of this world."

Being Friends

A key element of our commitment to one another is the quality of our friendship. Being friends means that we are connecting, sharing, and caring about one another. We are in each other's corner, looking out for one another, and sharing most aspects of our lives together. Here is guidance:

> "The Lord...hath made woman and man to abide with each other in the closest companionship, and to be even as a single soul. They are two helpmates, two intimate friends, who should be concerned about the welfare of each other. If they live thus, they will pass through this world with perfect contentment, bliss, and peace of heart, and become the object of divine grace and favor in the Kingdom of heaven."[53] 'Abdu'l-Bahá

> "...[M]arriage should lead to a profound friendship of spirit...."[54] On behalf of Shoghi Effendi

When our marriage is challenged, it can feel like we have lost our friendship. The ability to talk about everything and feel like we are loyal and caring companions may have lessened. Here is sharing about why friendship in marriage is valuable to these two people:

"Friendship is what makes us enjoy being with our partner. Friendship helps my marriage partner and I communicate, and want to spend time together, be of service, and work toward common goals."

"To provide a fortress for well-being, a defense from the harshness of the outside world, if marriage partners are friends first, then they become aware of each other's strengths and weaknesses and help the other grow at their own pace."

In marriages throughout history, friendship has often not been a factor that couples and families have taken into consideration. However, many experts now recognize its value:

> "...[H]appy marriages are based on a deep friendship. By this I mean a mutual respect for and enjoyment of each other's company. These couples tend to know each other intimately—they are well versed in each other's like, dislikes, personality quirks, hopes, and dreams. They have an abiding regard for each other and express this fondness not just in the big ways but through small gestures day in and day out. ... Friendship fuels the flames of romance because it offers the best protection against feeling adversarial toward your spouse. ... In the strongest marriages, husband and wife share a deep sense of meaning. They don't just 'get along'—they also support each other's hopes and aspirations and build a sense of purpose into their lives together."[55] John M. Gottman and Nan Silver

> "Usually the friendship aspect of one's marriage gets buried over time, under the burdens and responsibilities of life, work, and family. When asked if they feel like they are friends, the average couple would say yes. But then it gets complicated. They might realize that they don't always treat one another as they would their same-sex friends. They think of having a night out 'with friends' as somehow different from a night out 'with my spouse.' Some couples assume that they must be friends simply because most of

the time they act friendly toward one another and they don't think of each other as enemies. But friendship is more than friendliness. (You can be friendly toward a neighbor you rarely see.) Friendship is in many ways the foundation of a marital relationship. Happy couples realize that. Less happy couples usually have forgotten it."[56] Paul Coleman

"Highly happy couples aren't just spending time together because they are happy; a big part of the reason they're so happy is that they are spending time together! When these couples are in a season of being at odds with each other—when they are experiencing friction or hurt feelings—they solve it by spending more time together instead of less. ... Just as proximity leads to the closest friendships, proximity in marriage leads to the closest couples. The cause is spending quality time together; the effect is happiness. ... [T]hey act as if their marriages are, first and foremost, friendships. And not just any friendship. A happy spouse looks at the other person as their best and closest friend—a friend they want to stay close to no matter what."[57] Shaunti Feldhahn

Working Through Extended Family Experiences

Our marriage and children connect to an extended family, and the relationships we have had with family members in the past and have now, can affect the health and functioning of our union. "Family" can be a broad term that includes in-laws, half, step, adopted, and foster members.

We can identify benefits of being part of our families of origin, generating gratitude in our hearts. When we recall special memories, we might remember our family sharing fun activities, a parent comforting us after a disappointment, or a grandparent sharing timeless wisdom. Perhaps our parents have financially assisted with our education. Maybe they are wonderful grandparents to our children.

As we reflect, we will discover that we gained both positive and negative learning from our families. Even where there are many negatives, we may now see how we grew from the difficulties. When we consider our biological parents, it's wise to recognize that without them, we would not exist, nor would we be who we are. If we were adopted, fostered, or had other parent or caregiver experiences, these are also an opportunity for reflection and learning to see how the experiences shaped us and influence us today.

Each generation learns from the one before, and each one can improve on what happened in the past. Courage and perseverance are needed to move toward healing, to experience gratitude for blessings, and to take thoughtful action to greatly enhance our present and future happiness.

We may have already addressed and resolved mental or emotional issues that resulted from childhood experiences. However, there may still be lingering ones that are affecting us in our marriage, from which we can still heal, learn, and grow. For example, many adults are affected by their parents' poor relationship and subsequent divorces. If our parents divorced, we may have had to learn that their choice to split up was their decision alone. It was not our fault, and it does not mean there's anything wrong with us. We do not have to follow their path, and the relationship we have with them as an adult can be one of our own choosing. We may have also experienced violence or abuse as a child, and words or actions in our partner can remind us of early trauma and trigger a stress, anger, grief, or anxiety reaction in the present.

As we resolve and heal, we are less likely to repeat harmful childhood patterns with each other or our children. We can notice how our partner reminds of us a parent in positive or negative ways and separate our reactions in the present from experiences in the past. We may also more readily recognize where we missed observing healthy parental interactions, and we may choose to get to know and observe other couples for more positive modeling.

Unresolved emotions and harmful thinking patterns tend to re-surface over time, potentially causing negative interactions between us. There are, of course, many ways to heal. Effective healing and personal growth depend on our search for insights, inner strengths, circumstances, available resources, and inclination to seek assistance.

Experts such as Harville Hendrix advise those in a challenged marriage, "When two people treat each other the way they did in happier times, they begin to identify each other as a source of pleasure once again…".[58] Hendrix encourages couples to share with each other a few positive and specific ways their partners can please them. Carrying these out and interacting with a spirit of goodwill toward each other can help us to move back toward being friends and allies. This improvement in positive interactions opens the possibility of healing childhood wounds and being caring adults with each other in the present.

The healing actions listed below have assisted many people. We can assess whether each one related to family members of all types is wise and healthy for us to do or not:

- Pray for the healing of pain or challenges we have from experiences with them
- Pray for unity with them
- Show love to them through our actions, while keeping ourselves healthy
- Appreciate the emotional, material, and spiritual gifts we've received from them, and express our gratitude to them

- Initiate positive communication with them, where this is wise and safe, and seek to understand them
- Stop all negative forms of communication with them
- Spend time with them, if this contributes to healing
- If interactions with them in the present are very unhealthy, it may be necessary to spend time apart from them
- Pray for forgiveness for them for any of their behaviors that disrupted our lives; pray for forgiveness for ourselves, if we acted harmfully in situations
- In particularly painful situations, search our hearts for reasons to be grateful for the learning and growth that resulted from the experiences, particularly if we see where the learning has benefited others
- Seek professional help where needed
- Write a letter to them; after reflection and if written with wholehearted effort toward increasing unity, prayerfully read it aloud to them and discuss it, or send it to them—if these actions would be fruitful; alternatively, write it and then tear it up or burn it, to visualize the resolution of this issue and provide a sense of closure

Even if our family members are no longer alive, or we are unable to contact them, we may still benefit from trying some of the reflections and activities above.

Couple Actions

1. Grow a plant, flower, or tree from a seed or seedling. Note and reflect on what we need to do so the plant thrives and matures. How does this organic growth concept relate to growing the strength and health of our marriage?

2. Identify a place in our home and arrange and decorate it as "sacred space". Reflect on our views of what is sacred and

why. How can we effectively use this space for spiritual activities that benefit us and our family?

3. Identify one activity of our lives that is very physical and choose a spiritual quality to begin pairing with it.

4. Each of us share a brief story about how a friendship contributed positively to our lives. Identify aspects of friendship in the stories that we want to incorporate into our marriage.

5. Each of us make and share a list of three specific positive actions we would appreciate receiving from each other. We will carry these out for an agreed period and then reflect together on the outcome.

6. Review the list of family healing actions in the chapter. Choose one or two to carry out as needed. If more actions are needed, develop a plan to carry them out.

Couple Reflection and Consultation

1. What does it mean to us to participate in a "sacred" institution? How can we act to increasingly sanctify it?
2. How does fairness (justice) contribute to our unity? What do we want to improve?
3. How does equality contribute to our unity? What do we want to improve?
4. What are our views of and feelings about the effort needed to maintain our marriage?
5. When have we seen sacrifice or selflessness positively affect our married life? Are we both taking these types of actions, or is there an imbalance? How could we address any imbalance?

6. What examples do we see in our life where we integrate physical and spiritual factors?
7. What are some of the qualities of a good friend?
8. Why is friendship important in marriage?
9. What signs are there in our marriage that we are friends?
10. How is it benefiting us to be friends?
11. What aspects of friendship do we want to strengthen?
12. What are we grateful for from our growing-up years? From our parents now?
13. Where are we tested in maintaining unity with family members? How can we improve this?
14. What behaviors do we each do that remind us of poor patterns in our parents? How do we respond to these? How could we shift the patterns in a positive direction? Are we able to forgive our parents for their behaviors? Forgive ourselves for contributing to family disunity? How could this healing affect our marriage?
15. How can we continue to heal from any negative experiences while growing up or with family members throughout our marriage and now?

Chapter 7: Preserving Our Marriage

Keeping Our Marriage Alive

The Research Department of the Universal House of Justice speaks about "the importance of preserving the marriage bond."[59] When we think about the concept of "preserving", it can mean to keep it alive or in existence and to make it lasting and protected from harm or injury. We can pray for the preservation and protection of our marriage and family:

> "Immeasurably exalted art Thou, O Lord! Protect us from what lieth in front of us and behind us, above our heads, on our right, on our left, below our feet and every other side to which we are exposed. Verily Thy protection over all things is unfailing."[60] The Báb

Bahá'u'lláh says that marriage is a "fortress for well-being and salvation".[61] Fortresses are known to have many characteristics, and here someone provides perspectives on this concept:

"A radical change the Bahá'í Teachings call for is in our perspective on the nature and purpose of marriage. We often think of marriage as a 'fortress for (our own) well-being.' This view, definitely the predominant one in our society, is a self-centered approach. The Bahá'í Writings imply that God created marriage for the betterment of the whole human race. If we do not recognize this, our efforts to make ourselves happy will only lead to our misery.

"In general, a fortress is often not a place of peace and tranquility. A fortress is often a stronghold in a battlefield, a particularly strategic spot on the landscape that requires protection from enemy forces. As I understand Bahá'u'lláh's vision for a spiritual World Order, there is no school more

important than the family, no teachers more necessary than the mother and the father, and no pupils more worthwhile and critical than the children. That strategic spot on the landscape is none other than the future of these kids.

"It's the family's responsibility to secure their children against the manifold forces of evil in the world by imbuing them with the love of God and the knowledge of His teachings for this Day. These children will, in their turn, grow up to be the redeemers of humanity, the dawn-breakers of a peaceful world civilization, the bricklayers of a great peace beyond our wildest dreams. As the challenges and difficulties of the world they inherit from us must increase, so we need to empower them to surmount heights we could never dream of, and surpass us in all the paths of service to God and humanity. That is the primary goal of this 'fortress' for the 'well-being' of the whole human race.

"This fortress, if it understands its role properly, should constantly devote itself to the good of all people. Each member of the family needs to be aware of his mission as a servant of God and humanity and work unitedly with the others to expand the borders of the country of God's Love. A spiritual family will naturally collectively arise to promote spiritual thought and action. Children can be progressively encouraged to share their spirituality with their fellow human beings from the time they are first able to speak and reason. The parents can first lead their children by example, and then systematically instruct them as to how to do what they are doing. Action is the primary text in this school, and words but supplements to it."[62]

This quotation continues the theme:

"… [Y]oung women and men become acutely conscious of the exhortations of the Supreme Pen to 'enter into wedlock' that they may 'bring forth one who will make mention of Me amid My servants'…. …This generation of

youth will form families that secure the foundations of flourishing communities. Through their growing love for Bahá'u'lláh and their personal commitment to the standard to which He summons them will their children imbibe the love of God, 'commingled with their mother's milk', and always seek the shelter of His divine law."[63]
Universal House of Justice

Marriage and Family As a Service

As we assess the strength of our marriage fortress, the Bahá'í teachings give us some guidance on setting priorities and the importance of having a broad view of service that includes marriage and family:

"... [T]he importance of marriage lieth in the bringing up of a richly blessed family, so that with entire gladness they may, even as candles, illuminate the world."[64]
'Abdu'l-Bahá

"... [T]he unity of your family should take priority over any other consideration. Bahá'u'lláh came to bring unity to the world, and a fundamental unity is that of the family. Therefore, we must believe that the Faith is intended to strengthen the family, not weaken it. For example, service to the Cause should not produce neglect of the family. It is important for you to arrange your time so that your family life is harmonious and your household receives the attention it requires."[65] On behalf of the Universal House of Justice

"... [E]very aspect of a person's life is an element of his or her service to Bahá'u'lláh: the love and respect one has for one's parents; the pursuit of one's education; the nurturing of good health; the acquiring of a trade or profession; one's behavior towards others and the upholding of a high moral standard; one's marriage and the bringing up of one's children; one's activities in teaching the Faith and the building up the strength of the Bahá'í community, whether this be in such simple matters as attending the Nineteen Day Feast or the observance of Bahá'í Holy Days, or in more demanding tasks required by service in the administration of the Faith; and, not least, to take time each day to read the Writings and say the Obligatory Prayer, which are the source of growing spiritual strength, understanding, and attachment to God."[66] Universal House of Justice

As we develop a marriage that serves us and our family, we can also look outward to serving others as encouraged by the Universal House of Justice. Sometimes outward service develops us and our marriage, and sometimes we must do strengthening first; there is no exact formula. Here is guidance:

"He hopes that from now on you and your dear husband will be able to serve the Faith unitedly and devotedly together, as that is the highest form of Bahá'í cooperation in marriage."[67] On behalf of Shoghi Effendi

"Shoghi Effendi described 'service' as 'the true basis' of family unity and called upon the family members to 'arise with renewed effort to teach the Faith'. The Guardian's secretary writing on his behalf to one couple who had 'jointly undertaken a most successful teaching tour' stated: 'This bond of common service to the Cause which is so closely uniting your hearts...has proved such an effective solution of your personal problems.' And the hope was expressed that this 'bond' would be 'further cemented by the passing of years' and through the couple's 'increased and joint participation in the teaching work'."[68] Research Department of the Universal House of Justice

Marriage and Our Well-Being in the Physical World

Couples share their approaches to physical well-being in their marriages:

"We have discovered after some 40 years of marriage that walking is enjoyable to both of us, a way to spend quality time together, and exercise for our physical well-being."

"We enjoy making time to play together, to make love, to just be. We create regular islands of time just to enjoy each other. We strive to be affectionate every day, providing gentle touch that isn't always sexualized."

"We have searched to learn what gives us health and well-being. For example, good food, healthy diet, proper and regular exercise, encouraging each other to maintain healthy practices, and regular check-ups with our doctor and dentist. We make sure that the house is maintained, there is physical comfort, and we deal with maintenance problems as they arise. We keep the cars maintained for safety. Making our environment beautiful, orderly, and clean impacts on our physical well-being. We appreciate a comfortable bed and a quiet environment without TV being on during the day. We keep physically busy with maintenance of the home, as well as house cleaning, which can give us a good physical workout. Whenever possible, we get out into the fresh air, enjoying canoe trips, bicycle riding, and long walks."

Managing our energy is one aspect of physical well-being that can often affect our interactions. Each of us has our own "energy battery", and each of us has actions to take and not take to maintain the energy at a level for optimal functioning.

If we need time alone to re-charge (sometimes referred to as being an introvert), then it's wise to ensure that we look after that need. It's good to communicate about the need in a way that doesn't cause the other person to feel hurt or abandoned. If we need time with other people to re-charge (sometimes referred to as being an extrovert), then we may need time with friends or out at a spiritual or social occasion. Sometimes it will work to do this together, but not always.

If our batteries get too low, it's easier for conflict to occur. Our thinking can become scattered or foggy, our decisions are lower quality, and our actions are less focused. We feel generally exhausted or at least struggle to be as active as we want. Someone shares their experience:

"We have a commitment to attend the community Nineteen-Day Feast together. We participate in the spiritual readings and community consultation. However, consistently part-way through the social portion, my husband often insists on leaving. I get upset at him, and we end our time with the community in disunity. Now that I'm starting to understand that he is an extreme introvert, I'm realizing that by the time we are into the social portion, his energy battery is running close to empty, particularly if he's had a full day at work first. This insight is assisting me to be more compassionate toward him when he expresses a need to leave. Understanding this aspect about him also prompts me to arrange for some quiet time for him before we go."

As we evaluate our personal and marriage well-being, and as we consider our level of activity with work, home, and community service, we can assess what is important (high, medium, or low), what is urgent for us to participate in, and how much energy will be required. We can then consciously plan how to keep our batteries charged and our marriage well-being and family unity protected.

If we are more inclined to re-charge alone, we may also have the tendency to need internal thinking time before talking about an issue together. If we prefer to be with others to re-charge our energy, we may be more inclined to process a matter externally with words. Allowing each other this different approach, if applicable, can be vital for harmony in consultations.

Marriage and Our Spiritual Well-Being and Salvation

As Bahá'u'lláh was quoted at the beginning of the chapter, marriage is connected to our "salvation". This is a word that has a complexity of meanings and concepts associated with it, such as spiritual well-being, eternal life, and grace from God. Here are reflections from some couples on this concept of spiritual well-being:

"In the recited verse at the union of marriage Bahá'u'lláh asks us to say, 'We all, verily, abide by the Will of God'. What is the Will of God? Well, one way we could think of it is as divine education. It's everything: every atom, every event, and every person we learn from. This learning develops our souls in understanding, applying, and realizing God's will for us, as reflected in His Word and Reality, and we are perpetually becoming who we are destined to be.

"A husband or wife ought to be that person who walks with us on that path, who is a true partner in spirit, or soul companion. It's not necessarily a destined person, as in the 'only one soulmate' myth, but there are certain souls who have similar capacity, have developed key qualities, are going in the same direction, and with whom we have a shared vision and complementary path of service. We must serve together, and we must learn how to communicate truthfully and wisely. A true marriage serves the Bahá'í Faith and humanity."

"When our daughters were toddlers, we began morning family prayers. Our understanding was that if we wanted our children to grow to love and depend on prayer, we needed to be examples for them. In the process, our own marriage was more

unified. We were also committed that when one of us was traveling, we knew that we were praying for each other and that we were united on a spiritual plane though not physically. Service to the Faith, whether teaching activities, community gatherings, or children's classes, was the center of our family life. When having to make choices, teaching opportunities was the priority."

"We carve out a time, usually a weekend morning, where we dedicate a half hour to an hour to focus on our marriage. We are currently reading the book 'Mindful Matrimony' by Raymond and Furugh Switzer. One of us will read aloud. If there is a phrase or sentence that makes us pause, we stop and enter into a discussion or even a consultation. One week we discussed the spiritual mission of marriage and how it takes work from both of us to truly develop each other's spirituality. We truly relish the intimacy of this time together, and it has taken the discipline and practice of setting the time aside to achieve such depth."

"There are three practices we do that keep our marriage strong and healthy. One is reading the Family Life compilation (2008). Another is setting aside time each week for a consultation to raise more challenging issues. This gives us a time for prayer and when we can lovingly consult. The third is that we serve together."

"Marriage is a fortress where through prayer, encouragement, love of each other and the love of God, necessary virtues are acquired and cultivated for the development of our soul and for the betterment of this world."

"A fortress for well-being can provide health, stability, nurturing, reflection, action, consultation, and a love bond that extends to heightened prayerfulness. Involvement in key community activities then offers us the possibility of accessing

part of God's grace. This involvement enables us to transcend our own limitations, and how much more so in a healthy, spiritually blessed marriage. Such a fortress is a protection from the challenges of this world."

Couple Actions

1. Use a large piece of paper and draw a fortress to represent us and our marriage, and then draw and write in marriage and family activities that could happen within it. Circle the activities that we are currently doing. Put a box around the activities that we would like to add. Consult about how and when to add them.

2. Establish a weekly or monthly family devotional gathering. Consult about whether to have only our family present, whether to invite others with the family hosting, or to alternate. Consult as well about who will do the necessary home and hosting preparation activities.

Couple Reflection and Consultation

1. How do we relate our marriage to the metaphor of a fortress?
2. How do we see our marriage as a fortress for us as a couple? As a family?
3. How do we see our marriage as a fortress for others?
4. What are some aspects of our marriage that we think are contributing to our "well-being"? (consider physical, mental, emotional, and spiritual factors) Where could we improve? How?
5. What are some aspects of our marriage that we think are demonstrating "salvation"? Where could we improve? How?
6. What connects us spiritually? Where could we improve? How?

7. What is our attitude toward service within our home for each other? For our children?
8. What is our attitude toward offering hospitality to others? Toward participating separately in service activities in the community? Participating together?
9. What service attracts us to participate in together as a couple? How could we carry it out in harmony? How could we involve our children?

Chapter 8: Communicating with One Another

It's often a challenge for couples and families—and every human being—to communicate smoothly. We gain our experience with communication from our families and friends while growing up, the culture around us, and through relationship experiences. Sometimes we build positive skills through these experiences, and sometimes we learn poor habits or miss learning important ways of communicating. Each of us in a marriage comes with a history, so the blend together can make communication tough to navigate.

Sometimes we may be happy with how our interactions go, and at other times not so much. The skillfulness with which we handle these interactions directly affects the quality of our lives. When our words lead to disunity and pain, our stress levels spike upward. The more our communications with one another build unity and understanding instead, the stronger our relationship will be.

With practice, we can improve and even excel at communicating with one another. We can contribute to harmonious communications when we provide each other enough time to speak, and we listen with respect. This quotation may inspire us:

> "When the light of faith is kindled in the lamp of the heart and soul, its spreading rays illumine every limb of the body. When this resplendent light shineth forth through the medium of the tongue, it is made manifest in the powers of speech and utterance. When its beams fall upon the eyes, insight and true vision are revealed, and when it stirreth the ear, it bestoweth attentive hearing. When this light sheddeth its radiance upon the mind, it leadeth to the recognition of the All-Merciful, and when it setteth aglow

the limbs, it findeth expression in purity and the worship of God."[69] 'Abdu'l-Bahá

Here is a goal to aim for:

"Communication that comes from the heart has the ability to transform. Heart-to-heart communication helps us get past our separate realities to the common ground of mental health. It helps our thinking evolve and helps us see issues in a different perspective. When two people are communicating heart-to-heart, they always feel more respect and caring afterward than before they spoke."[70] Richard Carlson and Joseph Bailey

When Communications Go Poorly

Despite all good intentions and hopes for a peaceful relationship or home, most couples find that they are challenged at times with difficult or hurtful communications. We may end up in disagreements or fights without meaning to or wanting to, and we struggle to understand what went wrong. Disunity in our marriage results from these types of negative and destructive words and interactions.

It's wise for us to realize that each of us has a responsibility to apply self-discipline to govern our words and related behaviors. We can effectively observe what words and behaviors contribute to harmony and which ones escalate into conflict between us and thereby reduce couple connection. We must remember that we are two adults and not parents to each other. We can also observe the effect of our words and behaviors on our children and see where the outcome is beneficial or harmful. As we observe our interactions, we can understand where change needs to happen.

Some negative interactions that may be issues between us at times are listed below.

- Excluding from important decisions
- Robbing of the opportunity to help or be of service
- Questioning judgment
- Giving advice without asking first if it's welcome
- Ignoring advice
- Implying or accusing of inadequacy
- Making unrealistic demands of time and energy
- Overreacting
- Ignoring needs
- Focusing on what did not get done; ignoring what did
- Withholding praise
- Using a harsh tone
- Valuing others' needs as more important
- Undermining wishes
- Condescending
- Name-calling
- Belittling work
- Showing little or no interest in their interests
- Criticizing family
- Criticizing in front of others
- Ignoring
- Interpreting them to others
- Comparing
- Dismissing
- Being sarcastic
- Focusing on own unhappiness
- Expecting other to make them happy
- Making "you" blaming statements
- Globalizing
- Generalizing
- Therapizing[71]

(Summarized from Patricia Love and Steven Stosny)

Research conducted at The Gottman Institute with couples shows that these are some highly damaging behaviors:

1. *Harsh Start-up:* Sudden, negative attack or sarcasm, a form of contempt.
2. *Criticism:* Negative words about personality or an attack on the character of a partner; example, "You are so irresponsible."
3. *Defensiveness:* Reacts and blames a partner; example, "I am not! You are always picking on me!"
4. *Contempt:* Puts partner down through body language, or words that are sneering, sarcastic, patronizing, or self-righteous; example, "You're such an idiot! "Can't you do anything right?"
5. *Stonewalling:* Withdraws to avoid communication, thereby shutting partner out.
6. *Flooding:* Recipient of harsh criticism and contempt often experiences a protective reaction where physical symptoms overwhelm (flood) the person for about 20 minutes, and effective communication shuts down.[72] (Summarized from John Gottman and Nan Silver)

Any character attack, severe criticism (rather than a calm complaint), or stubborn insistence on one's own opinion or approach will cause the darkness of disunity. When these behaviors occur during couple conversations or consultation, it sabotages a positive outcome.

When Communications Go Well

Below is an overview of how we can communicate with one another effectively.

"In the case of dialogue, with conscious effort we can choose to stay with the experience our partner is describing—even though it may feel like a blow to us—without becoming defensive, even if the events being described contradict our memory of them. This does not mean that we agree with what our partner says or how she or he remembers events. Rather, we are staying in our partner's world, disciplining ourselves to stay present and see things as he or she does, according to the way he or she remembers things. Everybody makes sense in their own world, and the feelings they may have are legitimate. Listening well, therefore, puts us into the supportive position of being able to validate our partner's feelings. What they share with us in these dialogues is of vital importance if we desire to be intimately connected to them.

"In order to keep our attention on our partner, it may help to internally 'mirror' everything they say, to get and feel their meaning. We can take this even further and, at intervals, verbally repeat to them what we are hearing, or at least the essence of it, and ask them if we are 'getting it'. This outward mirroring, or paraphrasing, not only clarifies for us that we are understanding them as they want to be understood (which is what listening is all about); they receive the added comfort and feeling of safety of knowing that they are being heard. This helps and enables them to go deeper into their experience, revealing even more of their world to us, bringing a closer and more intimate connection. It also helps the sender to understand themselves better and perhaps gain a new and objective perspective of their own feelings as they hear them mirrored back.

"After the sender has conveyed all that is in their heart around the issue and has been heard and mirrored by the receiver, if the receiver then wants to respond to things that have been said, a conscious shift of roles is appropriate. This can go back and forth several times, if necessary, but it is important not to get muddled about who is in what role, so that listening is always taking place, protecting the safe and sacred space between husband and wife from the destructive effects of arguing back and forth.

"In summary, the goal of receiving is to understand completely the truth about what the other is experiencing, sensing, understanding, feeling, associating, remembering or fearing, and/or what she or he usually does when having such feelings, and to convey to the other with words, body language and tone of voice that we are 'getting them', that they are making sense (because all feelings are real and legitimate and everybody makes sense from their own point of view). A further goal is to be able to imagine how they are feeling and to empathize with them."[73] Raymond and Furugh Switzer

The Bahá'í teachings ask us to pay attention to many factors to ensure our communications are beneficial and not harmful. Communication is multi-faceted, including such elements as what we say or write, our ability to listen well, and the quality of our understanding. Consider these principles:

"Content, volume, style, tact, wisdom, timeliness are among the critical factors in determining the effects of speech for good or evil. Consequently, the friends need ever to be conscious of the significance of this activity which so distinguishes human beings from other forms of life, and they must exercise it judiciously. Their efforts at such discipline will give birth to an etiquette of expression worthy of the approaching maturity of the human race. Just as this discipline applies to the spoken word, it applies equally to the written word...."[74] Universal House of Justice

Spiritual principles and character qualities affect virtually every communication, verbal or non-verbal, that occurs between the two of us. The purity of our motives, the degree of our truthfulness, the level of respect for ourselves and each other, the strength of our characters, the depth of our equality, and much more guide every expression. Excellence in all our interactions is usually enhanced the more character qualities we can include, such as patience, respect, and compassion. [See more about character in Chapters 11 and 12.] One of the many spiritual qualities that can gentle our communications is courtesy:

"O people of God! I admonish you to observe courtesy, for above all else it is the prince of virtues. Well is it with him who is illumined with the light of courtesy and is attired with the vesture of uprightness. Whoso is endued with courtesy hath indeed attained a sublime station."[75] Bahá'u'lláh

Here is how one couple describes and practices courteous communications:

"We have developed a consistent practice in our marriage of 'checking-in' with each other for periodic updates. These maintain our close connection with one another. We can assess our progress and direction on decisions we have made related to a project, activity, or issue. We gain understanding of each other's thoughts, feelings, desires, and beliefs when we ask open-ended questions in an encouraging and respectful tone that prompt sharing. Some examples of questions we use are:

- *'How are you doing?'*
- *'How did your day go?'*

- *'How can I be supportive?'*
- *'What do you see are the next steps of our project?'*
- *'What unexpected demands are pressing on you that are important for me to know?'*
- *'What do you need from me, if anything, at this point?'*
- *'It will be a big day ahead for you. How do you feel?'*

"Consistent validations of character qualities, a mindful presence, thoughtful observation, and sharing promptly keep us emotionally and spiritually connected. We make better decisions and avoid disunity. We are tuned into the pace and important aspects of each other's lives in a helpful and friendly way. This has been especially important for us when parenting young children and when we are doing home renovation projects."

Personal "check-ins" with each other may be in person, but they can also include texts and calls, especially as we are transitioning from one activity or place to another. As we greet and leave one another, communication can also be in the form of a hug or a kiss.

Here is a summary of some pointers for positive sharing and listening experiences:

- Make sure the listener is available and attentive before beginning to speak; ask "Is this a good time?"
- Minimize distractions like electronic devices or children having immediate needs
- Start communications softly and gently
- Set aside biases, prejudices, and judgments
- Ask kind and respectful questions to discern and understand the speaker's words, needs, feelings, fears, and concerns; one method: "We do this by asking cup-emptying questions starting with 'what,' 'when,' and

'how'—never 'why,' which puts each other on the defensive."[76] Linda Kavelin Popov

- Apply self-discipline by patiently listening and not interrupting or finishing each other's sentences, which creates a safe space for someone to speak
- Listen attentively, summarizing understanding back to each other and clarifying the communication as needed
- Express caring and compassion as appropriate, sincerely encouraging the other's sharing using positive facial expressions and gestures
- Speak for oneself instead of the other
- Interact in partnership as teammates, working with shared effort toward discerning truth and understanding one another better
- Sincerely affirm and show respect toward the speaker's value and contribution, using positive and acknowledging words
- Avoid words, tones of voice, or actions that communicate control, domination, or an adversarial position
- Take pause breaks when a communication is escalating toward dissension, arguments, or conflict, and resume at an agreed time and place
- Set new goals for how to communicate and act with one another

As we engage in learning-in-action with our relationship, trying out new words and actions as part of the process, some things will go smoothly, and some things won't. A communication practice that can be useful as we reflect with each other is:

- "What worked well for me was _____, and I really appreciated it."

- "What did not work as well for me was _____, and here's what might work better."

This wording keeps us in learning mode and tends to be less likely to trigger defensiveness in each other.

If we automatically feel defensiveness kick in with any interaction, we can:

- Take a deep breath and release it slowly
- Recognize it as an opportunity to listen and learn, saying "Can you tell me more about this?" or something similar
- Summarize back to each other what we think we are hearing and understanding
- Clarify as needed

Reducing what prompts defensive reactions and stopping defensive reactions quickly, both assist our communications to proceed, build understanding, and reach effective conclusions.

Sharing Our Words

The relationship between us is a unique and very intimate one, different than with others. It's likely that we know sensitive things about each other that no one else knows. Every topic related to the past, present, and future comes up in our communications.

Both of us have equal voices to speak and listen dynamically to reach an outcome we are both happy with. As we increase our ability to respect one another as equal partners, the quality of our communications improves, and we have more ability to influence and encourage each other in positive directions. Here is guidance:

> "Divine Justice demands that the rights of both sexes should be equally respected since neither is superior to the other.... Dignity before God depends, not on sex, but on

purity and luminosity of heart. Human virtues belong equally to all!"[77] 'Abdu'l-Bahá

Science has shown that men's and women's brains function differently. We are also different people with different training and learning related to communication. These factors often lead to each of us having different needs and patterns with:

- Speaking: speed, pace, and number of concepts included at one time
- Listening: focus and amount of content
- Processing/Thinking: amount of time needed and the method used (ex: verbal, written, quiet reflection)

When we begin with believing that neither of us is right or wrong and rather coming from different perspectives that we need to understand, it's easier to be patient with our communications. We can also sometimes see ways to respond to a difference playfully and with acceptance and humor rather than with criticism or frustration.

Listening Carefully to One Another

We appreciate when our partner is listening with the goal of understanding us. When we see we have been heard, we feel respected, relaxed, confident, validated, and connected to each other. With effective listening, we build understanding about what is really happening with each other, and this sharing contributes to our friendship, intimacy, and unity. Conscious listening contributes to effective consultation and problem solving together, which then reduces or prevents conflicts between us.

Below is an example of listening from a description about 'Abdu'l-Bahá that may be one we can follow.

"To the questioner He responded first with silence—an outward silence. His encouragement always was that the other should speak and He listen. There was never that eager tenseness, that restlessness so often met showing most plainly that the listener has the pat answer ready the moment he should have a chance to utter it.

"I have heard certain people described as 'good listeners', but never had I imagined such a 'listener' as 'Abdu'l-Bahá. It was more than a sympathetic absorption of what the ear received. It was as though the two individualities became one; as if He so closely identified Himself with the one speaking that a merging of spirits occurred which made a verbal response almost unnecessary, superfluous. As I write, the words of Bahá'u'lláh recur to me: 'When the sincere servant calls to Me in prayer I become the very ear with which he heareth My reply.' That was just it! 'Abdu'l-Bahá seemed to listen with my ears."[78] Howard Colby Ives

Below are three levels of conscious listening that can move us closer to 'Abdu'l-Bahá's example:

- *Level One:* Listen for content—Be able to give a concise and accurate summary of what we heard the speaker say.
- *Level Two:* Listen for the emotions—Be able to hear the emotion under the words of the speaker.
- *Level Three:* Listen for the speaker's wants and needs—Be able to hear beneath the words and the emotions for what the speaker is really asking for and needing.[79] (Summarized from Kathlyn Hendricks and Gay Hendricks)

Of course, it's also beneficial when the speaker can articulate their emotions, wants, and needs.

Character qualities such as self-discipline, patience, empathy, and compassion influence our effectiveness as listeners. Strengthening these qualities reduces interrupting and enables us to better see the topic from our partner's point of view. We will have the best outcomes when we accompany one another and avoid competing verbally or interrupting.

Being in a close relationship with someone often gives us greater sensitivity to one another's thoughts and emotions, and sometimes we can guess what the other is thinking. However, it's unwise to make assumptions about what each other thinks, feels, needs, or wants without directly asking and listening. Sometimes we can get upset when the other doesn't "read our mind" and know what to do for us, but the ability to do mind-reading is a relationship myth, and the principle in the Bahá'í teachings is to use communication and consultation to discover the truth.

Acknowledging and Encouraging

Our sincere and loving words have great power to influence and encourage one another. They can inspire us to move in positive directions, be creative, achieve goals, try new types of service to others, and much more. When we see the best in each other's hearts, minds, and souls, our words of affirmation can strengthen each other's experience of self-respect, one of the keys to happiness. These types of communications are constructive when we are open to them, and they expand the possibility of each other achieving more than we ever dreamed. They soften our hearts. Here is some guidance:

> "We can never exert the influence over others which we can exert over ourselves. If we are better, if we show love, patience, and understanding of the weakness of others, if we seek to never criticize but rather encourage, others will do likewise…."[80] On behalf of Shoghi Effendi

When we use *Character Quality Language™* to affirm specific qualities in each other, it builds love, appreciation, and happiness between us, particularly when we include specifics about the actions each other did, and we are sincere. Here are some simple examples:

- "Thank you for being (Helpful, Flexible, Truthful…) when you…."
- "I appreciate your (Courage, Respect, Patience…) when you…"
- "I love how (Accepting, Enthusiastic, Encouraging…) you are!"

Having someone notice our use of a character quality encourages us to continue. It's often easier to criticize than to see and appreciate what someone does well. It takes practice to look consciously for someone's positive actions and speak specifically about them, but it's worth the effort and very affirming for everyone involved. Using character words recognizes the gems of our hearts and souls.

Couple Actions

1. Choose an issue that is causing us some challenges and take turns sharing back and forth about it, with the listener summarizing periodically to check for understanding. The goal is to understand each other's views, not necessarily to solve the issue currently.

2. Individually, observe and make notes of when we say or do something that seems to prompt defensiveness or conflict from the other. Set personal goals for reducing these behaviors. Then practice, observe, and adjust as needed.

3. Take turns acknowledging each other for something that happened recently using Character Quality Language. Reflect together on how it feels to receive such positive words.

4. Pray, consult, and agree on some of the communication practices we commit to using consistently. We can begin to compile the list now and then keep adding to it over a few weeks. Once we have a completed list, we can consider creating a visual reminder to post in our home.

Individual and Couple Reflection and Consultation

Communication Patterns and Preferences: Reflect separately first and then together on the current health and well-being of our communication patterns and methods, what is working well, and what we want to improve. Prompting statements are below, but it may also be useful to use such methods as journal writing, artwork, poetry, or spreadsheets. If this assessment process feels overwhelming to us, then we can spread it out over an agreed timeframe or focus on one aspect of our communications that we want to improve.[81]

Consider: It may enhance your ability to complete this activity if you study the words that describe feelings in Chapter 10 that follows.

Assessment:
1. I think excellent communication between us is important because: ____.
2. I feel happy when the following actions and outcomes occur in our communications: ____.
3. I feel frustrated or unhappy when the following actions and outcomes occur in our communications: ____.
4. When I'm speaking to you, I need you to do the following so that I'm clear you are listening to me: ____. (Examples:

stop doing other things; look at me; paraphrase back to me what you think you heard me say; ...)

5. When someone listens to me respectfully, I feel ____, and I am likely to respond in this way: ____.
6. When I do not think that someone is listening to me respectfully, or he/she interrupts me, I feel ____, and I am likely to respond in this way:
7. These phrases are encouraging to me: ____.
8. These phrases are discouraging to me: ____.
9. I feel honored and appreciated when I hear phrases like this from you: ____.
10. It seems as if there is a power struggle or domination going on between us when this happens or is said: ____.
11. When I'm having difficulty talking about something, it assists me if you: ____.
12. When we appear to be starting to have a disagreement or fight, I would like us to take the following steps to prevent it from becoming a serious or destructive conflict or resulting in disunity: ____.
13. It upsets me when you speak to me in this tone of voice:
    This is when it usually seems to happen: ____.
    This is my interpretation of what it means/feels like: ____.
14. When someone speaks to me in anger or yells at me, I feel ____, and I'm likely to respond this way: ____.
15. When teased, I feel ____, and I'm likely to respond this way: ____.
16. When criticized, I feel ____, and I'm likely to respond this way: ____.
17. Criticism toward me is especially hurtful when it's about these topic areas: ____.
18. When encouraged, I feel ____, and I am likely to respond this way: ____.

19. When someone acknowledges my best qualities and notices them in action, I feel: ____, and I am likely to respond this way: ____.
20. When I'm telling a story or joke, and you fill in part of it and tell it along with me, I feel: ____, and I am likely to respond this way: ____.
21. When I am telling a story or joke and someone tries to hurry the ending or share the ending before I get to it, I feel ____, and I am likely to respond this way: ____.
22. When I think you expect me to know what you are thinking, I feel ____, and I'm likely to respond this way: ____.
23. When you do not know what I'm thinking but you act as if you do, I feel ____, and I'm likely to respond this way: ____.
24. When I think our discussion has become like a debate in a courtroom, I feel ____, and I'm likely to respond this way: ____.
25. When you or someone else repeatedly tries to dominate a discussion by claiming intellectual superiority, I feel ____, and I'm likely to respond this way: ____.
26. When you remind me to do something, I feel ____, and I'm likely to respond this way: ____.
27. When you remind me more than once to do something, I feel ____, and I am likely to respond this way: ____.
28. When you do not do what you promise, I feel ____, and I'm likely to respond this way: ____.
29. When I feel I must remind you of a promise, I feel ____, and I'm likely to respond this way: ____.
30. When it seems that you are more interested in being right than solving a problem, I feel ____, and I'm likely to respond this way: ____.

31. When I slip into thinking that I'm right and you are wrong, these thoughts and actions shift me into openly listening to you and respecting your point of view: ____.
32. When we talk about serious subjects, I feel ____.
33. When there is a need for serious consultation and there are decisions to be made, I prefer to be in the following settings: ____.
34. It does not work for me to try to have serious discussions when I'm in the middle of doing the following things: ____.
35. If feel like communications on and use of social media affect our lives in these ways: ____.
36. I think we have issues about confidentiality and privacy when these topics are shared with others: ____.
37. It would assist me to feel unified in our communications if we resolve to take the following constructive actions: ____.

Couple Reflection and Consultation

1. Based on both our answers above and our discussions, what have we learned about our communication patterns? What are we happy about? What are our concerns?
2. What specific actions will we take, or what changes will we make, to improve our communications?
3. What are some areas that we want to reassess about our communication in the future?
4. When will we do the reassessment? (Set a reminder in place.)

Chapter 9: Understanding, Managing, and Expressing Feelings

As we increase our capacity to be aware of, manage, and express our feelings, also known as emotions, we are more able to be compassionate, mature, and healthy in our interactions. Our development of emotional intelligence contributes to our marriage well-being. Consider this:

> "...[E]motionally intelligent couples are intimately familiar with each other's world. I call this having a richly detailed love map—my term for that part of your brain where you store all the relevant information about your partner's life. Another way of saying this is that these couples have made plenty of cognitive room for their marriage. They remember the major events in each other's history, and they keep updating their information as the facts and feelings of their spouse's world change. ...Couples who have detailed love maps of each other's world are far better prepared to cope with stressful events and conflict."[82] John M. Gottman and Nan Silver

Expressing Many Feelings

It contributes to our friendship and the quality of our consultation in marriage when we discover, share, and understand each other's feelings. A variety of feelings is often a sign of vitality. Our feelings influence how we:

- Perceive the situation we are addressing
- Express our thoughts
- Make decisions
- Create and carry out possible solutions

We improve our life together and reduce conflict when we increase our skill with the factors listed below.

- Staying aware of our current and underlying feelings
- Understanding what has prompted our feelings, including differentiating between whether it was something from the past or the present
- Maintaining self-control and adjusting—not letting the feelings be in charge instead of us
- Being able to express intense emotions calmly, clearly, and safely, releasing or calming them through such activities as prayer, meditation, or constructive physical action as needed
- Wanting others to understand our feelings and vice versa
- Being able to compassionately empathize with another's feelings
- Being able to interact easily in social, close friend, marriage partner, and family settings

Someone shares her experience:

"My commitment to experiencing my feelings began many years ago when training as a psychologist. I learned that what you resist persists, and that repressed or suppressed feelings have damaging impact on your health and well-being and this often drives people into counseling or therapy, or they simply fester in unresolved, unhappy, health- and relationship-damaging ways. My training resulted in believing strongly in the importance of processing your feelings.

"What does 'processing your feelings' mean? It means experiencing them, bringing them into conscious awareness so you can feel them, look at them, explore them, think them over, realize insights about them, release them...any or all of the above, wherever the process takes you. When people experience their feelings in these kinds of ways, they lose their punch. Feelings are transitory by nature. They come...and they go...IF you allow yourself to experience them. But, if you tell yourself any kind of message that blocks your feelings or causes

them to get pushed away, they will keep popping up one way or another to grab your attention, sometimes at inopportune times or in inopportune ways. Telling yourself 'I shouldn't feel that way', or, 'I'm carrying on too much about this', or 'I'm being too sensitive', or even, 'Not now' seriously impedes your ability to experience your feelings and may ultimately, make it difficult to access those feelings.

"And, there's even more to this: if you deny or push aside Feeling A, it's likely to have a negative impact on Feeling B. This is because denial is a primitive coping mechanism, which means that it doesn't simply target the one feeling you want to block off, or lessen, it causes collateral damage to others. So, if you want to have access to happiness and joy and other 'good stuff'...open the door to feeling the tough stuff like loss, sadness, hurt, fear, loneliness, pain, despair.

"So, how do you open the door to experiencing your feelings? The key to giving yourself full access to them is to forgo labeling them as 'good' or 'bad', or otherwise pushing them around in any way: Let them simply be."[83]

Here is guidance:

> "... [T]he function of language is to portray the mysteries and secrets of human hearts. The heart is like a box, and language is the key. Only by using the key can we open the box and observe the gems it contains."[84] 'Abdu'l-Bahá

Generally, the quality of consultation in our marriage improves when we acknowledge and share our feelings about a topic early in the process. Expressing feelings does not mean attacking each other with anger or any other emotion. It does mean saying what feelings are happening and why so that understanding between us builds.

We benefit from recognizing shifting feelings in ourselves and each other as new conversations arise or when situations change. Disunity can occur when we don't honor or acknowledge each other's feelings, or when one of us remains silent and withdrawn for an extended period. Withholding feelings or thoughts and then speaking up later when it's too late to address the issue, usually causes frustration and problems. This could include saying things like, "Well, I didn't think that idea would work" or "I felt uneasy about that action" after it occurs.

A simple practice can be for one of us to say, "It seems like you are feeling ____. Is that true? Can you share with me what's going on?" We need to say this without accusation or judgment and then allow there to be silence until a response comes. A follow-up practice can be to say, "Is there anything else you need to say?" This ensures our inner cup has emptied. We may need to stop at times and summarize back to each other what we think we have heard. When we check for understanding, we quickly correct information and let each other know we are carefully listening.

Sharing feelings and striving for understanding are different from our feelings clashing with each other and conflict escalating. Consider this:

> "It is important to note that truth emerges after the 'clash' of carefully articulated views (which may well be expressed with enthusiasm and vigor), not from the clash of feelings. A clash of feelings is likely to obscure the truth, while a difference of opinion facilitates the discovery of truth."[85]
> Research Department of the Universal House of Justice

Knowing the Words That Apply

One challenge with understanding feelings, however, is that we may not yet be skillful with the words to label them. Marshall B. Rosenberg, PhD, guides people through the challenges of understanding and identifying feelings. He encourages specificity, which would have us state that we are "happy", "excited", or "relieved", rather than saying we feel "good". Being specific contributes to understanding and clarity.

Some of the words we might use for our feelings when our needs are *being met* are:

- Adventurous
- Affectionate
- Amazed
- Amused
- Aroused
- Calm
- Curious
- Energetic
- Fascinated
- Happy
- Mellow
- Moved
- Optimistic
- Proud
- Relaxed
- Surprised
- Thrilled
- Wonderful

Some of the words Dr. Rosenberg suggests for our feelings when our needs are *not being met* are:

- Afraid
- Angry
- Annoyed
- Anxious
- Ashamed
- Bored
- Concerned
- Confused
- Resentful
- Disappointed
- Discouraged
- Embarrassed
- Hurt
- Irritated
- Jealous
- Overwhelmed
- Pessimistic
- Sad[86]

With some practice, we may be able to quickly identify our feelings and name them, sometimes with assistance from each other. Alternatively, we may notice that our feelings only become clear to ourselves while sharing them with a partner or consulting. We may easily and intuitively identify feelings, or we may need gentle and exploratory questions to sort them out. Often one or both of us may also need time and space alone to allow feelings to surface and clarify. When we see that we struggle with identifying feelings, it can be useful to write down an incident and then list the feelings related to it, perhaps with assistance from another person.

Observing Feelings

It's wise for us to avoid making assumptions or judgments about each other and to simply inquire and honor how each other feels. It's unwise and likely contentious to:

- Tell the other person how they are feeling
- Project our own feelings onto the other
- Tell each other that we should or should not be having a certain feeling

Our tone of voice, facial expressions and body movements, and volume are also powerful cues about our thoughts and feelings. If we pay close attention, we can begin to observe our own feelings. If we listen carefully, we can also usually tell if our partner is feeling upset, happy, angry, excited, or annoyed. When someone's words, facial expression and body movements, and tone of voice do not align, it's likely we will believe their tone. It's wise for us to fact-check what we are noticing by asking gentle questions.

As we increase our skill with aligning our feelings and words, our trust in each other increases. When there is trust, it's also easier to offer one another gentle feedback and communicate effectively about our concerns.

How we express and understand each other's feelings can also link to cultural factors, or even voice accents. It's also possible that our unique personalities affect how we express feelings, and this causes misunderstandings.

Exploring all these factors together during a calm time may uncover and resolve factors that have been causing us issues. One couple shares these experiences:

"Over the years there are so many ways we non-verbally communicate our love and affection—a look, a smile, a touch—even when with friends. We have learned that the tone of our voice can communicate more than the words we may say when we are disgruntled, anxious, frustrated, or happy. We discovered that it's better to consult about an issue when in a positive frame of mind rather than when disgruntled, anxious, frustrated, or unhappy because those feelings color the issue. That also gives time to pray, reflect, and consider options."

At times what is happening for us emotionally has nothing to do with each other but instead relates to other happenings in our lives. Tuning into our own feelings and then sharing with each other that something has triggered feelings and that our partner is not the source, can relax us a bit. Perhaps a neighbor's accident causes some grief related to a family member dying in an accident in the past. Maybe a clerk was rude in a store and anger is simmering. Something happened at work, and there is fear of job loss. We can listen to each other, so we better understand the feelings and let them calm down. A man shares this experience:

"We received the news that close friends of ours were getting a divorce after they had been married only a few months. We were both concerned about them, but I could tell that my wife was particularly shocked and upset. It had only been a few months since her parents had decided to separate. She reacted to this new circumstance by blending her feelings about both experiences together inside of her.

"We had to decide how we were going to respond to the news from our friends. We especially wondered how we might

be able to remain friends with them without taking sides. It was a very painful couple consultation, and my primary role initially was listening to my wife, accompanying her, and helping her release her feelings and thoughts.

"She began by sharing memories of good times we have had with our friends and with her parents, and concerns about both. She shared anger, frustration, and grief. When she got quiet, I waited for a few moments and then asked, 'Is there anything else you need to say?' We repeated that process over and over until she cleared out her mind and heart. Only then could we begin to consult about the actions to take with this new situation."

Expressing Our Feelings

When the feelings that arise are between the two of us, it's often more difficult to handle them well. We need to keep practicing with how to convey our feelings in a constructive way that doesn't hurt each other. Sometimes we suppress our feelings until the best time, but what happens is they begin to leak out in unclear ways that confuse each other. Alternatively, they pile up and become an ugly mess when they do come out. It may be useful to have a routine time each day or each week to check in and sort out any issues that have arisen. Sometimes though issues arise and must be handled right then. Here is one couple's story:

"When we speak, we are aware of how our words include not only the idea we are trying to convey, but also how we feel about it. With this awareness, we take the time to let our speech be as skillful as it can be, while trusting that the other one will listen attentively. We speak our minds, and we let go of what we have said.

"As we listen proactively, we are aware of our own internal reactions, arising thoughts, and feelings. However, we also

know that the process of consulting allows a time and space for us to present what each of us feels is needed and helpful. This allows our minds to stay relatively quiet while the other speaks. We can truly hear what is being said as we consider our own opinion and formulate a response.

"Our consultation in marriage then, is a process of being aware of our own feelings as we speak and as we listen. There is a sense of great support in knowing that our marriage partner is openly aware as we do this. For example, I recently returned home from a week-long business trip. My wife was exhausted from caring for our sick four-year-old son for three days.

"When we had a few minutes to sit and catch up with each other and consult about what would happen the next day, we needed time to share our feelings. My wife said, 'I was very scared I was going to have to take him to the hospital without you here', and 'I was so upset that you didn't call last night to check on us.'

"With mindful listening, I was able to acknowledge her feelings of loneliness and fear about handling this challenge on her own, without jumping into being defensive. She could then hear me as I shared, 'I was very frustrated that there was not a cellphone signal along the route we were driving last night. I was very concerned about both of you and hoping you could feel my prayer support.'

"Listening to each other's feelings helped us re-connect. We also realized that we were both too tired to consult about plans for the next day. All we needed right then was to agree on how to look after our son for the next few hours."

Here are some steps that may be useful to follow:

1. Acknowledge and name the feelings we are experiencing
2. Determine what has likely caused the feelings

3. Assess or consult about what to do about the feelings using these types of questions:

    - Is there action to take?
    - Is there a problem to address with someone?
    - Are the feelings coming from an old situation and once recognized that they are not part of the present circumstances, can they be released?
    - Is there physical activity to do that will calm the feeling so it's easier to think about it?
    - Do we need to give ourselves some time to understand what we are feeling and why?
    - Is the feeling causing us or others harm?
    - Is the feeling brief and temporary, or has it been with us for a while and needs help from others?

The "Nonviolent Communication" method is designed for people to share and receive observations, feelings, needs, and requests both honestly and peacefully. The example below demonstrates "I-statements", where the speaker is careful to speak for themselves and not be accusatory with statements starting with "you". It may be useful to us to read more about this method Marshall Rosenberg created, so we can use it most effectively (https://www.cnvc.org/). A simplified view of the basic communication process is:

- SEE: We observe and share the concrete actions in another person that affected our well-being.
- FEEL: We identify and share how we feel about what we observed.
- NEED: We notice and share the needs, values, desires, and so on that led to our feelings.

- REQUEST: We communicate (not demand) a specific request of the other person that is clear and positive that if they carry it out will enrich our life.

Here is an example: "I'm noticing that you are getting involved in a lot of community service activities, and we are spending less time together. I'm feeling lonely and missing you, and I'm feeling frustrated that many tasks at home are not being done. I value our marriage relationship, and our children really benefit from your time and attention. I request that we consult together before you say yes to service activities outside our home, so we can ensure together that there is balance." The couple can then go into a problem-solving consultation.

Navigating Negative Feelings

If we label feelings as bad or feel shame about them, we will be tempted to ignore or suppress them. However, they will be difficult to hide. Here is some guidance:

> "Verily the most necessary thing is contentment under all circumstances; by this one is preserved from morbid conditions and from lassitude. Yield not to grief and sorrow: they cause the greatest misery. Jealousy consumeth the body and anger doth burn the liver: avoid these two as you would a lion."[87] Bahá'u'lláh

> "Love the creatures for the sake of God and not for themselves. You will never become angry or impatient if you love them for the sake of God. Humanity is not perfect. There are imperfections in every human being, and you will always become unhappy if you look toward the people themselves. But if you look toward God, you will love them and be kind to them, for the world of God is the world of perfection and complete mercy."[88] 'Abdu'l-Bahá

"You ask how to deal with anger. The House of Justice suggests that you call to mind the admonitions found in our Writings on the need to overlook the shortcomings of others; to forgive and conceal their misdeeds, not to expose their bad qualities, but to search for and affirm their praiseworthy ones, and to endeavor to be always forbearing, patient, and merciful."[89] On behalf of the Universal House of Justice

The Better Marriages organization recommends that couples make decisions when they are not angry about how they want to behave when anger arises. They suggest:

1. "STOP! Do not attack. Anger creates defensiveness...and encourages counter-attacks, causing anger to increase and spread beyond the immediate issue.

2. "LOOK! Acknowledge anger. Couples make an agreement to view anger as a normal emotion. Each partner then agrees to acknowledge anger rather than suppress it, and to share how they feel with the other as soon as possible. Sharing is done with an 'I feel' statement.... Clarify with your partner how you interpreted what happened.

3. "LISTEN! Look behind the anger. Anger is typically a secondary emotion. The feelings labeled as anger are often deeper feelings—hurt, taken for granted, trapped, used, overloaded. Couples must look behind the anger...and deal with these other feelings if they are to manage anger. ... When you get angry, consider these questions: What happened just before the incident? What else was I feeling (fatigue, hunger, frustration, overwhelmed, insecure, etc.)? Did this situation remind me of something in my background? Looking behind the anger may not be possible until emotions have 'cooled'. It is hard to think

clearly and sort out feelings in the heat of a conflict. Silence or a 'time out' can be useful for a short period. But be careful that silence is not used as a weapon against your partner! Refusing to talk increases anger rather than resolving it. When tempers have cooled, partners can take turns stating what each is feeling while the other listens without interrupting. In this way, feelings can be clarified and heard."[90] A.C.M.E./Better Marriages

The same feelings can have a positive or a negative interpretation, depending on the circumstances:

"In the innate nature of things there is no evil—all is good. This applies even to certain apparently blameworthy attributes and dispositions which seem inherent in some people, but which are not in reality reprehensible. For example, you can see in a nursing child, from the beginning of its life, the signs of greed, of anger, and of ill temper; and so it might be argued that good and evil are innate in the reality of man, and that this is contrary to the pure goodness of the innate nature and of creation. The answer is that greed, which is to demand ever more, is a praiseworthy quality provided that it is displayed under the right circumstances. Thus, should a person show greed in acquiring science and knowledge, or in the exercise of compassion, high-mindedness, and justice, this would be most praiseworthy. And should he direct his anger and wrath against the bloodthirsty tyrants who are like ferocious beasts, this too would be most praiseworthy. But should he display these qualities under other conditions, this would be deserving of blame."[91] 'Abdu'l-Bahá

It's important to get professional counseling when our feelings are seriously troubling and unresolved. There is a difference between feelings that arise normally every day and serious ones that occur and stay for long periods and that are best addressed by a mental health professional. [See Chapter 2 and Appendices C and D for more on this topic.]

The Bahá'í teachings also include turning to medical doctors as needed. Here is guidance to a physician:

> "Praise be to God that thou hast two powers: one to undertake physical healing and the other spiritual healing. Matters related to man's spirit have a great effect on his bodily condition. For instance, thou shouldst impart gladness to thy patient, give him comfort and joy, and bring him to ecstasy and exultation. How often hath it occurred that this hath caused early recovery. Therefore, treat thou the sick with both powers. Spiritual feelings have a surprising effect on healing nervous ailments."[92]
> 'Abdu'l-Bahá

How Detachment Helps

Sometimes when we are feeling very emotional, the character quality of detachment can facilitate us taking a step back, calming our feelings, and taking a more neutral look at what is happening. Below are some indicators that someone is practicing detachment well. He/She:

- Empathizes with others without making their feelings their own or suffering because of the actions or reactions of others
- Thinks rationally and clearly with some emotional distance and focus; responding according to the known facts without exhibiting personal bias, strong emotions, or preconceived expectations
- Gathers information, seeks input from others, and examines the facts related to a project, situation, or person without premature judgment or participating in backbiting or gossip

- Seeks spiritual solutions to issues
- Releases desires, dreams, or expectations that are unrealistic or unattainable, grieving as needed in the process of letting go
- Accepts a present situation with equanimity, even if it's difficult, uncomfortable, or not what they would have chosen
- Frees themselves from unhealthy or unwise attachment to people, incidents from the past, physical objects, and desires
- Releases overly strong fears of losing something or someone
- Bases choices on current circumstances rather than solely on previous experiences
- Understands and accepts the limitations of others and their own

Here is someone's reflection about detachment:

"I find this situation between us extremely challenging. I have come to realize part of my frustration lies in my trying to 'suppress' feelings in hopes of become detached. Now, I think the way to navigate this period is through acceptance, gratitude, and reflection. Accepting that these feelings and inclinations are natural frees me from becoming critical of myself and allows for honesty in my reflections on the matter. Gratitude for the test allows me to use the experience as a tool to 'learn' about detachment, so that I can further develop this virtue."

Happiness and Laughter

We may find it beneficial to lighten up a bit and laugh together more to smooth our communications and link us in unity. It can build connection between us if we are playful and humorous with each other at times (not sarcastic humor that has an underlying cutting message!), as well as spend time together relaxing and enjoying an activity or date. When we build connection this way, it can be easier to respond to whatever is going on in our lives.

Many people associate spirituality with being serious all the time. However, a very effective way to bring about positive feelings and happiness throughout our life journey is through genuine humor. Our ability to be content, joyful, and grateful, no matter what the circumstances are, will be a strong power in keeping us connected in marriage.

'Abdu'l-Bahá, the eldest son of Bahá'u'lláh, who was known at times as "The Master", is the person we are to look to as an example of how to live. There are many stories where we can read about His spiritual qualities and choices, one of which was His excellent sense of humor. He often joked and told stories. Here is an example: "In New York City a young supporter of tax-reform asked, 'What message shall I take to my friends?' The Master laughed with delighted humor: 'Tell them to come into the Kingdom of God. There they will find plenty of land—and there are no taxes on it!'"[93]

'Abdu'l-Bahá also provided this encouragement:

> "... [L]augh, smile and rejoice in order that others may be made happy by you."[94] 'Abdu'l-Bahá

Of course, humor also comes with a caution, as hurting hearts is not the intent:

> "... [W]hile laughter should not be suppressed or frowned upon, it should not be indulged in at the expense of the feelings of others. What one says or does in a humorous vein should not give rise to prejudice of any kind. You may recall 'Abdu'l-Bahá's caution 'Beware lest ye offend the feelings of anyone, or sadden the heart of any person....'"[95]
> 'Abdu'l-Bahá; On behalf of the Universal House of Justice

Here is guidance about the balance for us to create in our life:

> "One of the signs of a decadent society, a sign which is very evident in the world today, is an almost frenetic devotion to pleasure and diversion, an insatiable thirst for amusement, a fanatical devotion to games and sport, a reluctance to treat any matter seriously, and a scornful, derisory attitude towards virtue and solid worth. Abandonment of 'a frivolous conduct' does not imply that a Bahá'í must be sour-faced or perpetually solemn. Humor, happiness, joy are characteristics of a true Bahá'í life. Frivolity palls and eventually leads to boredom and emptiness, but true happiness and joy and humor that are parts of a balanced life that includes serious thought, compassion and humble servitude to God are characteristics that enrich life and add to its radiance."[96]
> On behalf of the Universal House of Justice

Here is some sharing about this topic:

"Laughter is a healing medicine for the soul, mind, and heart. Laughter melts away imagined differences and brings to the forefront that we are actually all related in a very real way. It unites us. Joy for me is about detachment from the changes and chances of this world. Joy is a kindness to ourselves and to others. When I am experiencing joy, I have more energy, I find life more pleasing and funnier in general. I am more compassionate and better able to empathize with others. I am able to serve others with grace and cheerfulness. I find it easier to think of others' needs and forget my own selfish wants. Others are happier around me when I am happy and joyful!"

"I have been tuning in more to what naturally boosts my level of happiness and joy. Really, I think of it as my 'joy level,' since

the joy that comes from accepting the will of God is stable and always there for me to access. Whenever I feel that joy ebbing (like when I see so much injustice and disunity), I become aware that I am becoming attached to worldly things. Now I have some tools to reconnect my soul to the grace of God! Prayer and reading quotations from the Bahá'í writings and from other faiths, as well as uplifting words of other people, are among these tools. Nature is and has always been a big one for me too. Water is intensely relaxing for me, and so is being around trees and birds."

Other authors comment on the link between laughter, joy, and spirituality:

> "Laughter is a spiritual practice. ... The transformative nature of any spiritual discipline comes with regular practice. When done consistently, it can eventually change our lives. If we make time to invite joy into our lives each day, we will become more aware of joy and laughter in our lives and in the world. Eventually, laughter will become an innate part of who we are."[97] Susan Sparks

> "Cultivate humor as a higher path—a cosmic contentment that is truly lighthearted and full of joy. You will lighten the lives of others simply by the radiance of your good humor. Even the briefest laugh reminds us that we have available a kind of spiritual gold anytime, anywhere."[98] Stephen Post

Couple Actions

1. Identify the specific positive and negative feelings that could arise in each of the situations listed below:
   a. There has been an injustice in our neighborhood; in our workplace; in our country
   b. We go out on a date to a concert for our wedding anniversary
   c. We have been asked to carry out a specific community service
   d. One of us burns and ruins a special dinner
   e. One of us is participating in a physical or spiritual fasting process (or other spiritual practice), and the other is not
   f. We take our first vacation in five years
   g. We unexpectedly receive a large sum of money
   h. We become parents (or grandparents)

2. To expand our skill in identifying feelings, think about different scenarios from our life, and then practice a few times with saying: "When I see or hear ____ (or when ____ happens), I feel ____."

3. Identify two low conflict issues in our relationship or home, one each, and take turns addressing each issue using Non-Violent Communication as a method to share our concerns. The receiver should summarize back to the speaker what they understood from the communication, ensuring this happens every few sentences, so we don't lose track of what to say. Then we can engage in problem solving consultation to determine a resolution.

4. Go to the https://www.5lovelanguages.com website and use the assessment there to determine the ways we both

prefer expressions of love from the other. [An alternative is to obtain one of the 5 Love Languages books by Gary Chapman.] Consult about a few simple ways to improve our expressions of love and begin carrying them out. Reflect on what is working well and where a shift in direction is needed without becoming critical about what has not happened in the past. It can be fine to try out all of the Love Languages, but strive to be consistent with at least carrying out regular actions to match each other's primary Love Language.

5. Read the story that follows and then carry out this practice of finding and sharing something funny from our day regularly for a week or so. Assess the effect of it on us and others. "It is good to laugh. Laughter is a spiritual relaxation. When [we] were in prison...and under the utmost deprivation and difficulties, each of [us] at the close of the day would relate the most ludicrous event which had happened. Sometimes it was a little difficult to find one but always [we] would laugh until the tears would roll down [our] cheeks. Happiness...is never dependent upon material surroundings, otherwise how sad those years would have been. As it was [we] were always in the utmost state of joy and happiness."99 Reported to be from 'Abdu'l-Bahá

6. Create a "Love Map" (Idea Source: John Gottman): It's important and potentially vitalizing for couples to know one another well through observing, sharing, and listening. The goal of this activity is to map out our marriage partner's life as we know him/her now. Then we will fill in the gaps together—without making negative comments about what each other was not aware of. Each of us begins with our own piece of paper and some writing or drawing

utensils, and we will do the first part of the activity individually. On the paper, we will describe our marriage partner in words and drawings in whatever creative way works for us. We could draw a tree, squares, circles, pictures, or anything else that creatively displays our partner's life and then add words to it. Here are some examples, in no order, but we can go beyond these as needed:

- Who he/she is striving to be
- Feelings most easily expressed
- Feelings most difficult to acknowledge and express
- Wounds in the middle of healing
- Upcoming events
- Views about children and parenting
- Profession(s)
- Favorite activities, service choices, and high priorities for spending time
- Best friends
- Current fears, stresses, and worries
- Common irritants
- Purpose(s) in life
- Philosophies/practices of parenting
- Life dreams
- Religious/spiritual beliefs and activities
- Basic philosophy of life
- Favorite music, games, movies, TV shows...
- Most special times in life
- Childhood traumas/stresses
- Major aspirations and hopes
- Would do with a major sum of money
- What does to re-charge energy
- Dream vacation spot

Example: A husband could draw a circle for "Current fears, stresses, and worries" and list in the circle about his wife that she is concerned about: "Daughter Molly's school report card, adjusting to her new job, and her mother's health". A wife could draw a circle for her husband's "Major aspirations and hopes" and write in the circle: "Getting a promotion, teaching son Jason how to coach a baseball team, retiring and traveling at age 65".

Couple Discussion: When we have both completed our maps, then share them with each other, discuss them, and add to them. Discuss: What were the surprises? What did we appreciate learning? Were we able to learn without becoming upset that our partner didn't know something important about us? Do we feel confident we know one another better? That we know one another well?

Related Activity: Now draw a map together of our marriage. What activities do we do together? What does our parenting or grand-parenting look like? What are our goals, services, and activities as a couple? What do we do separately with agreement from the other, and these activities enrich us and our marriage? What significant concerns are on our minds and hearts? What are the joys we feel?

Individual Reflection

1. What feelings do I experience most often? How do I express those feelings? In what ways would I prefer to express those feelings?
2. What negative thoughts and feelings do I hold toward my marriage partner? Am I willing to address them constructively or let go of them and put them in the past? What needs to happen to achieve this? What would I replace them with?

3. What do I want my marriage partner to know about me that I have not shared before?
4. What makes me laugh?
5. How do I share laughter with others?

Couple Reflection and Consultation

1. What feelings most often arise between us?
2. How do we usually express our feelings? What do we want to learn to do differently?
3. How can we ongoingly stay familiar with what is most important to each other?
4. How do humor and laughter affect us? How could we increase them between us? In our family? With our friends?

Chapter 10: Utilizing Consultation As a Couple

Note: This chapter provides many perspectives and options for consulting as a couple. This can feel overwhelming at the beginning, especially if you are unfamiliar with the concept of consultation. It will take time and practice to develop the approaches that work best for you. Consulting as a couple (or family) is different in many ways than experiences you may have had in administrative meetings. Your emotional link and physical closeness, as well as there just being two of you, are factors that influence this difference. Please read what is here, try out the ideas, experiment with your own, learn, and persevere. The investment in your harmony is vital.

Some Purposes of Consultation

Consultation builds our understanding of each other's perspectives and can also lead us to make excellent and unified decisions as needed. Our consultations as a couple and family can be formal at times when an issue is very serious. However, our process is usually informal and an excellent way to manage our lives and household. We engage in it consciously with a clear agreed purpose, so it's not casual conversation, but it often occurs in a casual setting. Here is a perspective:

> "Consultation is a method for finding out the truth, solving problems, deciding on the best course of action, preventing difficulties, and generating new ideas and plans. It is a tool for equitably sharing power and decision-making between two or more people."[100] Khalil A. Khavari and Sue Williston Khavari

When unity is already present, it contributes to the quality of consultation, and consultation can also build unity. It's a way of saying "I really value your opinion on this, I value you, I love you, and we are one." Here is guidance:

> "... [C]onsultation is of vital importance, but spiritual conference and not the mere voicing of personal views is intended. ...[C]onsultation must have for its object the investigation of truth. He who expresses an opinion should not voice it as correct and right but set it forth as a contribution to the consensus of opinion, for the light of reality becomes apparent when two opinions coincide. A spark is produced when flint and steel come together. Man should weigh his opinions with the utmost serenity, calmness and composure. Before expressing his own views he should carefully consider the views already advanced by others. If he finds that a previously expressed opinion is more true and worthy, he should accept it immediately and not willfully hold to an opinion of his own. By this excellent method he endeavors to arrive at unity and truth."[101] 'Abdu'l-Bahá

> "Whether concerned with analyzing a specific problem, attaining higher degrees of understanding on a given issue, or exploring possible courses of action, consultation may be seen as collective search for truth. Participants in a consultative process see reality from different points of view, and as these views are examined and understood, clarity is achieved. In this conception of the collective investigation of reality, truth is not a compromise between opposing interest groups. Nor does the desire to exercise power over one another animate participants in the consultative process. What they seek, rather, is the power of unified thought and action."[102] Office of Social and Economic Development at the Bahá'í World Centre

Someone shares:

"Detaching from being 'right' is a big adjustment piece that needs to happen before effective consultation and unity can happen. One of my challenges in life is the very human tendency to want to be 'right' most of the time, which has me at times decide what the outcome should be before we even begin to talk. This communicates to my partner that their input is unnecessary or invalid and that my mind is closed to alternative perspectives. Consultation teaches me, instead, that there is sharing and blending of our perspectives and then choosing the path that seems the best and most true for both of us. When we make a decision and carry it out in unity, then we have the ability to see where we are going astray and where we have our feet placed firmly on a positive path. If we try to move forward without unity, the result is harmful and painful, and it's impossible to see the truth. There is also definitely no place for either of us saying 'I told you so' as we reflect on how a decision is being carried out, because we made the decision together."

Another person says:

"I resisted the whole idea of consultation for a long time. To me it felt like it robbed me of my independence. I thought it meant that my own thinking was faulty, or that I wasn't capable of deciding something on my own. Sometimes I thought it was about getting permission from my wife to do something. I did what I could to avoid consulting, until I realized that my wife was in a lot of pain from this choice. She saw it as an attitude of disrespect toward her, that I didn't value her ideas and opinions or trust her. She felt very disconnected then from some important decisions that I made solo, and that disconnected us. And, honestly, some of those decisions could have used her wisdom. I've learned to value our unity, and with

gradual practice, I'm better at making joint decisions. It's taken courage, humility, and more to participate, but I'm glad to have made progress."

As we build harmony by working through an issue together, it contributes to our well-being. Bahá'u'lláh says:

> "No welfare and no well-being can be attained except through consultation."[103]

> Here is more guidance:

> "Consultation bestoweth greater awareness and transmuteth conjecture into certitude. It is a shining light which, in a dark world, leadeth the way and guideth. For everything there is and will continue to be a station of perfection and maturity. The maturity of the gift of understanding is made manifest through consultation."[104] Bahá'u'lláh

> "... [W]hen a problem ariseth, or a difficulty occurreth, the wise should gather, consult, and devise a solution. They should then rely upon the one true God, and surrender to His Providence, in whatever way it may be revealed, for divine confirmations will undoubtedly assist. Consultation, therefore, is one of the explicit ordinances of [Bahá'u'lláh]."[105] 'Abdu'l-Bahá

> "Man must consult on all matters, whether major or minor, so that he may become cognizant of what is good. Consultation giveth him insight into things and enableth him to delve into questions which are unknown. The light of truth shineth from the faces of those who engage in consultation. Such consultation causeth the living waters to flow in the meadows of man's reality, the rays of ancient glory to shine upon him, and the tree of his being to be adorned with wondrous fruit. The members who are

consulting, however, should behave in the utmost love, harmony and sincerity towards each other. The principle of consultation is one of the most fundamental elements of the divine edifice. Even in their ordinary affairs the individual members of society should consult."[106]
'Abdu'l-Bahá

Someone shares:

"Sometimes there is no question—a decision cannot begin to be made without prayer and sorting through the options verbally together. The decision is blocked, stunted, and ill-formed otherwise. It feels uncomfortable, like a shirt pulled over my head but it's inside out and backwards. Any actions I take cause me to trip and falter. It's like I am traveling without directions and headed for the wrong destination. If I hold something back in consultation, I walk away feeling dissatisfied, with something stuck in my mind, heart, and soul. Sometimes I feel resentful when my partner doesn't ask for my thoughts and feelings, so I don't share them, or I share them with a tone of voice or in a way that doesn't move the consultation forward. I don't rest well until I fully express myself."

Setting Up the Environment

Over time we are learning the types of environments we both prefer for consulting and what level of privacy is needed, especially if we have children. Sometimes we like walking outdoors. At other times we prefer comfortable seats in our home along with cups of tea or coffee. Occasionally we consult while doing routine tasks, but we must be cautious that this doesn't interfere with listening.

Sometimes looking directly at each other can create a strong feeling of connection; sometimes less direct eye contact and more sitting or walking side-by-side can encourage a discussion to flow more comfortably. Often men feel direct eye contact is confrontational, while women often appreciate direct eye contact and trust a man more when he looks at her. So, we can experiment and vary our approaches to see what works for both of us at various times.

At times it's good for our children to hear us consulting and problem-solving peacefully, but for sensitive topics it's better if we arrange to be alone. A couple shares:

"We have been married for about 12 years. Most evenings, we eat together in our home with our two children, who are now ages 10 and 7. From the time they were quite young, we started the practice of settling them with quiet activities after dinner. This gives us time to retreat to a private spot in our home. We share the events of our days with one another and consult as necessary about anything on our minds.

"Our consultations as a couple often include such topics as these:

- *"Between us, whose time commitments will best allow for driving the children to after-school activities this week?"*
- *"We have our appointment with the financial planner coming up in two weeks. What issues do we think are the most important ones for us to consult about with her? What preparations do we need to make?"*
- *"We are hosting this month's married couples' group on Saturday evening. When will we finish up our reading assignment? How will we get the house cleaned and refreshments arranged?"*
- *"I'm concerned about my medical test next week, and I would be calmer with you there. Is it possible for you to adjust your work schedule so you can go with me?"*

"Certain questions have assisted us as we consult, and they seem to shorten the time required for consultation. These questions are:

- *What do we want to see happen?*
- *Does either of us have any strong preferences related to the topic?*
- *Are there any goals we are trying to meet?*

"We learned early on in our marriage that we both tend to be irritable and negative when we are tired and hungry. Serious talk before dinner always ended in sharp words. The children have learned that we are better parents when they give us this quiet time after dinner. We are committed to showing the children that it's possible to discuss issues with calm voices and peacefulness. We are not always successful, but most of the time we are. When we are done, then we focus on the children's needs until they are in bed for the night."

It's important for us to remember that there is no set form given in the Bahá'í Writings for consultation in a group, between a couple, or within a family. Some couples we know consult daily about most matters; others weekly only about very important topics. Some couples consult about every detail of their lives; others delegate some decisions to each other. We are confident that we will learn through experience what flows best for us. We also know we must be aware that even when we have established a rhythm of how and when to consult together, disruptive circumstances or problems may arise. It's good for us to be flexible and set a new pattern in place as needed.

Timeliness

Excessive delay in raising important issues, or suppressing communications, usually results in an escalation of challenges later. This does not include taking a pause break to calm down, which can be quite beneficial. Problems also arise when anyone involved decides before consulting what the outcome should be or what decision should be made. The time for making decisions is after we have fully shared our thoughts, views, and feelings. As we raise ideas, solutions that neither of us conceived of begin to unfold and develop. Some of the outcome likely comes in the form of inspiration from God or Bahá'u'lláh; some of it comes from the intersection of our input and the building of new perspectives between us.

Sometimes a couple acts first and then realizes consultation ahead of time would have been a good idea, because the result was conflict. Here is one couple's story:

"We both love to be helpful to each other. However, we have learned that it's wise and respectful to consult with each other before jumping in with unasked-for assistance. One incident made this understanding clear for us.

"We were both working in the yard in different places. I went up the ladder with an electric trimmer and began cutting off branches of a tree. I let them fall to the ground. My husband saw what I was doing, came over, and began moving around the base of the ladder while gathering up the fallen branches.

"Unfortunately, he bumped up against the ladder, which distracted me, causing me to cut the electrical cord with the trimmer. This tripped the power off to our whole home, and I came close to falling from the ladder. 'I can't believe you did that! Why couldn't you have waited until I was done?!' I was angry and upset.

"Later that day, after we calmed down and we were able to talk about the situation, my husband said, 'I'm sorry for getting in the way and causing the accident.' I responded with, 'I forgive you. And...I'm sorry I yelled at you.'

"We consulted about what had happened and discussed how to prevent a repeat incident. We realized we had skipped consulting with each other about responsibilities before going outside to work. I was also able to share that it would have worked better for me if we had consulted briefly about the timing of the help before it started."

Real consultation can only occur in the presence of respect—a genuine respect for each other's opinions, feelings, preferences, and contributions.

Attributes and Skills Needed

We will consult most effectively when we both have excellent communication skills [See Chapters 8 and 9.]. Consider this:

> "The tone of collaborative dialogue is friendly. Even when the topic is a serious one, the tone still feels cooperative, as if you have placed your problem on a table and the two of you have sat down side by side to try to solve it. You feel that you are confronting the problem together, rather than that you are confronting each other.
>
> "Another tip-off that dialogue is collaborative is that you feel a sense of forward movement as you accumulate shared understanding. Adversarial dialogue feels repetitious. When dialogue is cooperative, with each successive comment you feel movement toward a shared plan of action."[107] Susan Heitler

You can improve the quality of your dialogue and have it feel mutually participatory in four key ways:

1. **Symmetry:** Equalizing voice volumes, your amount of speaking, and speech speed rates; focusing on issues related to each of you

2. **Short segments:** Speaking only a few sentences per speaking time
3. **Specifics:** Giving details and not just generalities
4. **Summaries:** Occasionally reviewing or summarizing the points that have been made[108]

(Summarized from Susan Heitler and Abigail Hirsch)

You can accompany and encourage each other throughout a consultation with responses such as:

- That's a good idea!
- I see what you mean.
- That's an interesting way of looking at it.
- That's a unique perspective!
- I'm glad we have different perspectives, let's see how we can use them to create a good solution.
- I would like to reflect on that.
- Let me see if I understand.
- I think I need a bit more explanation.
- Perhaps we could take a break and come back to this later?
- Could we pray, and then talk about it some more?
- What are the spiritual principles that apply to this situation?
- It seems as if it would be good to get some more facts.
- I am still confused—can you please explain it again with new words?
- Please, help me to understand.
- That was helpful to me to hear!

There are many facets of our individual behavior that can contribute to our consultations going smoothly. The Bahá'í teachings below share some of these when they talk about people consulting as a Spiritual Assembly.

"The prime requisites for them that take counsel together are purity of motive, radiance of spirit, detachment from all else save God, attraction to His Divine Fragrances, humility and lowliness amongst His loved ones, patience and long-suffering in difficulties and servitude to His exalted Threshold."[109] 'Abdu'l-Bahá

"The first duty of the members is to effect their own unity and harmony, in order to obtain good results. ... [T]heir second duty is to read the verses and communes, to be in a state of commemoration and mindfulness, that they may see each other as if in the presence of God."[110] 'Abdu'l-Bahá

"The first condition is absolute love and harmony amongst the members of the assembly. They must be wholly free from estrangement and must manifest in themselves the Unity of God, for they are the waves of one sea, the drops of one river, the stars of one heaven, the rays of one sun, the trees of one orchard, the flowers of one garden. ... They must, when coming together, turn their faces to the Kingdom on high and ask aid from the Realm of Glory. They must then proceed with the utmost devotion, courtesy, dignity, care and moderation to express their views. They must in every matter search out the truth and not insist upon their own opinion, for stubbornness and persistence in one's views will lead ultimately to discord and wrangling and the truth will remain hidden. The honored members must with all freedom express their own thoughts, and it is in no wise permissible for one to belittle the thought of another, nay, he must with moderation set forth the truth...."[111] 'Abdu'l-Bahá

"The second principle is that of detachment in consultation. The members...must learn to express their views frankly, calmly, without passion or rancor. They must also learn to listen to the opinions of their fellow members without taking offense or belittling the views of another. ...[C]onsultation is not an easy process. It requires love, kindliness, moral courage and humility. Thus no member should ever allow himself to be prevented from expressing frankly his view because it may offend a fellow member; and, realizing this, no member should take offense at another member's statements."[112] Universal House of Justice

"'Abdu'l-Bahá advises us that should it be found, in the course of coming to a decision, that discussion has become prolonged or given rise to disputation, consultation should be deferred and taken up at a more propitious time. ...Of course, it must be remembered that the purpose of consultation need not always be to arrive at a particular or final decision. Often the aim may simply be to engage in an exchange of views so as to help clarify a certain matter and bring about unity of vision. Further, you should recognize that, given current circumstances, there may be issues that cannot be resolved at present and which should be left for future consideration."[113] Universal House of Justice

Consultation requires that we behave with a level of maturity. However, learning about the requirements of consultation is necessary for maturation and unity to take place. Consider this:

"Consultation is no easy skill to learn, requiring as it does the subjugation of all egotism and unruly passions, the cultivation of frankness and freedom of thought as well as courtesy, openness of mind and wholehearted acquiescence in a majority decision."[114] Universal House of Justice

"Consultation has been ordained by Bahá'u'lláh as the means by which agreement is to be reached and a collective course of action defined. It is applicable to the marriage partners and within the family, and indeed in all areas where believers participate in mutual decision-making. It requires all participants to express their opinions with absolute freedom and without apprehension that they will be censured and/or their views belittled; these prerequisites for success are unattainable if the fear of violence or abuse are present."[115] Universal House of Justice

A wife shares:

"Discerning what decisions to make in a marriage, and how to make them effectively so they maintain and create unity, is an ever-present, ever-evolving process. Alone, our ability to discern the truth and to make the best and wisest decisions possible is restricted and limited by our single frame of reference. Together, we open up the channel for the gifts of understanding, clarity, and forward motion. Our marriage grows and matures as we increase our effectiveness with consulting together. When I try to do it alone, the board meeting in my head thinks it knows everything and has it all worked out. However, when I pause and look at all the mental chatter, I realize just how frustrated I am with the solo process and conclusions. My thoughts often spin in a circle and don't flow out into meaningful directions.

"When we consult, all thoughts and feelings matter. They not only matter, but they are vital to the outcome. However, all the chatter in my head also must calm down so I can truly listen to the wisdom of my husband. He doesn't usually think like I do, and that's a good thing! He listens well though and drops starbursts of wisdom that focus on what's important or clarifies where my thinking is off base. Sometimes we are

delightfully surprised to find out we are already thinking alike. The more deeply we listen to one another, practice self-discipline, and apply communication skills, the better the consultation process goes.

"Sometimes consultation is easy, but at other times it's very difficult. Sometimes I keep saying what I think, but my partner has a different perspective. We pop in from time to time and visit the topic, but one or the other of us retreats. It seems like there are too many things in the way of clarity, or we just must wait patiently for something to fall into place. At times we need to involve others in the process. I often want to agitate for the matter to be settled 'now' rather than waiting. But sometimes readiness must come first. Readiness can be about many things:

- Letting go of hurt feelings
- Increasing our compassion for one another
- Working through forgiveness of some action one of us has taken
- Gathering the facts
- Hearing other perspectives
- Gathering strength to deal with the outcome"

Each of us may take different pathways and lengths of time to process thoughts and feelings. One of us may do this privately and internally, and the other externally through talking. One may be direct and the other more circular. Alternatively, we may have similar approaches. Our success at consulting requires us to learn how to adjust to each other's needs and styles, as well as make requests for different approaches as needed. Someone shares:

"It's a new feeling to create a partnership striving for physical and spiritual union, as I have been used to making my life decisions on my own for the last 30 years. Rarely have I

consulted with others about decisions in my life. Now I need to remember to consult with my new marriage partner about decisions affecting us both. We have done quite well in letting decisions evolve, starting at one decision then modifying it with more information and input, a creative process, one that shows we can be flexible."

Someone shares their views on consultation and the spiritual and creative process involved:

"I love the feeling inside when all the pieces of a consultation come together and we are inspired to form a united decision, where the direction feels clear and definite. There are no hidden facts or feelings held back waiting to explode with some unexpected trigger. It's like putting the last piece of the puzzle in place and seeing the whole picture. Our minds and hearts were open to cooperating and collaborating, and the truth and benefits of a choice became clear. It's joyful when there's agreement, and we can both wholeheartedly support the decision. And, it's usually a decision far greater, stronger, and with more wisdom than I could ever have created on my own.

"In fact, thoughts and creative ideas flow out of me in consultation that are completely new to me. At times, I have no conscious thought about what I will express until my mouth opens and out comes something that works perfectly. It comes alive as I speak it. This tells me that inspiration has a place in consultation too.

"For consultation is no mere exchange of thoughts between two or more people. It's actually discourse with the spiritual energies that circle round us and assist the words to touch, bump, mingle, grind, caress, and finally blend into a coherent whole. It's the process of listening, not just to one another, but to the guidance God promises when we try to discern His Will and align our lives to it.

"Ultimately, consultation brings the institution of marriage to its maturation and fulfillment, generating the light of unity with every consultation and every decision."

As we develop our skills in consulting, the process becomes smoother, we build better understanding, and there is more synergy and creativity in our decision-making. Consultation frees us from using strictly linear thinking and makes the best use of both of our styles of working through issues. Someone shares about their process:

"I married later in life and gained a young adult stepdaughter with the marriage. Shortly after we married, she contacted us about spending a week with us in our small apartment. My husband would be away at work all day, every day of her visit. I was in a state of panic because of my difficulties communicating with her.

"I knew I wouldn't be able to fake it for an entire week! I also knew that things kept inside have a way of blowing up in the worst possible ways. There was no way around it. I had to tell my brand-new husband that I didn't want to be alone with his 'baby' girl.

"I said some prayers and asked if we could consult. He knew it was important, because the word 'consultation' has special meaning for us. We sat kneecap-to-kneecap. I began to cry, and I said to him, 'Honey, I apologize so much, and I know I'm about to disappoint you, but I have to tell you the truth. I am really uncomfortable being around your daughter. I'm just not sure how to manage while she is here.'

"I thought that this could be the end of us. To my shock and amazement, my dear husband burst out laughing! He, too, had the same difficulty communicating with her, and he, too, was nervous!

"It was wonderful knowing that neither of us was alone and could offer comfort and support to one another with the visit, which turned out fine.

"It was even more wonderful to learn that no matter how difficult the topic of our consultation, we could each participate in the process of finding a unified plan of action. We knew we would be heard, that understanding could be achieved, and that our marriage would be stronger for it. We now have a strong marriage, and consultation is at its foundation."

Following the Will of God

When we pray and consult together, we are always conscious that ideally the outcome will be blessed and guided by Bahá'u'lláh and God. Consider this quotation:

> "Your desire to follow the Will of God in all things in your life is highly praiseworthy and will, indeed, as you have experienced, bring spiritual confirmations. However, the House of Justice stresses that the avenue by which one receives guidance is not confined to inspiration, which can, in fact, be highly misleading.
>
> "God has endowed human beings with more than one way of receiving guidance in the decisions we have to make, as 'Abdu'l-Bahá has explained. There are the Holy Writings, in which are clear directions for the way in which we should live; if an inner voice prompts us to act contrary to the explicit teachings we can be sure that, far from being an inspiration from God, that inner voice is the expression of our own lower nature, and should be disregarded. There is also the gift of intelligence and good judgement—the faculty which distinguishes man from the animal kingdom; God intends us to use this faculty, which can be a powerful instrument for distinguishing between true inspirations and vain imaginings. There is the power of prayer through

which we strive to purify our motives, to seek the Will of God and to implore His guidance and assistance. There is also the law of consultation, one of the distinguishing features of this great Revelation."[116] On behalf of the Universal House of Justice

Someone shares:

"When my husband and I were going through a very challenging time, it seemed that no consultation, discussion, argument, or anything, was going to resolve the issues. I learned that when someone believes you have an ulterior motive, or that your opinion is self-serving, it does not matter whether you use reason, scripture, or science. Your marriage partner cannot listen, because the trust is not there. We were at that spot, where nothing I could say or do mattered, and I thought nothing would penetrate or alter his thinking.

"I realized that all I could do was stop talking and pray for my husband to see. After a week or so of holding my tongue and praying diligently, I discovered that it was my eyes that began to see differently! As I began seeing things differently, and I began changing, then, and only then, did I notice that he began seeing our situation differently. It was as if through silent prayer, we met halfway. It was then I learned that sometimes consultation in marriage needs to be primarily between us and God."

Deferring to Each Other

There can be times during consultations when we may not agree with each other about a matter and may consultatively agree to defer to one or the other of us. We may also consultatively agree on certain instances when we can act independently without returning to consult together about a matter. If consulting or agreeing to defer to one of us does not produce harmony, then we may be best to involve someone else in helping us reach agreement. Guidance about these matters is below.

> "...[W]ives, in some cases, have a tendency to exert an unjust degree of domination over their husbands, which, of course, is not right, any more than that the husband should unjustly dominate his wife.
>
> "In any group, however loving the consultation, there are nevertheless points on which, from time to time, agreement cannot be reached. In a Spiritual Assembly this dilemma is resolved by a majority vote. There can, however, be no majority where only two parties are involved, as in the case of a husband and wife. There are, therefore, times when a wife should defer to her husband, and times when a husband should defer to his wife, but neither should ever unjustly dominate the other. In short, the relationship between husband and wife should be as held forth in the prayer revealed by 'Abdu'l-Bahá which is often read at Bahá'í weddings: 'Verily they are married in obedience to Thy command. Cause them to become the signs of harmony and unity until the end of time.'"[117] Shoghi Effendi

> "... [T]here are times when the husband and the wife should defer to the wishes of the other. Exactly under what circumstances such deference should take place is a matter for each couple to determine. If, God forbid, they fail to agree, and their disagreement leads to estrangement, they should seek counsel from those they trust and in whose sincerity and sound judgment they have confidence, in order to preserve and strengthen their ties as a united family."[118] On behalf of the Universal House of Justice

Here is one couple's experience:

"Deferring without first fully exploring an issue doesn't work if we are attempting to live within the character qualities of integrity and honesty. However, occasionally, one of us does not feel strongly about what we are consulting about, and so we defer to the choice the other feels is best. There is no majority vote in a marriage, so at times when we try repeatedly and still cannot see the best choice, we may again defer to something one or the other thinks might work. This is not about dominating each other, however. We are together on the decision and carry the choice out in unity."

Consulting Together

We might spend only a few minutes together and reach a decision on a topic at hand. The process could be longer as we spend a few days or months working through an issue step-by-step. We may discover it works to build regular consultation into a routine, such as having tea together after dinner. We may add to our dialogue with telephone calls, texts, or emails. One retired couple we know consults as they play a daily game of dominoes, and a decision arrives gradually through multiple interactions. Being flexible with our process is a good strategy when we are advancing into new growth opportunities. We need to allow for time to research options or to seek counsel from others that may enhance our understanding. Someone shares:

"The most productive way I have found in my marriage for building closeness and learning about each other is practicing consultation together. We assist each other to share freely with one another. Through consulting together, we have learned each other's weaknesses and strengths and how to be partners to one another. However, we didn't start out being that skillful.

"Before I married my current husband, I had a serious relationship with another man. It took me a long time to see how his words toward me eroded my self-respect and self-confidence. He would say things like 'You don't have a useful thought in your head,' or 'Where did you come up with that stupid idea?'. I sought counseling after the relationship ended, which brought me healing and prepared me for a new relationship and for marriage.

"In spite of the counseling, the past still caused a challenge when I entered into this marriage. Early on, I instantly tensed up when my husband and I began consulting. I was on guard, fearing that he might criticize me. Instead of paying attention to the topic and what I might say, I watched his facial expressions anxiously and listened for an insulting tone of voice. I wanted to spot any upcoming negativity, so I could run away. Obviously, our consultations as a couple did not go well!

"Thankfully, my loving husband realized that we were going astray, and he made some suggestions. 'Sweetie, how about we spend time with me just holding you and telling you how much I love you before we start talking. We could even try consulting with you in my arms!' Being newlyweds, however, sometimes that turned into a distraction!

"We have found, however, that holding hands or sitting knee-to-knee while we talk often helps. Sometimes he rubs the tension out of my shoulders. I've gradually built trust in his kindness and gentleness and learned to relax, listen, and participate much better."

Someone else shares about the process of consultation in their marriage:

"We use consultative communication as a core of our relationship. We talk often and nothing is off limits in our discussions. We present and openly discuss our thoughts and ideas and work to find the most skillful path forward in our

relationship, our home, as parents, and as individuals. Our communication is loving and respectful, whether we agree or not. We do not accuse or blame each other when things are tough, or when we disagree.

"The foundation of our relationship is mindfulness. We each have a strong meditation and mindfulness practice, and this provides us each with the tools to see things in a way that is very conducive to consultation and a caring relationship. Mindfulness is the process of looking inward to see what is really happening inside us in a situation. With mindfulness, one comes to see that the external world is not the problem. The only problem is our reaction to what is going on in the world around us. We come to see clearly that it's our internal self-talk, judging mind, desires, and aversions that are the roots of our suffering. And when we suffer this way, our ego feels threatened and reacts with fear and rejection, and we close down to others. Mindfulness breaks this pattern.

"While the external world provides a stimulus, it's what we do with that stimulus that determines how we feel and how we treat others as a result of what we are feeling. When we learn this deeply, experientially, there is an inner stability—a sense of peace and tranquility—that has the capacity to hold all the stimuli in our lives as they happen. When we act from this place of stable tranquility, we speak and act skillfully. Our words and actions are rooted in compassion, generosity, and wisdom. When we respond to the events in our lives without this stable tranquility and clear seeing, we are much more likely to be reacting to our own desires, our fears and aversions, and to the confusion that comes with an unsettled mind. Strong relationships can be built on stable and peaceful minds. Reactive minds tend to create erratic and unsettled relationships.

"This calm and peaceful place of mindfulness, then, is the foundation upon which we have built our relationship. We each

take responsibility for our own thoughts, feelings, and actions. When one of us is feeling frustration, anger, fear, or any other afflictive emotion, we both recognize that those feelings belong to the one who is feeling them. As such, the other person does not take on the negative feelings themself, nor do they need to be defensive or guilty. Instead, the one who is not feeling the afflictive emotion can be present to the needs of the one who is feeling the emotion. We listen without judgment or commentary, without trying to solve the issue for the other. We let the other feel what they need to feel, but are caring, supportive and loving. We call this 'being the space for the other person to happen in'.

"With the foundation of mindfulness, our relationship is a place of harmony and loving feelings most of the time. As with any relationship, there are times when we are at odds with each other (when neither of us is being mindful). In these cases, we each have the freedom to call a time out, to take a break until we are feeling more spacious. But even this is done with honor and respect—no blame, judgment, or animosity is attached to the need for a little time.

"The relationship that has grown out of our mindfulness is a safe space, a refuge, a 'fortress for well-being'. Each of us has the implicit awareness that in this relationship it's okay to feel what you need to feel and express what you need to express. The other will (most of the time) be the space that holds what you need to express. The space is loving, non-judgmental, and boundless. It feels as though the love, the caring and the intimacy are greater, as there is less of 'me' standing in the way of being present to the other person.

"Consultation seems to arise organically out of a mindful relationship. Mindfulness invites us each to consider what is most skillful first, and to realize that we do not need to cater to every desire and aversion that arises within us. This is the basis

of consultation—one can put forward an idea, thought, or opinion, and realize that it does not belong to 'me'.

"When we speak, we are aware of how our words include not only the idea we are trying to convey, but also the emotions that are attached to the idea—how we 'feel' about the idea. With awareness, we can take the time to let our speech be as skillful as it can be, while trusting that the other one will hear us from that spaciousness spoken of earlier. We speak our mind and then let go of it.

"When we listen, we just listen. We are aware of any of our own internal reactions, arising thoughts and feelings, but we are aware that these have no power when we just open to them and let them be. This allows the mind to stay relatively quiet while the other speaks. We can truly hear what is being said before we form our own opinion and formulate our response.

"Our consultation then, is a process of being aware of our own feelings as we speak and as we listen. There is a sense of great support in knowing that the other is spacious as we do this."

Approaches to Consider

It's wise for us to remember to flexibly try out various elements and approaches enough times to know what is useful. If conflict arises, we can take a pause break or try something new, such as writing down a thought and passing it to the other, and then go back and forth this way for a while. We can try consulting outdoors on a walk or in some other venue. We can succeed with practice.

A Simple Outline

Here is a list of elements that we can consider:

1. Focus on achieving harmony.

2. Pray together.
3. Clarify the topic or purpose of the consultation.
4. Mutually share about the topic and ask questions to build understanding, stopping to reflect or pray again as needed.
5. Assess if more time or fact-finding are needed.
6. Make a unified decision if timely and needed.
7. Carry out the decision or move forward with greater understanding.
8. Reflect and assess the decision or situation, adjusting our approach as needed.

More detail is below.

Possible Couple Consultation Guidelines[119]

Some aspects of consultation include:

- Open and unified communication between two (or more) people before making decisions or taking action
- A prayer-centered approach that includes a desire to be guided by facts, others' perspectives, spiritual principles, and religious quotations that inform the decision-making process, where relevant for those consulting
- Focusing on the truth and ideal outcomes—understanding each other and clarifying each person's thoughts, feelings, views, preferences, requests, goals, and beliefs
- Each person contributes equally to the process, sharing information, offering opinions for consideration, and seeking to understand and gain new insights from different perspectives—even those which appear to clash with other ideas
- Each person proceeding with a flexible and open mind, receiving new information and shifting to incorporate new understandings

- The group/couple harmonizing its purposes and directions to reach a mutually-agreeable decision about the best course of action (or no action), often resulting in a solution of higher caliber than any being considered at the outset; Even if a decision or plan doesn't produce the desired results or appears to have been misguided, when made and carried out in unity, it's usually quickly corrected through further consultation

Suggested Guidelines for Couple Consultation

The guidelines below summarize many aspects of this chapter and may improve consultation in our marriage. Creating an atmosphere of openness, objectivity, and humility will empower us to successfully resolve issues.

While this process is presented below in a formal, sequential way, in real life it need not, and usually will not, follow this order. Couples often consult in casual and relaxed settings—during a walk, while driving, during a meal, or while working on a project together. Therefore, we can view these guidelines as hints or tips that may or may not be useful, depending on the situation. While they are outlined in a matter-of-fact manner, they can sometimes require considerable emotional and mental effort to yield the best outcomes. Also, it's common for advice about consultation to include saying a prayer first. This can be beneficial; however, when consultation is happening in the middle of action, it may be difficult to stop in the moment and pray.

At the Beginning

1. **Prepare in Advance:** Find or prepare any applicable background information and relevant facts. Take care of any personal needs, such as eating or sleeping, before we engage in what may be a difficult conversation. Pray and

prepare ourselves to be open and detached, eager to come to a common solution that we can commit to together.

2. **Assess Timeliness and Privacy:** Assess whether it's timely to address the matter—sometimes there is an immediate need, sometimes it's better to set a time in the future. Protect our privacy when appropriate; for example, we may not want to have a difficult consultation with other people around. Consider whether working through an issue would be good for others to see, especially children—sometimes it is, sometimes it is not.

3. **Focus:** Agree together on the purpose and/or goal of the consultation, and refrain from bringing up unrelated issues. Stay aware of thoughts, views, preferences, requests, goals, beliefs, and feelings that we may wish to or are wise to share. Also stay aware of how and when we express these, so we encourage rather than discourage someone else from sharing as well. Try to stay centered on coming to a solution by sharing in a unified manner and avoid manipulating each other or the outcome.

4. **Explore Openly:** Strive to understand the problem at a deep level. Detach from any particular outcome and be open to learn. Each person considers which of their values and beliefs—and those of their partner—are relevant to the situation. Allow the creative process to generate solutions that neither of us planned ahead of time.

5. **Begin with Love and Unity:** It's helpful to take some action to build a loving and unified connection before consulting, such as prayer or holding hands; incorporate these practices as needed throughout the consultation. Remember that our individual interests are interwoven with our couple and family interests.

Throughout the Process

1. **Include Others:** When needed and appropriate, include other people, particularly those affected by the situation and outcome or those who have expertise related to the issue. Involve relevant children when appropriate for their age, maturity, and the topic. Be clear in our own minds—and with any children—about whether they are only sharing their views, thoughts, and feelings, or whether they will also participate in the decision-making part of the process.

2. **Share and Listen:** Share opinions, perspectives, and ideas frankly, honestly, respectfully, and in a moderate manner. Invite each other to fully share what is on our minds and hearts. Search for truth and do not stubbornly insist upon our own views—recognizing that each of us has something to offer and that the solution will often arise from "the clash of differing opinions". Listen patiently, attentively, and compassionately, and check in with each other to ensure that we are understanding each other throughout the process. Take a break when we need it—to clear our heads, reflect, say a prayer, meditate, eat, sleep, walk, or whatever else is needed.

3. **After Sharing, Let Go:** At the heart of consultation is relinquishing our own agendas, egos, and investments in the outcome in recognition that a shared solution is the desirable result. To help with this, we might imagine that we release our ideas and contributions into an imaginary central area where neither of us "owns" them. They belong to both of us—not individually but collectively—and we can modify them as needed. As we gain new perspectives, we create mutual solutions. [Hint: It can be useful to put an actual, physical bowl or other container between us to

symbolically and metaphorically "receive" our words. If we are struggling in expressing ourselves, we can also write down our thoughts and exchange them through this bowl.]

4. **Practice Equality, Respect, and Fairness:** Participate equally, with all contributions worthy of respect. Avoid domination, blame, repeated complaints, abuse, or threats that would sabotage the process or force any one decision or outcome to happen. Ensure that we consider each other's perspectives with fair-mindedness. Resolve not to cause or take offense at each other's words. If either of us notices we're repeating things we've already said, it's likely that we don't feel heard. It may be helpful to write key points down and share them, or have the other person reflect back a summary of what they think they've heard and see whether there is understanding. Reflecting understanding is not the same as coming to agreement, but once someone has said back to us what they think we are trying to convey, we can clarify our perspective as needed. It can also set our heart at rest that we have been heard—regardless of the outcome that follows. This is an important tool in any communication process, but particularly so with loved ones.

5. **Search for a Diversity of Solutions:** Share clear information, in an honest, calm, courteous, loving, and open-minded way. Search for new insights and facts and apply any pertinent information to the issue. Welcome both agreement and clashes of differing *opinions*, which can lead to a spark of truth and keep us focused on finding solutions. On the other hand, avoid a clash of *feelings*, which can obscure or hide the truth, and cause hurt. We will, of course, experience emotions, but stay aware of their impact, as they may hinder the effectiveness of the discussion, and be aware when sharing feelings may

enhance the discussion instead. For example, sharing that, while we feel frustrated, we also feel deep respect for the other person and want the best outcome, can relieve tension in a situation. On the other hand, feeling anger or frustration and expressing that as an attack will likely derail the effectiveness of the consultation.

6. **Monitor the Quality:** Encourage and affirm each other's positive participation and progress. Pause if serious disunity begins to arise and do what is needed to calm down and rebalance before consulting further. Be thorough. Avoid rushing decisions that need more time.

Making a Decision

1. **Make a Unified Decision:** Settle matters in harmony and love and conclude with a unified decision. Aim not necessarily for perfection, but for the best possible decision from among the options available. Ensure that we assess whether the decision will serve our marriage and family well.

2. **Defer As Needed:** At times after consulting about an issue thoroughly we may still struggle to find an agreed-upon solution. At other times, we may note that one of us has more expertise on the matter, or one of us does not have a strong opinion about the issue. When these situations arise, one of us may choose to defer to the other's opinion. This is still a unified consultative decision that we will benefit from carrying out together as couple.

3. **Seek Additional Help:** If we find it impossible to reach a unified decision and this is causing disunity, seek out sincere, trustworthy people whose judgment and wisdom we respect. This may include family members, friends, or experts. Invite them into the consultation and ask for their

input on the issue as a means of preserving the well-being of our marriage and our family.

Carrying Out the Decision

1. **Share Responsibility:** Commit to carrying out the decision wholeheartedly and in unity. Agree on the best ways to carry out the decision, such as what will be done together and what will be left up to individual initiative and judgment. Execute the agreed-upon actions with a learning-in-action mindset, to discover the merits of the decision.

2. **Set up Support Systems:** Recognize that we will likely have to persevere for it to be clear that the decision was the best one. Put in place a system of accountability that we both agree will assist the decision to be carried out smoothly and consistently. This system could include calendar notifications, cell phone reminders, text reminders, specific goals with dates assigned, checking in with each other periodically, or anything else that works for us.

Pause for Reflection and Assessment: Reflect on what is happening and assess any progress, successes, or difficulties. Determine the next stage in carrying out the decision or whether a new, modified decision is needed instead. Capture any learning that occurred and avoid criticism or blame about anything that happened. Focus on the next best unified actions to take.

The method below can be useful when a couple wants to consult about a specific issue.

Building Understanding and Making Unified Decisions Through Consultation—Possible Approach After Agreeing on a Focus Topic (Susanne M. Alexander and Philip L. Donihe)

Process Notes:

- The intent of consultation is building understanding; it also often includes making unified decisions.
- Pause for prayer and/or silent meditation before or during the consultation; be open to inspiration throughout.
- All contributions to the consultation belong in the middle to all involved; they no longer belong to the person who said them, so ideas mingle, and everyone is free to work on the best outcome.
- At times we may find it useful for the listener to summarize what the speaker said to check for understanding and provide opportunity for clarification.
- At times, we may ask ourselves the question, "Is there anything else to say?" and then pause for quiet reflection.

Part 1

- Clarify the Topic to Address
- Choose one person to make notes while the other talks; switch as needed
- Put each item below as a heading on a separate piece of paper/index card
- The process does not need to be linear; jumping around the items while sharing is fine

1. Principles/Values That Apply to the Topic
2. Concerns Each of Us Has
3. Feelings About the Topic or Circumstances Related to the Topic
4. Facts that Relate to the Topic
5. Possible Approaches/Solutions to Consider or Reject

6. Vision/Perspectives of the Desired Outcome
7. Decision Made (if Applicable)
8. Actions to Take, Who Is Responsible, and When to Be Completed by

Process Consideration: Unrelated topics may arise to address at another time. Make a note of them on a separate document, but do not be distracted by discussing them.

Part 2:

1. Choose timing for when to review actions and progress
2. Reflect and identify actions that are working well and why
3. Reflect and identify actions that will be good to stop doing and capture any learning from them
4. Plan for building on effective actions; Next steps
5. Choose timing for re-review

Couple Actions

1. Choose a topic and use the "Building Understanding and Making Unified Decisions Through Consultation—Possible Approach After Agreeing on a Focus Topic" framework.

2. Identify an issue that will benefit from others being involved in the consultation. Invite them and use this same framework or an agreed different approach.

3. Assess the possibility of having regular family meetings with our children. What roles could be useful? What pre-planning is needed? What guidelines would contribute to an orderly meeting? Note: Researching family meetings on the internet will provide suggestions and lessons learned from others.

Couple Reflection and Consultation

1. What do we appreciate about our consultations?
2. What skills and attributes could we strengthen to improve the quality of our consultations? How will we do this?
3. What environments seem to be best for us when consulting?
4. What methods of consulting are useful for us?
5. What occurs in consultations between us that are most successful? In ones where other family members are involved?
6. Do we have any issues that would be best to invite others to join us for addressing them? How will we invite them? How will we explain the issue to them? Will we need to explain to them what consultation is?

Parallel Track 2: Growing Our Individual Capacity

Note: This section is generally for individuals in a marriage. Please ensure that as a couple you are also studying "Parallel Track 1: Sharing with One Another", when you are ready.

Chapter 11: Honoring Our True Selves

Striving for Self-Respect and Happiness

When tests arise within a marriage, we can struggle with how we feel about ourselves. At times we behave in positive ways, but at other times we become unhappy and our words and behavior reflect this mood. The nature of the tests and how we speak and act can diminish our self-respect and self-confidence.

When we value our words and actions because they align with God's teachings and reflect our nobility as human beings, our self-respect increases. Our happiness is vitally linked to this self-respect. When we are happy:

- It's easier to influence happiness in others
- We are more likely to find useful ways to be of service in the world
- It can be easier to contribute to strengthening our marriage.

This quotation illuminates these concepts:

"... [M]an's supreme honor and real happiness lie in self-respect, in high resolves and noble purposes, in integrity and moral quality, in immaculacy of mind."[120] 'Abdu'l-Bahá

Self-respect increases as we develop our capacity for knowing and loving God, ourselves, and others. As we develop our capacity for self-respect and love, we strengthen our ability to be of selfless service to others, which can be viewed as the highest expression of the best of ourselves. This service can include the thoughtful and kind actions we offer to our marriage partner and children.

Daniel C. Jordan in his pamphlet "Becoming Your True Self" writes:

> "The loving capacity includes not only the ability to love but also the ability to be loved—to attract love. We cannot have lovers without loved ones. If we do not know how to be loved or cannot accept it, then we frustrate others who are struggling to develop their capacity to love. Not accepting someone's love is very frequently experienced as rejection and does untold amounts of damage, particularly in young children."[121]

One person shares:

"I think that we are all on the road toward being better people illumined by the teachings of Bahá'u'lláh. Some seem to be further along the road and others not so far, but as long as we are striving along this path, there is hope that we will continue to improve. People can contribute to us by noticing our small achievements and improvements and overlooking our shortcomings."

Our Dual Nature

We all have a higher spiritual nature and a personal responsibility for developing it, while at the same time subduing our lower, material nature. We have the capacity to develop an almost endless number of character strengths, the attributes or virtues that God has placed within our higher nature. These quotations amplify this concept:

> "Having created the world and all that liveth and moveth therein, He, through the direct operation of His unconstrained and sovereign Will, chose to confer upon man the unique distinction and capacity to know Him and to love Him—a capacity that must needs be regarded as the generating impulse and the primary purpose

underlying the whole of creation.... Upon the inmost reality of each and every created thing He hath shed the light of one of His names, and made it a recipient of the glory of one of His attributes. Upon the reality of man, however, He hath focused the radiance of all of His names and attributes, and made it a mirror of His own Self. Alone of all created things man hath been singled out for so great a favor, so enduring a bounty."[122] Bahá'u'lláh

"In man there are two natures; his spiritual or higher nature and his material or lower nature. In one he approaches God, in the other he lives for the world alone. Signs of both these natures are to be found in men. In his material aspect he expresses untruth, cruelty and injustice; all these are the outcome of his lower nature. The attributes of his Divine nature are shown forth in love, mercy, kindness, truth and justice, one and all being expressions of his higher nature. Every good habit, every noble quality belongs to man's spiritual nature, whereas all his imperfections and sinful actions are born of his material nature."[123] 'Abdu'l-Bahá

"Self-sacrifice means to subordinate this lower nature and its desires to the more godly and noble side of ourselves. Ultimately, in its highest sense, self-sacrifice means to give our will and our all to God to do with as He pleases. Then He purifies and glorifies our true self until it becomes a shining and wonderful reality."[124] On behalf of Shoghi Effendi

"... [T]he complete and entire elimination of the ego would imply perfection—which man can never completely attain—but the ego can and should be ever-increasingly subordinated to the enlightened soul of man. This is what spiritual progress implies."[125] On behalf of Shoghi Effendi

Aspects of our lower nature, such as selfishness, jealousy, or laziness, can interfere with our self-improvement process. When our marriage becomes difficult, often it can seem easier to dwell in our lower nature, which, in turn, diminishes our self-respect. We focus on the poor behavior of our partner, tell others about our grievances, and focus entirely on their faults or mistakes. We magnify everything negative our partner did in the past and ignore the positive they do in the present. We stop reflecting on our own behavior and what we need to improve. When we behave in these ways, conflict is likely, and positive progress forward is difficult to achieve.

Marriages and families benefit when there are many more positive interactions than negative ones. Consider this:

> "If we Bahá'ís cannot attain to cordial unity among ourselves, then we fail to realize the main purpose for which the Báb, Bahá'u'lláh and the Beloved Master lived and suffered.
>
> "In order to achieve this cordial unity one of the first essentials insisted on by Bahá'u'lláh and 'Abdu'l-Bahá is that we resist the natural tendency to let our attention dwell on the faults and failings of others rather than on our own. Each of us is responsible for one life only, and that is our own. Each of us is immeasurably far from being 'perfect as our heavenly father is perfect' and the task of perfecting our own life and character is one that requires all our attention, our will-power and energy. If we allow our attention and energy to be taken up in efforts to keep others right and remedy their faults, we are wasting precious time."[126] On behalf of Shoghi Effendi

Someone reflects:

"In marriage, mutual growth will occur when each partner recognizes the other's qualities, praises them always, and

encourages them in that path. Developing qualities that one already possesses will ease the acquisition of more qualities, and in a couple, the qualities of one partner can be learned by the other. As for the weaknesses, qualities like patience, avoiding fault finding, and forgiveness will permit the couple to overcome them or live with them. These qualities could be learned or strengthened in marriage. That's how a couple fosters each other's spiritual progress."

A challenge that arises in our lives when we lose self-respect is that we feel unworthy of having others think well of us, or we believe the lies of abusive others. When we respect ourselves and believe we are worthy of God's love and of positive occurrences, we can engage in personal transformation and make progress forward. [For more on abuse, please see Appendix C.]

Consider: A negative view of what's going on with oneself, a partner, a marriage, or a family can at times increase when individuals focus on negative happenings in the world. This could include spending significant time on social media reading negative commentary, or it might be watching negative happenings in politics or in the news of the world. Discussing politics or backbiting about politicians can be particularly divisive in a home. It's wise for us to carefully observe what external factors are affecting us, referring to the appropriate guidance from the institutions on the topics as needed.

Our Essential Nobility and Character

As we recognize that we are worthy of love and respect, we progress forward in life, honoring our essential nobility as human beings with a body, mind, heart, and soul. As we honor our nobility, we can begin to see that we are a "mine rich in gems of inestimable value."[127] (Bahá'u'lláh) There are many tools and principles for purifying our characters with positive choices that aim us toward excellence. We can fully engage in transformation:

> "At the very core of the aims of the Faith are the establishment of justice and unity in the world, the removal of prejudice and enmity from among all people, the awakening of compassion and understanding in the hearts of all men and women, and the raising of all souls to a new level of spirituality and behavior through the vitalizing influence of divine Revelation. The course set forth by Bahá'u'lláh for the attainment of these aims is the double task of simultaneously building an ideal society and perfecting the behavior of individuals. For this dual and reciprocal transformation He has not only revealed laws, principles and truths attuned to the needs of this age, but has established the very nucleus and pattern of those institutions which are to evolve into the structure of the divinely purposed world society."[128] On behalf of the Universal House of Justice

When we are in a mode of action and learning, striving to improve ourselves, we tend to produce positive results, increasing our self-respect. It's possible to look honestly and objectively at what we are doing well and where we need to focus our self-improvement efforts.

Individual Actions

1. Choose two actions to take that we think will contribute to increasing our self-respect. What was the outcome? What continues to build our self-respect?

2. Choose one action to take that we think will show respect for another person. What was the outcome? What actions will we now take that will consistently show respect for this person?

3. For 2-3 days, track what negatively influences our thoughts, mood, behavior, and interactions with others. Reflect on where we can change and begin to create an increase in positive occurrences instead.

4. Reflect on what seems to prompt us to feel happiness or joy. Choose one action that demonstrates both self-respect and happiness and carry it out. What was the result?

Individual Reflection

1. How has being disrespectful to myself affected me?
2. What do I specifically respect about myself?
3. What increases my self-respect during times when I doubt my self-worth?
4. When has my experiencing self-respect had a positive effect on others in my life?
5. When has my self-respect seemed to link to happiness?
6. What assists me to look at myself as a noble human being?

Couple Reflection and Consultation

1. How does it affect our relationship when we each respect ourselves?
2. How does it affect us when we don't like our own behavior toward the other?
3. What do we respect and value in each other?
4. What ways can we speak to each other that demonstrate respect?
5. How does it affect our relationship when we each show respect to the other? How does speaking this way affect our children? Others?

Chapter 12: Seeing and Polishing Our Character Gems

Understanding Character

Knowing and applying our character strengths, the qualities of our higher nature, can increase our self-respect. Our character strengths contribute in positive ways to our relationships of all types, including our marriage, and to our family and community. We can define character as:

- The sum of the qualities we develop throughout life as we make choices about how to speak and act; our characters affect most of our words and actions
- The spiritual essence of who we are as human beings; the qualities of God mirrored in us (ex.: courage, thoughtfulness, dependability...)
- Our moral compass or ethical strength that provides the unwavering drive to choose what is right, even when that choice could cause us difficulties, and even if no one else is watching or knows what we are doing

Reputation is what others think about us. Character is who we truly are—the heart and soul of us. We have significant ability to practice character qualities with others for their benefit and ours, as well as to transform the qualities that are weaker. We can build a good reputation by demonstrating character strengths, which are also known as virtues.

Below are quotations from the Bahá'í teachings about character and its importance.

> "The light of a good character surpasseth the light of the sun and the radiance thereof. Whoso attaineth unto it is accounted as a jewel among men. The glory and the

upliftment of the world must needs depend upon it."[129] Bahá'u'lláh

"How resplendent the luminaries of knowledge that shine in an atom, and how vast the oceans of wisdom that surge within a drop! To a supreme degree is this true of man, who, among all created things, hath been invested with the robe of such gifts, and hath been singled out for the glory of such distinction. For in him are potentially revealed all the attributes and names of God to a degree that no other created being hath excelled or surpassed."[130] Bahá'u'lláh

"The most vital duty, in this day, is to purify your characters, to correct your manners, and improve your conduct."[131] 'Abdu'l-Bahá

"Education must be accorded the greatest importance; for just as diseases are highly communicable in the world of bodies, so is character highly communicable in the realm of hearts and spirits."[132] 'Abdu'l-Baha

"The great thing is to 'live the life'—to have our lives so saturated with the Divine teachings and the Bahá'í Spirit that people cannot fail to see a joy, a power, a love, a purity, a radiance, an efficiency in our character and work that will distinguish us from worldly-minded people and make people wonder what is the secret of this new life in us. We must become entirely selfless and devoted to God so that every day and every moment we seek to do only what God would have us do and in the way He would have us do it. If we do this sincerely then we shall have perfect unity and harmony with each other. Where there is want of harmony, there is lack of the true Bahá'í Spirit."[133] On behalf of Shoghi Effendi

We develop and refine our characters over time as we:

- Pray
- Follow the Bahá'í teachings
- Learn about character qualities
- Try out new actions and activities
- Experience, learn, and grow from challenges
- Listen to our inner voice of conscience and feelings of shame or guilt and take preventive or corrective action
- Make amends to others we have hurt; ask for forgiveness
- Make choices to strengthen our qualities, say new words, and take new actions
- Put ourselves in environments and with people who encourage and accompany us with making beneficial changes

No one is perfect. We are probably strong in some character qualities and unskilled or uncertain about practicing others. We develop each quality according to our own willingness, choices, and efforts. We have the capacity to improve. The stronger our character qualities, the better we function in the world. Here is the challenge to remember:

> "On the one hand, the high standard of conduct inculcated by Bahá'u'lláh's Revelation can admit no compromise; it can, in no wise, be lowered, and all must fix their gaze on its lofty heights. On the other, it must be acknowledged that, as human beings, we are far from perfect; what is expected of everyone is sincere daily effort."[134] Universal House of Justice

We can make our best effort to know and develop ourselves. Here is some sharing:

"We are enthusiastic about learning the skills associated with having a good marriage. Because we've both had failed

marriages in the past, we are trying not to repeat the same mistakes. This is hard work because it requires self-reflection and increased self-knowledge, which at times can be quite painful."

"We are mirrors of each other; we reflect each other's light. So, we recognize strengths and shortcomings as they resonate with our own character development. Therefore, we consciously recognize virtues that we value and have developed in ourselves. Correspondingly, when we perceive that another lacks a virtue, it's an opportunity for us to reflect on our own development of that virtue. I find that accepting this concept helps me with both detachment and humility. And, I am less likely to judge my marriage partner or others."

Balancing Our Character Qualities

We can further expand our understanding by learning to apply the principles of balance and moderation in how we practice character qualities:

> "A good character is in the sight of God...and the possessors of insight, the most excellent and praiseworthy of all things, but always on condition that its center of emanation should be reason and knowledge and its base should be true moderation."[135] 'Abdu'l-Bahá

Moderation is the middle way—an excellent balance. Moderating a character quality *does not mean doing it half-way*. It means recognizing the other complementary qualities and behaviors that lead to wisdom in action. We may think of this as applying "helper" qualities—where one quality helps another quality—to produce a better, more balanced outcome. Here are some examples:

- Flexibility can be helpful when we are being purposeful, because while we strive to complete tasks, flexibility reminds us that sometimes circumstances change, or we need to adjust to the needs or preferences of others

- If we want to practice orderliness, including the quality of respect prompts us to reflect and consult about how our actions might affect our family members

Sometimes we apply a quality and are surprised that the outcome is negative instead of positive. It's an opportunity to look at whether we were excessive with it or used it at the wrong time or place. When we apply a character quality to a situation, if we notice that the result is hurt, harm, disunity, or a problem of some type instead of benefit, it's possible that pairing another quality with it would have changed the outcome. We can then apply another quality the next time to practice moderation and balance.

Individual Actions

1. **Assess and Understand My Character Qualities:** This activity will get us started on an individual development process if we are not doing one currently. It's just the beginning, as we will continue to develop all our qualities throughout life. After we have increased our individual understanding, depending on the state of our relationship, we may also choose one or two qualities to strengthen together as a couple. [Below is a self-assessment. If you prefer, there is a validated instrument available called the Character Foundations Assessment™ that can also be paired with an online development system. See the Contact Information at the end of the book to arrange to take the assessment and meet with a certified practitioner for insights and a development process.]

    - Set up a chart on an electronic device or in a notebook of the qualities listed below to increase our understanding of some of our strengths and to identify areas for improvement. Definitions are provided to build our understanding. There are many more possible qualities that could be listed; if we have any additional ones that are important to us, then we can add them to the list.

- Take whatever time we need to be thorough. We may or may not be able to do this activity all at once, especially if we feel overwhelmed or begin to be very self-critical. We can honestly rate ourselves on each character quality by using the 5-point scale provided below. Individually write down the number we think is accurate next to each quality. As we do this, we can also pay attention to whether we use our character strengths with everyone. It can be useful information to note if we use them with others but not in our marriage with each other.

  1 – I rarely use this quality, so my words and actions can often cause problems
  2 – I use this quality only occasionally, possibly causing problems
  3 – I understand this quality, and am strengthening it; sometimes resulting in positive outcomes
  4 – I am becoming more consistent in practicing this quality, usually with positive outcomes
  5 – I practice this quality consciously and consistently

- Looking at our list of qualities again, note four that we most want to develop or build upon—at least for now. The qualities we rated 1, 2, or 3 may offer good choices, as they are in a currently weaker state. Reflect on what specific actions might strengthen them and try out a few.

Some Character Qualities from CharacterYAQ™:

1. **Adherence is** following guidelines, rules, agreements, and laws created to protect relationships, safety, and order; staying faithful to promises made to others.
2. **Compassion is** demonstrating a unique capacity to listen deeply to others about their situations; understanding others' feelings; caring for others' well-being; and seeking ways to ease someone's pain and suffering in mutually satisfactory ways.
3. **Creativity is** drawing on ideas, inspiration, or imagination from many sources to develop or produce something new; being resourceful, intuitive, and solving problems in unique and beneficial ways; and immersing in a problem or situation, looking broadly for insights and connections, allowing for breakthrough ideas and solutions to emerge.
4. **Dependability is** making and keeping commitments, completing agreed tasks, honestly managing resources and money, handling information wisely, and cleaning up after mistakes.
5. **Excellence is** achieving high standards and a superior quality of work, effort, appearance, relationships, and personal development; learning and improving from experiences; and continually raising and meeting expectations.
6. **Flexibility is** being open to change and surprises, adjusting and adapting to life as it happens; being nimble in responding to different people and situations; and considering new and different approaches, methods, ideas, and viewpoints.
7. **Friendliness is** demonstrating an outgoing and positive social attitude and reaching out to connect and build relationships with people; and gracious and warm consideration for others by interacting with polite

manners, respectful gestures, thoughtful actions, and tactful language.

8. **Honor is** having clear principles, beliefs, and positive intentions that guide actions to create beneficial change.
9. **Humility is** seeing and accepting one's whole self, including strengths, imperfections, abilities, accomplishments, failures, and needs in modest and realistic perspective; offering one's time, knowledge, and talents in a self-effacing way; and being willing to accept the knowledge, skills, and help of others.
10. **Joyfulness is** maintaining a happy, optimistic, and uplifting attitude; energetically celebrating the best in relationships, work, and service; and looking at the positive side of circumstances.
11. **Justice is** making careful, independent, and proactive observations of other's actions; initiating decisions, agreements, or actions based on clear facts that are free of bias or prejudice; ensuring fair rewards and appropriate natural consequences or agreed corrective actions occur; and setting appropriate boundaries in relationships.
12. **Moderation is** recognizing and avoiding extremes in use of time, words, actions, and other choices; accomplishing variety, balance, and positive outcomes in such aspects as rest, work, reflection, community service, and leisure activities; and effectively applying and adjusting a level of intensity of focus and action to both accomplish goals and protect relationships and well-being.
13. **Orderliness is** living and working with a sense of harmony; creating uncluttered, well-organized, clean, and shareable spaces; developing systems that allow for easy finding; and systematically planning improvements, tasks, and projects.
14. **Perseverance is** applying energy, effort, and resources toward worthwhile goals until achievement is attained; being committed to the long-term future benefit of actions

done in the present; and using willpower to overcome challenges or adversity as they arise.

15. **Purposefulness is** pursuing and fulfilling meaningful long-term personal goals, commitments, aspirations, and needs; contributing ideas, words, and actions; and participating primarily in vital activities that contribute to desired outcomes.
16. **Reflection is** calm self-awareness, understanding, and assessment; inwardly exploring actions, circumstances, thoughts, feelings, and perceptions; seeking inspiration; and analyzing to learn the best approaches for improving situations.
17. **Respect is** interacting with all people and what they value with fair treatment, dignity, consideration, and esteem; and recognizing the best knowledge, skills, talents, and abilities of others.
18. **Self-Discipline is** maintaining the inner control to perform needed and important tasks in a timely way; consciously responding in appropriate ways; and choosing what is beneficial or productive and resisting what is harmful or distracting.
19. **Service is** acting selflessly and often sacrificially, directly or indirectly, and with positive intent; and providing time, knowledge, or resources to benefit others without expecting reward or recognition.
20. **Trust is** generously extending confidence; assuming the good intentions and actions of others; accompanying others through learning experiences that build skills and capacities; and giving and expecting appropriate confidentiality.
21. **Truthfulness is** recognizing and accurately communicating facts and feelings; independently seeking knowledge of people, circumstances, issues, and information.

22. **Unity is** consciously looking for and strengthening points of commonality, harmony, connection, and attraction; accepting differences; and working with others to build a strong and coherent foundation for oneness, love, fairness, commitment, inclusion, cooperation, and common goals.

Source and Copyright Note: The definitions in this list are the copyright of CharacterYAQ™ (characteryaq.com) and Susanne M. Alexander, W. Grant Peirce IV, and Johann S. Wong. None of the definitions should be reproduced or used for any purpose without written permission from the copyright holders. Thank you for your respect toward our work.

2. **My Character Development Plan:** Set up on an electronic device or in a notebook a chart that captures the elements in this example below for each quality to develop.

EXAMPLE
Quality to Develop: *Perseverance*
Why? *Because I often fail to finish my personal projects. Too often I allow obstacles or trying to be perfect to discourage me, I lose motivation, and I postpone action until "I have more time."*
Who Can Help or Encourage Me with This? *My friend ___, who told me he/she found some strategies for developing his/her virtue of perseverance.*
Development Goal (Desired Outcome): *I'd currently rank my perseverance at a 2 out of 5. If I could get that quality, when working on my projects, up to a strength of 4, I think I could accomplish much more in life.*

Development Actions:	**Start Date:**	**Assess Date:**
1. *I will create actionable goals and firm deadlines for when to complete 2 personal growth projects. I will make myself accountable to (my friend) or someone else for delivery of these results. I will make sure that at least 1 project is focused on service to others.*	*Date*	*Date*
2. *Talk with (my friend) or other friends whenever I feel discouraged; this will help me to address the obstacles so I can keep moving forward.*	*Date*	*Date*
3. *When starting work on each project, I will take a few minutes to pray for perseverance, focus, and determination.*	*Date*	*Date*
4. *Read inspiring quotations and stories about perseverance as part of my daily practice of reading the Bahá'í writings.*	*Date*	*Date*
Signs of Improvement: *After 1 month of doing this, I completed 1 of the 2 projects, and I am 75% finished with the second project. The service component of these projects has visibly helped the children in my community take charge of improving their lives and those of others.*		
New Actions to Take: *Keep up the accountability, talk to (my friend) more often about this—at least once every 2 weeks.*		

When the date arrives to assess our progress:

- Look over our notes
- Review our behavior
- Reflect on our words and actions
- Determine how much we advanced toward our goal
- Think carefully about how people responded to us—not only those we consulted with but also those we live with or encountered as we were striving to develop and demonstrate the quality

This assessment will give us a sense of our progress, which we can note in the "Signs of Improvement" section. If we want feedback in addition to our own self-assessment, we can approach people and ask for frank but kind comments. Is anyone noticing our positive changes? Are we getting enough useful feedback and encouragement?

Other Action Options

3. Choose a character quality from the list above that we want to increase our awareness of. For a week—or some other reasonable timeframe—be in situations with other people where we can observe their behavior. Track how others demonstrated or spoke about the quality and what the outcome was. When appropriate we can prompt a discussion with those we are observing about the quality we chose. Where did we see the quality appear? How often did it happen? When did the use of the quality surprise us? How did we practice this character quality, too? What thoughts do we have about our observations?

4. Choose a quality that inspires us and search for quotations from a variety of sources that increase our understanding of it. Create an artistic rendering of the quality that will be visible to us in our daily life. Consider a poster, screensaver

on a computer, meme, artwork, song, poem, photo, dance, or other expression. Involve children in the activity as appropriate.

5. Identify four specific and attractive gems we like—for example, diamonds, emeralds, sapphires, and rubies—and locate photos of them in a magazine or on the internet. Choose from the "Assess and Understand My Character Qualities" (above in this chapter) four of the character qualities we consider strengths, and match each of these to one of the chosen gems. As we practice each quality, visualize the beautiful gem we have associated with it. For example, we could associate a ruby with justice, and then every time we think or act fairly or advocate for justice on behalf of someone else, we could visualize a sparkling red ruby inside of us. We may find it useful to revisit these images weekly or monthly to assess our consistency with using this metaphor of gems to guide our words and actions.

Individual Reflection:

1. What are some noble character qualities that I respect as strengths of mine?
2. When has practicing a character strength brought me joy? When has this brought joy to others?
3. What interferes with knowing my own character? How can I overcome these challenges?
4. Who do I trust that knows me well and can assist me to gain further insights? How and when will I invite them to participate in this reflection process?
5. Which three of my character strengths could I apply to improve my relationships with my marriage partner and other family members?

6. What are the qualities I'm consistently assessing in my behavior and focused on strengthening? How will strengthening these bring benefit to my marriage? My family?
7. When have I balanced a character strength with another character quality to produce a more positive effect? Which pairings have been most effective?
8. When have I relied too much on a character strength and caused harm by not also using a moderating or "helper" quality? What will I do differently next time?

Couple Reflection and Consultation

1. What do we consider the most attractive character qualities in each other?
2. How does noticing and appreciating these qualities affect how we feel about each other?
3. When might feedback on each other's practice of character qualities cause disunity instead of benefit?
4. When do we find it difficult to use a character strength with each other? What makes it difficult? Would there be benefit in using it anyway?
5. When do we use a character strength to excess with each other and there is a poor outcome? What other quality might moderate or balance its use?
6. How could we positively influence character strengthening in each other?

Chapter 13: Transforming Ourselves Each Day

Accounting for Our Behavior Daily

God has given us free will, which allows us to make whatever character and behavior choices we wish. As we choose words and actions that are positive and that align with the Bahá'í teachings, it facilitates positive interactions with others. Our behavior does not and should not depend upon the behavior of others, even though it's easy to assume that link. Here are some quotations about doing daily and regular self-assessment and personal transformation:

> "... [M]an should know his own self and recognize that which leadeth unto loftiness or lowliness, glory or abasement, wealth or poverty."[136] Bahá'u'lláh

> "Bring thyself to account each day...to give account for thy deeds."[137] Bahá'u'lláh

> "Noble have I created thee, yet thou hast abased thyself. Rise then unto that for which thou wast created."[138] Bahá'u'lláh

> "... Every day, in the morning when arising you should compare today with yesterday and see in what condition you are. If you see your belief is stronger and your heart more occupied with God and your love increased and your freedom from the world greater then thank God and ask for the increase of these qualities."[139] 'Abdu'l-Bahá

> "... [Y]ou should not neglect your health, but consider it the means which enables you to serve. It—the body—is like a horse which carries the personality and spirit, and as such should be well cared for so it can do its work! You should certainly safeguard your nerves, and force yourself to take

time, and not only for prayer and meditation, but for real rest and relaxation. We don't have to pray and meditate for hours in order to be spiritual."[140] On behalf of Shoghi Effendi

The purpose of bringing ourselves "to account" is to better understand what we have done well and what we need to improve. It can be counterproductive if we allow a large negative response to be part of the process:

"[Excessive] Feelings of guilt and shame lead to depression and despair. This, in turn, generates a very negative self-image, and even the smallest problem can seem insurmountable. ... The distinguishing characteristic of a human being is his nobility of character. No matter what the circumstance or the condition, the underlying reality remains that of a nobility of character in the image of God Himself. Negative self-images have no place in a Bahá'í context, and self-abasement is contradictory and forbidden. Struggles and frustrations should be expected as the result of the nobility striving to express itself, and the spiritualization process in these instances must be directed towards strengthening this image of nobility, as opposed to a tendency to cripple oneself with guilt and self-flagellation."[141] Sharon Hatcher Kennedy and Andrew Kennedy

Someone shares about doing the daily process in a positive way:

"I'm focused on the present moment, staying true to myself, whole within my own core, doing an accounting every day, and doing the work around that. I'm grateful to be getting better acquainted with myself through the process too. I'm finding that through natural reflection following service, and through honest sharing, that humble learning occurs, in a palatable way. I feel an acceptance for who I am, as I am, which fosters

the natural desire to be better and work on those areas to improve myself."

Many people have sought help for addictions and problems, and they apply twelve steps of healing to their lives. A portion of those steps shown below addresses a path for individual change and may be useful to us:

- Step 4. Made a searching and fearless moral inventory of ourselves.
- Step 5. Admitted to God, to ourselves and to another human being the exact nature of our wrongs.
- Step 6. Were entirely ready to have God remove all these defects of character.
- Step 7. Humbly asked Him to remove our shortcomings.
- Step 8. Made a list of all persons we had harmed, and became willing to make amends to them all.
- Step 9. Made direct amends to such people wherever possible, except when to do so would injure them or others.
- Step 10. Continued to take personal inventory and when we were wrong promptly admitted it.[142]
  (Excerpt from the 12 Steps of Alcoholics Anonymous)

Here is some guidance about Step 5 above:

> "It is quite understandable that the matter of confession would raise some doubts in your mind as Bahá'u'lláh's injunction against confession is very clear. However, this step...is not confession with the idea of being absolved of one's sins, but is rather a step which helps in self-knowledge. Bahá'u'lláh has said 'True loss is for him whose days have been spent in utter ignorance of his self.'[143] Al-Anon as well as AA is a type of therapy, a therapy not based on medical practices but which stems from the need of human beings to solve their problems

using basically spiritual concepts. We cannot expect a therapeutic method to work if the problems it is designed to address are not spelled out.

"The inventory that is suggested as necessary would contain material relevant to the problems the alcoholic creates and the problems that those close to him create for him. This is not confession of sins as much as being as objective about your own personality and character. Sharing your evaluation of yourself with a close friend would not necessarily be a confession of wrong-doing to that friend as it would be asking someone who is more objective to help you come to a fuller understanding of yourself and your interactions with the alcoholic in your environment."[144] National Spiritual Assembly of the Bahá'ís of the United States

Engaging in Being Our Best

Self-assessment is rarely easy, but it can be great to understand ourselves and to grow. We can then better contribute to the lives of others and raise our children to have excellent characters. Once we recognize a character strength, we can:

- Feel a sense of authenticity when we practice it
- Feel excited and enthusiastic about having a positive quality we can apply throughout our life
- Remember to practice moderation; we can often make better progress with focusing on improving one or two qualities at a time rather than many at once

Here is this guidance:

"There is nothing more harmful to the individual—and also to society than false humility which is hypocritical, and hence unworthy of a true Bahá'í. The true believer is one who is conscious of his strength as well as of his weakness, and who, fully availing himself of the manifold opportunities and blessings which God gives him, strives to overcome his defects and weaknesses and this by means of a scrupulous adherence to all the laws and commandments revealed by God through His Manifestation [Bahá'u'lláh]."[145] On behalf of Shoghi Effendi

When we interact with each other, our family members, a manager at work, a community member at a gathering, or people we encounter in daily life, we can assess ourselves by asking questions such as:

- Were my intentions, words, and actions aligned and consistent with each other and with spiritual principles?
- What did I do that was effective? What positive effect did my choices have on me and on others?
- Which character qualities did I practice well?
- Where did I misstep? What would I do differently, if I could do it over?
- Would another character quality have made a difference if I had practiced it instead? For instance, did I practice justice, when compassion might have led to a better outcome?
- Could I have added in a second quality, such as flexibility or respect, to balance the first quality and thereby improve the situation?
- Did I behave ineffectively, or rather did the other person's difficulties or character lead to the negative outcome?
- If the interaction didn't go smoothly, what words or actions would I choose instead, to elicit a better outcome next time?

Someone reflects on the value of character assessment:

"A truthful evaluation of our own thoughts and character is a wholesome, healing step to take, for it's only when we are honest about ourselves that we begin to change and then have a profound effect on society. Prayerfully turning our attention to our own shortcomings and telling ourselves the truth need not have a negative or destructive effect; this is the beginning of a powerful, positive process when it is motivated by the love of God and the desire to be of service to humanity."[146] Hooper Dunbar

Improving Ourselves

No matter how difficult the circumstances, individual and marital transformation can happen with prayer, reading the Bahá'í teachings, reflection, consistent effort, patience, and help from others as needed. We can strengthen ourselves through many experiences, such as traveling, dealing with difficulties, carrying out service, and communicating with others and getting their input. Here is guidance:

> "What every believer, new or old, should realize is that the Cause has the spiritual power to re-create us if we make the effort to let that power influence us, and the greatest help in this respect is prayer. We must supplicate Bahá'u'lláh to assist us to overcome the failings in our own characters, and also exert our own will power in mastering ourselves."[147] On behalf of Shoghi Effendi
>
> "The power of God can entirely transmute our characters and make of us beings entirely unlike our previous selves. Through prayer and supplication, obedience to the divine laws Bahá'u'lláh has revealed, and ever-increasing service to His Faith, we can change ourselves."[148] On behalf of Shoghi Effendi

Someone came to a key realization:

"Early in marriage I was made to realize after all the prayers for detachment I said that the only person I can change is myself. I had to reconsider my attitudes and perceptions, as well as reassess my priorities."

Someone talks about how to accomplish personal growth:

> "Your choices matter, so make a commitment and choose a new path, even if you are uncertain about where it will lead you. Be aware—if the path is familiar, it is not a new one. Only if you give your effort your full 100% commitment, will you be able to assess its value effectively later. Involve others by telling them of your commitment and asking for their assistance—show them how it can benefit both of you. Call on the spiritual power of prayer and allow yourself to be guided forward.
>
> "Your commitment and choice to take a new path in your life will likely result in four to six weeks of turmoil; it will call for conscious awareness and regular effort before it begins to feel right. At the first difficulty along the path, you may be tempted to retreat to a more familiar path, but persevere, be determined, and hold your commitment with integrity. Guidance, confirmation, and support come when you are in action. Observe what is happening and be honest with yourself. Growth is positive change. Be patient, flexible, and graceful—change will come—little by little, day by day." [149] Dan Popov

Here is a perspective from a person engaged in shifting their life in a new direction:

"I knew that if I wanted to have a happy and healthy life, I needed to grow. Because of the positive changes I've made, I feel happier, I sleep better at night, I'm a better husband and

father, and I'm a better friend. I honestly don't think that I know one person who really changed because someone else asked them to and then was genuinely happy. It has to come from inside. I learned mindfulness meditation, I started dance classes (to overcome insecurity issues), I went back to reflection and prayer, and more.

Here is what I learned:

1. *Changing from a personal growth point of view (when the choice is mine and nobody else is asking me or expecting me to change) required me to leave my comfort zone and take risks. We develop defense mechanisms, and we draw imaginary lines that we're not willing to cross or that we don't let others cross. If we or others get too close to that line, or at the first sign of adversity, we come right back to our comfort zone.*

2. *The hardest thing about changing is admitting that there is something wrong with me. It's as if subconsciously it means that something is broken inside of me and needs to be fixed. If someone else asks me to change, then that feeling gets magnified.*

3. *On the lighter side, I'm discovering that the beautiful thing about change is that ultimately it's a choice. When I am brave enough to go past points 1 and 2, no matter how hard it is, how embarrassing it feels, or how much it hurts, ultimately the choice is mine. Now, if I learn something, fix something, or get any type of benefit from what I do, then the reward is totally worth the risk.*

4. *One hard thing about changing is that by doing so my relationships with a lot of people changed, including some of my best friends with whom I hadn't practiced the best habits. It took me a long time to realize that it was okay, even if it was tough.*

"I still have more growing to do, and more change is coming. Now that I have left my ego behind much more, I have extended my comfort zone way past where it was. I have let some old relationships go, and I now surround myself with people who bring out the best in me. I am looking forward to whatever the future brings—all the new lessons, the new experiences, and everything else that 'change' may bring into my life."

Striving for Integrity

Our growth contributes to our ability to strive for a high level of integrity with giving our word and carrying out spiritual actions and life commitments. Every time we keep a promise or commitment, we are operating in alignment with integrity. Every time we break our word, we move away from it. Since our lives are full of promises and commitments, it's an ever-shifting landscape and daily striving. Consider these perspectives:

> "A person's word can have value and power or it can be cheap and meaningless. Persons of integrity have a reputation for keeping their word. What creates a strong reputation for integrity is behavior that is congruent, or consistent, with what we say. People listen to those who keep their word, and people organize their own behavior around promises made. ... When [people] keep their word to each other, predictability results, which creates security and trust. They can rely on each other."[150] Sandra Gray Bender
>
> "A person has integrity when there is no gap between intent and behavior...when he or she is whole, seamless, the same—inside and out. I call this 'congruence.' And it is

congruence—not compliance—that will ultimately create credibility and trust.

"People who are congruent act in harmony with their deepest values and beliefs. They walk their talk. When they feel they ought to do something, they do it. They're not driven by extrinsic forces, including the opinions of others of the expediency of the moment. The voice they listen and respond to is the quiet voice of conscience. ... When you consistently demonstrate inner congruence to your belief system and to principles, you inspire trust in both professional and personal relationships. People feel you are strong, solid, and dependable, and that you are committed to live in ways that are certain to bring positive results and validate their confidence in you."[151] Stephen M. R. Covey

Including Gratitude in Our Lives

As we reflect on our lives and behavior, we can be grateful for opportunities to practice, learn, and grow. Perhaps we were flexible when a friend wanted to make different plans. Maybe we saw an accident happen and practiced compassion by stopping to help. We discovered we were able to be friendly to a difficult neighbor. All these and more are opportunities to thank God for His help. Someone reflected on Bahá'u'lláh's encouragement to be thankful when problems happen:

"I really believe that gratitude is key to being able to experience joy and that it's especially important to look for opportunities for gratitude during times of difficulties."

Gratitude to God encourages us to express thankfulness within our home:

"At home the only currency exchange is how you and your mate express your feelings about each other, and gratitude is an often-overlooked commodity. It's easier to say 'Thanks' when you're feeling good about your marriage. It's harder when you're dissatisfied. But gratitude, and its expression, is not just a *reflection* of a happy marriage; it is one of the causes."[152] Paul Coleman

These people comment on their experience of thankfulness between them and their partners:

"I've been sick with a head cold, and I've been sneezing and coughing. Everywhere I turned, there was a tissue box, waiting for me to cover a sneeze, cough, or drippy nose. I am REALLY grateful to my husband for all these tissue boxes, so I have repeatedly thanked him for this and for how well he takes care of me."

"My husband had a very difficult first marriage. Now that he's in a better marriage with me, he says he never wants to take me and everything I do for us for granted. He thanks me for even the little things. If I hand him a clean towel, cook a good meal, buy supplies, consult with him about his work, and so on, he usually says, 'thank you'. I feel appreciated and more willing to participate fully in our marriage. It also reminds me to thank him for all he does!"

"I've written in a journal most of my life. A few years ago, though, I shifted and started writing letters to God. Each day I express thanks for what happened the day before, make requests for guidance and assistance, and do my best to tune into what work and service I'm to do that day."

Individual Actions

1. Develop a daily habit of bringing ourselves (not our partner) to account, both what we have done well, and where we need to improve the next day. Some people find

it more effective to do a personal review after a night of sleep. Then we can determine what to do better that day.

2. Each day for a week, list three things we are grateful to God for, three things to ask forgiveness for, and three requests for Him to help us with. If we are comfortable with it, we can share the gratitude part of our lists with each other. Continue this practice if it's positive and effective.

3. Make one small (agreed) change in our home environment to see how long it takes us to get used to it. We could move a piece of furniture, move the location of a picture hanging on the wall, or put socks in a different drawer. Then we could make a different, more significant improvement in our physical space, such as organize a few drawers or a closet, paint a wall, or plant some flowers. How do we feel about the changes? What do we think about the amount of effort and adjustment required when something new happens? Would it feel different if we had no say or control over the change rather than these ones that are conscious decisions? How could we adjust when something happens outside of our control?

4. Addressing a habit:
   a. Identify a habit we want to modify or replace.
   b. Outline the expected benefits of the new or different habit.
   c. Write specific goals for our new behavior.
   d. Make a commitment to each other (or to someone else) to accompany each other, be encouraging, and hold each other accountable.
   e. Plan rewards for every week or whatever time interval is most useful.

f. Set up other reminders or incentives that will assist with fulfilling our commitment.
g. Set regular times on our calendars (daily? weekly?) and assess our progress toward the goal.
h. Celebrate progress.
i. Reflect on these questions: "What assists me to grow and change? How do creativity and perseverance strengthen me in this effort?"

Individual Reflection

1. What words and behaviors in my life seem to be in alignment with the Bahá'í teachings? Where am I struggling with this alignment? What will I do differently?
2. What is the current state of my well-being: physical, mental, emotional, and spiritual?
3. How could I increase my integrity with keeping promises and commitments?
4. How do I feel about being engaged in consistent personal transformation?
5. What am I grateful for in my life? In my marriage partner? In my family? In my home?

Couple Reflection and Consultation

1. How does it feel when we encourage each other?
2. What makes our adjustment to new behaviors in each other happen smoothly? To improvements in our marriage? To changes or improvements in our home?
3. What are we grateful for in our marriage? Our family? Our home? How does it affect our attitude toward each other and our environment when we practice gratitude? How might it benefit us to express gratitude to God daily?

Chapter 14: Being Kind to Ourselves

Dismantling the Need to Be Perfect

It may seem that striving for perfection should always have a positive outcome. However, sometimes we may slip into our lower nature and be unwise and immoderate. Instead of striving for excellence, we may start demanding perfection from ourselves—and others. This can result in magnifying our faults or weaknesses and minimizing our strengths and nobility. Consider this:

> "The only people who are truly free of the 'dross of self' are the Prophets, for to be free of one's ego is a hall-mark of perfection. We humans are *never* going to become perfect, for perfection belongs to a realm we are not destined to enter. However, we must constantly mount higher, seek to be more perfect."[153] On behalf of Shoghi Effendi

Sometimes we feel anxiety when we don't think we measure up to our own, other's, or God's standards and those in the Bahá'í teachings. When carried to excess, this anxiety becomes known as "perfectionism". It's problematic in our marriage and other relationships, because we always want to be right. This then interferes with humility and unity. It's also difficult to admit or be forgiving of mistakes, whether our own or those of others. It can also interfere with effective consultation.

If perfectionism is affecting our life together, we may:

- Experience an inner critical and judgmental voice saying our efforts are not good enough, even though there may be positive outcomes

- Frequently use words like "should", "ought", "must", "always", or "never" in relation to doing something
- Lose the ability to discern that we are doing something well
- Stop ourselves from trying something new, creative, or interesting
- Be hyper-conscious of never wanting to make a mistake or appear as a failure in front of others, which can make relationships very tense
- Put excessive weight on what others will think of us; as a result, we lose energy and then begin to fail, or become exhausted from working so hard and trying to be or appear perfect
- Resist asking others for help, out of concern for appearing imperfect
- Think that we are "bad" or "wrong", labeling our whole self as "bad" or "wrong" rather than a particular *action* as harmful and responding appropriately to correct our behavior
- Break away from God, as we cannot measure up to His standards
- Stop participating in spiritual or other community activities

Life experiences, especially those that are emotionally or physically painful or abusive, may lead a person to question their value as a human being. When people grow up with a lot of criticism from parents, or they have a highly critical partner, they can feel competent with daily responsibilities but lack confidence in their own worth. Those who instead received excessive praise from parents or others may be confident, but they lack the competence to work and serve others effectively. When people are exposed to a significant amount of criticism or unachievably high demands from others, they can often struggle to feel noble, worthy of love, or respected.

We develop (or sabotage) our capacity for knowing and loving God, ourselves, and others. Insisting on perfection from ourselves or others can block mutual understanding and the ability for others to love us as we truly are, including our vulnerabilities. In its essence, this means missing opportunities to build a connection of love and unity with God, each other, and with others around us.

As we develop our capacity for self-respect and love, we strengthen our ability to be engaged in selfless service to others, which can be viewed as an excellent expression of the best of ourselves. Someone comments:

"After many decades on this planet, I'm finally starting to let go of the deeply ingrained sense that God is a stern judge and only that. I'm striving to grasp the many meanings of God's love."

Another person reflects:

"I think it's important to note that there are many types of perfectionism. One is critical and judgmental behavior toward your own self. It results in procrastination and difficulties in starting or initiating anything, because there is the fear of failure and of not performing as perfectly as one would want. This often results in inactivity. The other type of perfectionism is where the person is hyper-productive, an over-achiever, and they constantly perform and initiate new projects without true balance in life. They tend to be workaholics, only satisfied with the best (otherwise the world falls apart), and they want to be the best person in most situations. They have a strong urge to control many situations and people."

Perfectionism results in living without joy. Do we erect walls or impose standards that interfere with happy and healthy relationships? Could this leave us feeling angry and alone? Can we accept that we are always worthy of being loved by God? Remember:

> "O Son of Being! Love Me, that I may love thee. If thou lovest Me not, My love can in no wise reach thee. Know this, O servant."[154] Bahá'u'lláh

There is no question that God sets high standards for us and encourages us to strive toward them. However, we will never perfectly meet them. The gift in having high standards is that we get better and better, benefitting those we live with and serve. Developing our character strengths will result in happier and more love-filled lives. Here is some guidance:

> "The Bahá'í community...makes no claims to perfection. To uphold high ideals and to have become their embodiment are not one and the same. Myriad are the challenges that lie ahead, and much remains to be learned."[155] Universal House of Justice

Someone comments:

"The ideal of being perfect is a fragile state, for it excludes the possibility of future growth. At its core is the concept that I must arrive at a point when I am perfect and do whatever it takes to hold onto that station. In this way, perfectionism is the antithesis of having a humble posture of learning. Recently, I have realized how debilitating my own propensity for striving for perfection has been on the quality of my life and on my emotional stability. Now, I believe that we should strive for excellence, which is being able to do the best we can in the moment, given our current capacity and the exigencies of the situation.

"Striving for excellence allows for my progressive improvement. The excellence mindset supports honest

reflection, because there is conscious awareness that the current condition is not permanent. Therefore, there is no need to feel shame or focus on perceived inadequacies or imperfections. Instead there is sense of curiosity during reflection, a detached acceptance of what is uncovered, and gratitude for the insights gained."

Here are suggestions:

"Authentic spirituality means giving up perfectionism for the rigorous process of developing ourselves one thought, one act, one day at a time."[156] Linda Kavelin Popov

"There is only one ultimate cure for perfectionism: it is as profound and yet as simple as the word *grace*. ... [T]his word has a special meaning: 'freely given, undeserved, unmerited, unearnable, and unrepayable favor.' God's loving acceptance of us has nothing to do with our worthiness. ... Grace is what God is and what God does when He meets the sinful and undeserving. Grace is a pure gift, free for the taking. The healing of perfectionism does not begin with some initial experience of grace in salvation or sanctification, and then move into a life lived by effort and perfect performance. The healing of perfectionism takes place in day-by-day believing, living, and realizing this grace relationship with a loving, caring heavenly Father."[157] David Seamands

Uplifted by Spiritual Forces

It's wise to avoid negative self-talk that weighs us down with destructive criticism. This looks like inner comments such as "I am so stupid!" or "Why don't I ever do anything right?!" If we are very self-critical—which is essentially training ourselves to always see what is wrong with us—we are more likely to be critical of each other or others around us. We are also less likely to notice and accentuate our strengths and those of others or see the spiritual beauty in each other. If negativity is an issue, it may be useful for us to study and strengthen the qualities of humility, mercy, and joyfulness. Here is guidance:

> "Let no excessive self-criticism or any feelings of inadequacy, inability or inexperience hinder you or cause you to be afraid. Bury your fears in the assurances of Bahá'u'lláh. Has He not asserted that upon anyone who mentions His Name will descend the 'hosts of Divine inspiration' and that on such a one will also descend the 'Concourse on high, each bearing aloft a chalice of pure light'? Step forth, then, into the arena where all His loved ones are equally summoned, equally challenged and abundantly blessed. For to teach, Bahá'u'lláh Himself affirms, is to do the 'most meritorious of all deeds'. And at this extraordinary moment in the history of the planet, nothing whatever is of more critical importance than inviting people of every sort and every gift to the banquet table of the Lord of Hosts."[158] Universal House of Justice

There is also this perspective:

> "The duty to obey the laws brought by Bahá'u'lláh for a new age, then, rests primarily on the individual believer. It lies at the heart of the relationship of the lover and the Beloved; 'Observe My commandments, for the love of My beauty,' is Bahá'u'lláh's exhortation. Yet what is expected in this connection is effort sustained by earnest desire, not instantaneous perfection. The qualities and habits of thought and action that characterize Bahá'í life are developed through daily exertion. 'Bring thyself to account each day', writes Bahá'u'lláh. 'Let each morn be better than its eve', He advises, 'and each morrow richer than its

yesterday.' The friends should not lose heart in their personal struggles to attain to the Divine standard, nor be seduced by the argument that, since mistakes will inevitably be made and perfection is impossible, it is futile to exert an effort. They are to steer clear of the pitfalls of hypocrisy, on the one hand—that is, saying one thing yet doing another—and heedlessness, on the other—that is, disregard for the laws, ignoring or explaining away the need to follow them. So too is paralysis engendered by guilt to be avoided; indeed, preoccupation with a particular moral failing can, at times, make it more challenging for it to be overcome.

"What the friends need to remember in this respect is that, in their efforts to achieve personal growth and to uphold Bahá'í ideals, they are not isolated individuals, withstanding alone the onslaught of the forces of moral decay operating in society. They are members of a purposeful community, global in scope, pursuing a bold spiritual mission—working to establish a pattern of activity and administrative structures suited to a humanity entering its age of maturity. Giving shape to the community's efforts is a framework for action defined by the global Plans of the Faith. This framework promotes the transformation of the individual in conjunction with social transformation, as two inseparable processes. Specifically, the courses of the institute [study circles based on Ruhi books] are intended to set the individual on a path in which qualities and attitudes, skills and abilities, are gradually acquired through service—service intended to quell the insistent self, helping to lift the individual out of its confines and placing him or her in a dynamic process of community building."[159] On behalf of the Universal House of Justice)

Individual Actions

1. Create a document or chart and record what is good about us, such as talents, skills, character strengths, abilities, friendship skills, professional skills, and so on. When we struggle with negative thoughts about ourselves, we can read this document as a reminder we are valuable human beings with gifts to offer others.

2. Pray to feel self-acceptance and to receive God's grace and forgiveness. How do we feel and respond after the prayer?

3. Engage in an act of service to one or more people. Reflect about what you did well, learned about yourself, and want to do better next time.

Individual Reflection

1. How do I relate to or react to reading quotations that ask me to strive for a very high standard?
2. How has striving for perfection benefited me? Harmed me?
3. What assists me to strive for excellence without demanding or expecting myself to be perfect?
4. What inner words do I use that are destructive? Which inner words feel constructive instead?
5. What situations or people have I withdrawn from due to perfectionism? Which ones do I want to re-connect with? What steps will I take?

Couple Reflection and Consultation

1. How can we strive for excellence without expecting each other to be perfect? How can we also offer this gift to our children?

2. What gifts and positive qualities do we honor and appreciate in each other? In the others who live with us? In others we see regularly?
3. How can we respond constructively to each other's mistakes? When is genuine humor beneficial in accommodating each other's mistakes?

Chapter 15: Directing Our Thoughts in Positive Ways

How Our Thoughts Affect Us

What we think about ourselves, each other, our marriage, our family, and everything else affects how we perceive our life and our experiences. When we think something negative, it causes our mood to darken, and we tend to see faults in others instead of their noble qualities. In contrast, when our thoughts are positive and uplifting, our mood rises, and we are more likely to feel joyful and see positive aspects of our situation and the people we interact with. Consider these quotations:

> "Guide them then, O my God, to the ocean of Thy good-pleasure, that in Thy Name they may immerse themselves therein, and that they may not be saddened by that which their own minds have conceived, nor grieved by all that they have witnessed in Thy path. Verily Thou art the All-Powerful One...."[160] Baha'u'llah

> "Joy gives us wings! In times of joy our strength is more vital, our intellect keener, and our understanding less clouded. We seem better able to cope with the world and to find our sphere of usefulness. But when sadness visits us we become weak, our strength leaves us, our comprehension is dim and our intelligence veiled. The actualities of life seem to elude our grasp, the eyes of our spirits fail to discover the sacred mysteries, and we become even as dead beings. There is no human being untouched by these two influences; but all the sorrow and the grief that exist come from the world of matter—the spiritual world bestows only the joy!"[161] 'Abdu'l-Bahá

The book *Mindful Matrimony* includes this perspective:

> "In order to see ourselves and our partners accurately, we need to search for the unconscious patterns and habits of thought that...derail our best efforts to create unity. In this process, we need to be present for each other, open and awake to the differing (and often complementary) version of reality our partner frequently presents to us. The process of being mindful and present to our partner in difficult times is an intrinsic challenge to our ego, which strives, when entering into conflict, to make the other conform to its expectations or, on the other hand, resentfully cave in. Our minds, especially in the intimate context of the marital relationships, tend to get triggered automatically, pulling us into regressive behaviors which cause ruptures in our feelings of connectedness."[162] Raymond and Furugh Switzer

Observing Our Thoughts

It takes practice to become aware of our thoughts. As we increase our consciousness of what we are thinking and the outcome, we begin to gain mastery over the power we give to our thoughts. We can also begin to see what might be ego-driven and what is spiritual. For example, if a person thinks, "I have so much to do that my partner and family are just going to have to wait", this may be the ego in charge. Once we observe and recognize our thoughts, we need to assess their validity and fact-find. Here are ways to do that:

> "God has endowed man with reason that he may perceive what is true. If we insist that such and such a subject is not to be reasoned out and tested according to the established logical modes of the intellect, what is the use of the reason which God has given man? The eye is the organ of sense by which we view the world of outer phenomena; hearing is

the faculty for distinguishing sounds; taste senses the properties of objects, such as bitter, sweet; smell detects and differentiates odors; touch reveals attributes of matter and perfects our communication with the outer world; yet after all, the circle and range of perception by the five senses is exceedingly limited. But the intellectual faculty of man is unlimited in its sphere of action."[163] 'Abdu'l-Bahá

Once we begin questioning whether the focus of our thoughts is true, we can then assess whether a spiritual principle might apply to turn around our thinking. For example, in the case of the person above who wanted their family to wait for attention, they could begin instead to have their thoughts be, "My work is important, but God is clear that a healthy marriage and family are vital contributions in the world. It makes sense for me to moderate my activities, so my home life gets the attention it needs." This shift in thinking leads to a shift in attention and actions. Here are additional quotations about how we use our minds and how powerful our thoughts are:

"O Thou the Compassionate God. Bestow upon me a heart which, like unto glass, may be illumined with the light of Thy love, and confer upon me thoughts which may change this world into a rose garden through the outpourings of heavenly grace."[164] 'Abdu'l-Bahá

"The reality of man is his thought, not his material body. The thought force and the animal force are partners. Although man is part of the animal creation, he possesses a power of thought superior to all other created beings.

"If a man's thought is constantly aspiring towards heavenly subjects then does he become saintly; if on the other hand his thought does not soar, but is directed downwards to center itself upon the things of this world, he grows more and more material until he arrives at a state little better than that of a mere animal."[165] 'Abdu'l-Bahá

"If you desire with all your heart, friendship with every race on earth, your thought, spiritual and positive, will spread; it will become the desire of others, growing stronger and stronger, until it reaches the minds of all men."[166] 'Abdu'l-Bahá

In the absence of facts, human beings tend to make assumptions to fill the gap. Then we react to other people based on these thoughts. Problems ensue, because we communicate based on what we have imagined and without fully understanding a situation. We might jump prematurely to conclusions; for example, upon seeing a receipt or bill for a purchase we don't recognize, we assume our partner is spending money inappropriately.

Alternatively, we might dwell on something small and build up a high level of anxiety or add in unverified information. For example, a wife might expect a husband home by a certain time. When he is a half hour late, she might start to imagine that he has been in an accident and is badly hurt. By the time he arrives home, she is highly anxious or perhaps angry. What happened, objectively, is that he was late. Her reaction is due to her thoughts, what she imagined might be happening.

In another situation, a husband might see a tool missing from the garage and start imagining someone stole it or a family member was careless with it. He becomes angry based on his imagination, and only later remembers where he left it. We interpret someone's frown that they are angry or unhappy at us, when perhaps they just remembered a task that they had forgotten to do the previous day. We look at dishes stacked on the counter and think our mate is lazy or inconsiderate. Perhaps they got caught up in a creative project, prioritized the children, or didn't feel well.

Bahá'u'lláh encourages us to be conscious of our unproductive thoughts and to seek protection from them:

> "Protect us, we beseech Thee, O my Lord, from the hosts of idle fancies and vain imaginations. Thou, in truth, art the Mighty, the All-Knowing."[167] Baha'u'llah

The vitality of a couple's relationship is often diminished through negative thoughts and judgments about each other. Consider this perspective:

> "Compatibility is a product of thought, a figment of the imagination. If we think a characteristic is incompatible, then we will get a negative feeling from that thought. The negative feeling is what we call 'incompatibility.' Were we to have a change of heart and think of the characteristic as good or unimportant, we would feel compatible again.
>
> "Compatibility is a matter of the heart. True compatibility is sharing a positive feeling. It is enjoying the time you spend together. ... The feeling of compatibility in a relationship will diminish when one person is troubled by thoughts about the other. ... When thoughts of incompatibility cross our minds, they signal that we are in a low mood. If we were in a high mood we would view difference from the positive end...." [Examples: Something in our partner is interesting and endearing rather than irritating or a problem.][168] George Pransky

For many people, it can be common to have thoughts that prompt us to feel "stressed" or "anxious". When we are highly stressed, there tends to be a negative effect on our health and relationships. The higher our stress level, the more it's wise to examine whether our ego is being triggered. There may be almost unconscious thoughts like, "If I'm this busy, I must be someone important" or "If I don't do this work myself, everything will fall apart". We tend to avoid asking others for help and shut out useful suggestions from loved ones. The "fortress for well-being" of marriage can become a place to avoid, because it's not feeding self-importance. Consider this perspective:

> "Stress is not something that happens to us but rather something that develops within our own thinking. From the inside out, we decide what is and what is not stressful. Events are not stressful per se; they are what we make of them."[169] Richard Carlson and Joseph Bailey

Turning Our Thoughts Around

When we remain calm and in the present moment, we can consciously pay attention to and evaluate our thoughts. Even urgent situations can then feel less stressful. Keeping control of our thoughts instead of using them to imagine negative scenarios or focus on criticisms makes us more effective in responding to all circumstances.

One of the ways we can influence our thoughts and subsequent interactions with each other is if we think of each other as equal adult partners. If instead we think like a parent, we are likely to try directing and correcting each other, which disrupts the emotional balance between us. We are likely to react like a child to a partner acting toward us like a parent. Part of this interaction can prompt us to react like we did to a parent who raised us. We are not parents to each other but partners.

Sometimes anxiety or stress can be a signal that we are not turning to God for help. When thoughts seem to escalate in a negative direction or spin out of control, we can fill our minds with spiritual content or focus our attention in more positive directions. Examples include:

- Listening to or singing the Bahá'í Writings set to music
- Repeating Allah'u'Abhá (The Greatest Name) a few times

- Focusing on a memorized prayer or quotation
- Praying
- Sitting and reading spiritual guidance
- Doing a kind act for someone
- Attending a devotional gathering
- Finding something to laugh about or prompting someone else to laugh
- Taking an action of self-care, such as showering or being out in nature or some peaceful place
- Doing vigorous exercise or some other physical activity

When we look for opportunities to focus our thoughts in a positive direction about our marriage partner, work, community service, or the world situation, it opens the possibility of creating positive appreciation, improvement, and transformation. Here is a reflection that may uplift us:

> "What is that mystery underlying human life which gives to events and to persons the power of...transformation? If one had never before seen a seed, nor heard of its latent life, how difficult to believe that only the cold earth, the warm sun, the descending showers, and the gardener's care were needed to cause its miraculous transformation into the growing form, the budding beauty, the intoxicating fragrance of the rose!"[170] Howard Colby Ives

Individual Actions

1. Choose a method of replacing negative thoughts with something uplifting and try it out every day for a week. Reflect on the effect of this and what I want to do going forward.

2. Pray for my heart to soften. Choose a positive thought about my marriage partner and repeat it to myself several

times each day for a week. It may be useful to think of something my partner does that I am grateful for. How did my attitude shift toward my partner?

Couple Actions

1. We can role-play and analyze the scenario below to build skill in distinguishing between what is happening, the interpretation that the other imagines, the behavior that results, and the effect on the communication between us. The person reacting negatively to what happened should say out loud what they are imagining in their mind for the other person to hear. Then we can talk through how to respond more effectively.

   Scenario: One person asks the other to stop at the grocery and buy small candles to decorate their child's birthday cake. The person arrives home without them. What goes through both of their minds, and how does this affect their communication? How could they communicate instead?

   Using an example from our own life, explore:
   a. What occurred
   b. What interpretations we gave to the circumstances
   c. What feelings arose
   d. How we behaved as a result
   e. How we could have viewed and responded to the situation in a more positive way

   What insights did we learn from this activity?

Individual Reflection

1. When have I noticed my thoughts leading me to positive actions? To negative ones?
2. What positive ways do I manage or reduce my stress level? My anxiety level?

3. What deliberate new thought patterns would lower my stress level and increase my happiness?
4. How does humor influence my thoughts and interactions?
5. How can I be more open and hopeful about beginning and sustaining new behaviors in myself and improving my marriage? What effect does it have when I am hopeful that our marriage can move in a positive direction?

Couple Reflection and Consultation

1. What powerful thoughts could we hold that would have a positive effect on our marriage? Our family?
2. How could we encourage each other to avoid adding negative meanings to our thoughts and responses?
3. What could we do to lower our stress levels?

Chapter 16: Easing Up on Controlling

Exploring Controlling Behavior

Some people naturally have personalities that are more inclined for them to be leaders, and they want control or strong influence over the activities of others. Others prefer to follow and let someone else lead. Yet others can flex and take charge or let others lead depending on the circumstances. Navigating this dynamic in marriage so that we are both comfortable with the balance of power and control takes careful attention, consultation, and flexibility so that we avoid conflict and chaos.

We both have strengths, but we need to learn when applying them is wise, and when we need to adjust our words and actions with each other for harmony. Sometimes when we are unhappy with each other, we try to dominate or control each other and outcomes, and this can cause disunity.

For some people, control gets commingled with perfectionism, and it's difficult to accept anything less than perfection from ourselves or others. Being more flexible and less critical usually bring greater joy and unity. We improve our relationship with God and with people in our lives.

Sometimes when we try to dominate or control each other, it's a reaction and attempt to "fix" what seems to be wrong. Partner-controlling can often result from our upbringing or previous life experiences. When something negative has happened in our lives that felt out of our control, our human reaction going forward is often to try exerting control on the people and events in our lives to prevent a similar occurrence or future problems. Couples can struggle repeatedly when these attitudes or feelings are dominant in either person:

- "Fear of the past repeating itself

- Fear of the future turning out wrong
- Attachment to having your way
- Expecting the world to be as you wish it were"[171] (Susan M. Campbell)

When a power struggle dynamic is happening between us, it can be a good practice to Inquire about the possible link to a childhood or previous partner experience. Then it's possible to consult about remedies.

Some people have a need to have and keep "control" as a survival mechanism. If this applies to us, then there is a deep distrust that if we don't strongly exercise control over people and events, they will not function "properly", the "right" way, or the way we want them to. What eventually develops is a hypervigilance to make sure that everything is going right and "our way" at all times, which is stressful and exhausting for everyone involved. The goal is to achieve a better outcome; however, the opposite often occurs instead. The person on the receiving end often ends up resentful and resistant.

Control and domination often make it harder to achieve equality or unity. Consider this perspective:

> "Equality...is a state of unity and integration. An equal relationship is characterized by the willingness and ability to be cooperative, generous, and other-directed. In the contemporary world, as humanity traverses its most problematic phase of adolescence, the quest for establishing equality between women and men has deteriorated into a virulent and destructive power struggle. Power, the very instrument that men have always used to achieve their self-centered interests, is now being sought by women to correct past and present injustices—hence, the potentially destructive power struggle found in most marriages. This situation should not be surprising. It

is the inevitable outcome of a mindset that gives power the most importance in human relationships."[172] H. B. Danesh

Note: Some people have mental or emotional illnesses or conditions that prompt them to exert high control. These are not addressed here and require professional counseling and specialized training. [See Chapter 2 and Appendix C.]

Bending Gently to the Will of God

Trying to always be in control can make it difficult for us to rely on the Will of God, something the Bahá'í wedding vow from Bahá'u'lláh puts at the center of marriage: "We will all, verily, abide by the Will of God". Trying to exert strong control over our partner and others can demonstrate a distrust not only in others but also suggests a lack of trust in God to provide what is best for us. Turning our will over to the Will of God then becomes a pitched battle where we don't want to give in. Here is an alternative perspective:

> "If it be Thy pleasure, make me to grow as a tender herb in the meadows of Thy grace, that the gentle winds of Thy will may stir me up and bend me into conformity with Thy pleasure, in such wise that my movement and my stillness may be wholly directed by Thee."[173] Bahá'u'lláh

Often underneath a wish to be in control is a deep—possibly unrecognized or unadmitted—fear of being found out to be inadequate, unworthy, or wrong. So, we may feel an intense need to be in charge and be right at times. When this occurs, there is no way to explore options, consider alternatives, defer to another, have more than one person be right about part of a matter, and so on. Our resistance can block the creative process of praying and consulting for understanding and solutions.

As we pray individually and together, we can tune into God as the Higher Power for both of us. As we both move toward Him, it can draw us closer together. As we pray for His guidance and help, it prompts us to feel humbler and more willing to accept that we don't have to have all the answers.

Balancing Individual and Couple Control

When we lessen our need to control situations, we can open the possibility for the following to occur:

- An attitude of learning; engaging in learning-in-action
- Being content with the Will of God
- Relaxing and authentically being ourselves, which includes self-acceptance and acceptance from each other
- Engaging in consistently developing ourselves with humility, purposefulness, and perseverance
- Practicing respect, love, and unity with others
- Serving others with thoughtfulness and humility
- Leading and parenting by example
- Handling situations with creativity and a sense of humor

As we turn to God and each other through consultation, we create a space between us for our ideas to mingle, and we can allow God to guide the direction of our decisions. Here is some guidance:

> "They must in every matter search out the truth and not insist upon their own opinion, for stubbornness and persistence in one's views will lead ultimately to discord and wrangling and the truth will remain hidden."[174] Shoghi Effendi

> "Once a decision has been reached, all members of the consultative body, having had the opportunity fully to state their views, agree wholeheartedly to support the outcome.

What if the minority view is right? 'If they agree upon a subject,' 'Abdu'l-Bahá has explained, 'even though it be wrong, it is better than to disagree, and be in the right, for this difference will produce the demolition of the divine foundation. Though one of the parties may be in the right and they disagree, that will be the cause of a thousand wrongs, but if they agree and both parties are in the wrong, as it is in unity, the truth will be revealed and the wrong made right.'"[175] Universal House of Justice

"Family consultation employing full and frank discussion, and animated by awareness of the need for moderation and balance, can be the panacea for domestic conflict. Wives should not attempt to dominate their husbands, nor husbands their wives...."[176] On behalf of the Universal House of Justice

When we make a unified decision, or there is a group decision involving us, we must agree that we will make a strong effort to make the decision work. This requires consistent and persevering action long enough to determine whether the decision was effective. If the solution works, great; if not, there is to be no blame, but rather we turn back to consultation to determine a new approach to the problem. Then we consistently persevere with the new approach so we can determine whether the new decision was effective. [See more about consultation in Chapter 10.]

Individual Actions

1. Pray, reflect, and observe our own words and actions. Identify one person or situation and stop trying to control what is happening. Be wise—this is not about stopping someone from doing something life-threatening or dangerous. Observe our inner responses and the responses of others involved. After some success with one

area, choose a second area of our life and back off from high control. Is there an opportunity to use humor toward ourselves or each other in this circumstance? What does prayer contribute? What do we observe happening in our life from lessening control that we appreciate? What is difficult or harmful? What adjustments do we need to make?

Individual Reflection

1. When do I try to control someone else or the outcome of something? What is prompting this action?
2. How is trying to control others or situations negatively affecting me? My relationships? What are my views and feelings of the outcomes?
3. What strategies will support me in lessening my control of others and situations? What would be wiser and healthier for me to do instead?
4. When is it still appropriate and wise to be in control of others or situations? With children or teenagers, when is it wise and useful to offer them choices instead of demands?

Couple Reflection and Consultation

1. How do we each feel and react when the other says and does things that seem dominating or controlling?
2. How might applying the principle of the equality of women and men reduce a tendency to dominate each other?
3. When has using consultation reduced conflict between us? What additional skill-building in this area would be useful? [See Chapter 10.]
4. When we picture our marriage and home with no very high-control behaviors happening, what would it look like? What seems attractive about this picture?
5. When is control over a situation wise and helpful? If we don't agree, who could help us see new perspectives?

Chapter 17: Developing Spiritual Habits

Exercising Our Souls

Just like our physical muscles need exercise and use, so does our soul:

> "... [F]or if the spiritual qualities of the soul, open to the breath of the Divine Spirit, are never used, they become atrophied, enfeebled, and at last incapable...."[177]
> 'Abdu'l-Bahá

When we consider the well-being of our souls, our spiritual selves, then there are specific actions that keep our vitality flowing. They involve following the teachings and laws of Bahá'u'lláh, such as in the quotations below.

> "The source of courage and power is the promotion of the Word of God, and steadfastness in His Love."[178]
> Bahá'u'lláh

> "Bahá'u'lláh has stated quite clearly in His Writings the essential requisites for our spiritual growth, and these are stressed again and again by 'Abdu'l-Bahá in His talks and Tablets. One can summarize them briefly in this way:
>
> - "The recital each day of one of the Obligatory Prayers with pure-hearted devotion.
> - The regular reading of the Sacred Scriptures, specifically at least each morning and evening, with reverence, attention and thought.
> - Prayerful meditation on the Teachings, so that we may understand them more deeply, fulfil them more faithfully, and convey them more accurately to others.

- Striving every day to bring our behavior more into accordance with the high standards that are set forth in the Teachings.
- Teaching the Cause of God.
- Selfless service in the work of the Cause and in the carrying on of our trade or profession.

"These points...represent the path towards the attainment of true spirituality that has been laid down by the Manifestation of God for this age [Bahá'u'lláh]."[179] Universal House of Justice

"It is not enough to proclaim the Bahá'í message, essential as that is. It is not enough to expand the rolls of Bahá'í membership, vital as that is. Souls must be transformed, communities thereby consolidated, new models of life thus attained. Transformation is the essential purpose of the Cause of Bahá'u'lláh, but it lies in the will and effort of the individual to achieve it in obedience to the Covenant. Necessary to the progress of this life-fulfilling transformation is knowledge of the will and purpose of God through regular reading and study of the Holy Word."[180] Universal House of Justice

There is a 19-Day Fast that occurs during March of each year, when Bahá'ís abstain from food and drink from sunup to sundown:

"For this material fast is an outer token of the spiritual fast; it is a symbol of self-restraint, the withholding of oneself from all appetites of the self, taking on the characteristics of the spirit, being carried away by the breathings of heaven and catching fire from the love of God."[181]
'Abdu'l-Bahá

"… [O]bligatory prayer and fasting produce awareness and awakening in man, and are conducive to his protection and preservation from tests."[182] 'Abdu'l-Bahá

When we're actively engaged in spiritual actions, we're more likely to feel happy, creative, energetic, and in harmony with others. Bahá'u'lláh's teachings focus on unity, and our spiritual practices align us with this spirit. Through caring for our souls, we more easily spot ways to be of service to others and carry them out in unity. Someone shares about caring for the soul:

"What is a soul and how does one take care of it? How does one seemingly upkeep something that cannot be seen? Where is the high shelf or enclosure to keep it out of reach, ensuring it's handled only by those who understand its value? And, if it can't be touched, how do we maintain, clean, and polish it?

"Typically, something we can't see, touch, or recognize with one of our five senses tends to fade from our awareness. In our walk within this world—the human experience—we commonly lose sight of our soul-essence, as our daily lives seem to require most of our attention and effort. It begins to recede behind a wall of what we'll often call reality. Our truest self, as a fragment of light from God, fades with disconnect and distance until it eventually seemingly disappears.

"I believe a great part of our journey is rediscovering our essence and advocating its purpose with steadfastness, aligning ourselves inwardly and outwardly. Consciously choosing to step onto this path is a brave action. Most people live their lives unconsciously (which simply means they're on autopilot) rather than clearly making choices they know are congruent with their soul, their sacredness."

Other important ways we may take care of our spiritual well-being are listed below.

- Engaging in thoughtful service to and with others
- Being creative
- Listening to or playing uplifting music (and avoiding music with sexual images or vulgar, derogatory, or hate-filled words)
- Spending time in nature—God's creation; cleaning-up or protecting the environment
- Sharing genuine humor, laughter, and stories with others
- Building excellent friendships
- Eliminating prejudiced thoughts and actions and contributing to the oneness of humanity
- Promoting and practicing the equality of women and men
- Increasing marriage and family unity

Building Strength and Growing Capacity

If we want to grow into being spiritually strong, it takes prayer, meditation, reading the Bahá'í teachings, and making daily efforts to align our lives with these teachings. We may also include reading the scriptures from other faiths. Here is some guidance:

> "As for thy mention of the Obligatory Prayer: in truth, anyone who readeth this with absolute sincerity will attract all created things, and confer new life upon the world of being. This servant beseecheth his Lord to assist His loved ones in that which will deliver them from this world's vicissitudes, its preoccupations, its frustrations, and its darkness, and will adorn them with that which shall under all conditions draw them nigh unto Him. He, verily, is the All-Possessing, the Most High."[183] Bahá'u'lláh

> "The obligatory prayers are binding inasmuch as they are conducive to humility and submissiveness, to setting one's face towards God and expressing devotion to Him.

Through such prayer man holdeth communion with God, seeketh to draw near unto Him, converseth with the true Beloved of his heart, and attaineth spiritual stations."[184] 'Abdu'l-Bahá

"When a person becomes a Bahá'í, actually what takes place is that the seed of the spirit starts to grow in the human soul. This seed must be watered by the outpourings of the Holy Spirit. These gifts of the spirit are received through prayer, meditation, study of the Holy Utterances and service to the Cause of God. The fact of the matter is that service in the Cause is like the plough which ploughs the physical soil when seeds are sown. It is necessary that the soil be ploughed up, so that it can be enriched, and thus cause a stronger growth of the seed. In exactly the same way the evolution of the spirit takes place through ploughing up the soil of the heart so that it is a constant reflection of the Holy Spirit. In this way the human spirit grows and develops by leaps and bounds."[185] On behalf of Shoghi Effendi

"The Twin Luminaries [The Báb and Bahá'u'lláh] of this resplendent age have taught us this: Prayer is the essential spiritual conversation of the soul with its Maker, direct and without intermediation. It is the spiritual food that sustains the life of the spirit. Like the morning's dew, it brings freshness to the heart and cleanses it, purifying it from attachments of the insistent self. It is a fire that burns away the veils and a light that leads to the ocean of reunion with the Almighty. On its wings does the soul soar in the heavens of God and draw closer to the divine reality. Upon its quality depends the development of the limitless capacities of the soul and the attraction of the bounties of God, but the prolongation of prayer is not desirable."[186] Universal House of Justice

"It is striking how private and personal the most fundamental spiritual exercises of prayer and meditation are in the Faith. Bahá'ís do, of course, have meetings for devotions...but the daily obligatory prayers are ordained to be said in the privacy of one's chamber, and meditation on the Teachings is, likewise, a private individual activity, not a form of group therapy. In His talks 'Abdu'l-Bahá describes prayer as 'Conversation with God', and concerning meditation He says that 'while you meditate you are speaking with your own spirit. In that state of mind you put certain questions to your spirit and the spirit answers: the light breaks forth and the reality is revealed." [187] On behalf of the Universal House of Justice

Sharing the Bahá'í Teachings with Others

The subject of teaching others about Bahá'u'lláh could fill volumes, and there are many available resources. Essentially though it's about:

- Learning the teachings
- Living them as best as we can
- While interacting with friends, colleagues, family, and others we meet, we naturally share about what we or someone in our family believes

Many people don't yet know that there is a new, wonderful Faith in the world with transformative teachings, and as we become excited about this, we will want others to know about it. Below are quotations of guidance:

"Every word that proceedeth out of the mouth of God is endowed with such potency as can instill new life into every human frame...."[188] Bahá'u'lláh

"In these days, the most important of all things is the guidance of the nations and peoples of the world. Teaching the Cause is of utmost importance for it is the head corner-stone of the foundation itself."[189] 'Abdu'l-Bahá

"Let him consider the degree of his hearer's receptivity, and decide for himself the suitability of either the direct or indirect method of teaching, whereby he can impress upon the seeker the vital importance of the Divine Message, and persuade him to throw in his lot with those who have already embraced it. Let him remember the example set by 'Abdu'l-Bahá, and His constant admonition to shower such kindness upon the seeker, and exemplify to such a degree the spirit of the teachings he hopes to instill into him, that the recipient will be spontaneously impelled to identify himself with the Cause embodying such teachings. Let him refrain, at the outset, from insisting on such laws and observances as might impose too severe a strain on the seeker's newly awakened faith, and endeavor to nurse him, patiently, tactfully, and yet determinedly, into full maturity, and aid him to proclaim his unqualified acceptance of whatever has been ordained by Bahá'u'lláh. Let him, as soon as that stage has been attained, introduce him to the body of his fellow-believers, and seek, through constant fellowship and active participation in the local activities of his community, to enable him to contribute his share to the enrichment of its life, the furtherance of its tasks, the consolidations of its interests, and the coordination of its activities with those of its sister communities. Let him not be content until he has infused into his spiritual child so deep a longing as to impel him to arise independently, in his turn, and devote his energies to the quickening of other souls, and the upholding of the laws and principles laid down by his newly adopted Faith."[190] Shoghi Effendi

As we pray and read, we can spot phrases to memorize, so we can share the exact words of the teachings. These can especially influence others' hearts.

The "essential requisites" of service and transforming behavior are covered in other parts of the book.

Individual Actions

1. Choose two prayers and say them consistently each day for a week. Note if they are easier or harder to say in different environments. Memorize the entire prayers or learn some phrases from them that are useful to carry in our minds.

2. Consistently pray one of the three daily Obligatory Prayers for a week, praying at a time when we are alone and private. If we have not already, focus on memorizing the Short Obligatory Prayer to be said daily between noon and sunset after washing our hands and face and turning toward Bahá'u'lláh's Shrine in Israel. The words are: "I bear witness, O my God, that Thou hast created me to know Thee and to worship Thee. I testify, at this moment, to my powerlessness and to Thy might, to my poverty and to Thy wealth. There is none other God but Thee, the Help in Peril, the Self-Subsisting."[191] (Bahá'u'lláh) Then put in place an ongoing reminder system so we stay consistent with saying one of them. In addition to one of these prayers, the following is to be done each day: "It hath been ordained that every believer in God, the Lord of Judgment, shall, each day, having washed his hands and then his face, seat himself and, turning unto God, repeat 'Alláh'u'-Abhá' ninety-five times."[192] (Bahá'u'lláh)

3. After reflecting on the quotations in this chapter, explore if any of the essential requisites are missing from our lives. Choose two to begin carrying out more actively over the

coming week. Create a reminder system to see how we're doing over the course of the week. After we have had some success, begin adding other requisites, one at a time, gradually over time. If increasing our ability to share about the Bahá'í Faith is one of our goals, this advice may guide us: "He suggests that you daily pray to Bahá'u'lláh to let you meet a soul receptive to His Message. The power of prayer is very great, and attracts the Divine confirmations."[193] (On behalf of Shoghi Effendi)

4. Learn about different types of meditation and experiment to see what works for us. There is no one method required in the teachings. Some people prefer to sit quietly, and others prefer to be more active, such as doing a walking meditation or a discipline like Tai Chi. This is some guidance: "There are no set forms of meditation prescribed in the teachings, no plan, as such, for inner development. The friends are urged—nay enjoined—to pray, and they also should meditate, but the manner of doing the latter is left entirely to the individual."[194] (On behalf of Shoghi Effendi)

5. We are wise to establish the habit of reading the Writings of The Báb or Bahá'u'lláh twice a day, as instructed in the teachings. We will likely wish to also regularly read the guidance from 'Abdu'l-Bahá, Shoghi Effendi, and the Universal House of Justice. We can purchase books from many locations, and there are many here to download: https://www.bahai.org/library/. There are also mobile phone apps with Bahá'í prayers, books, and quotations.

6. Consider going on pilgrimage to the Bahá'í Holy Places in Israel as a place to become spiritually connected and carry out intense prayers. The Bahá'í institutions can provide

instructions on how to apply to participate. If you have already gone on pilgrimage separately or together, then recall the experience and visualize being back in the Shrines.

Individual Reflection

1. What spiritual habits will empower my growth, well-being, and service to my marriage partner, our family members, and others?
2. What effect could it have on my progress in life and in our marriage if I am consistent with daily spiritual habits?
3. How do I describe my approach to and experience of prayer?
4. What is the experience like for me when I say the Obligatory Prayers? How does saying them daily relate to my spiritual life feeling faithful to God?
5. How could I be more prayerful every day, both in reading revealed prayers and increasing my conversations with God and Bahá'u'lláh?
6. What meditating do I do? How could I be consistent with it, if I'm not? Have I ever received wonderful insights after meditating? When I raise a question with my spirit, am I specific with what I'm seeking? Are the insights I receive related to my present or more applicable to my future?
7. Do I ever feel all this is too much, that the standard is too high or the demands overwhelming? Is it okay to talk about these feelings? Who can I share them with?

Couple Reflection and Consultation

1. What differences do we notice in our life on days when we pray separately and together and on days when these do not happen?
2. What are our thoughts about fasting together? What would sharing this experience look like for us?

3. Does it appeal to us to go on pilgrimage to the Bahá'í Holy Places in Israel together? How will we carry out this commitment? What other spiritually related places are we drawn to visit?
4. What else might draw us closer spiritually?

Chapter 18: Learning and Growing from Difficulties

Difficulties Are a Reality of Life

Life has challenges and difficulties. It just does. We can pray to be spared from major ones, but tests are part of life on earth, and they can be a means of waking us up. It's vital to improve how we respond and make use of tests in ways that foster our physical, mental, emotional, and spiritual growth. Here are perspectives on the purposes of difficulties:

> "Tests are benefits from God, for which we should thank Him. Grief and sorrow do not come to us by chance, they are sent to us by the Divine Mercy for our own perfecting."[195] 'Abdu'l-Bahá

> "The mind and spirit of man advance when he is tried by suffering. The more the ground is ploughed the better the seed will grow, the better the harvest will be. Just as the plough furrows the earth deeply, purifying it of weeds and thistles, so suffering and tribulation free man from the petty affairs of this worldly life until he arrives at a state of complete detachment. His attitude in this world will be that of divine happiness. Man is, so to speak, unripe: the heat of the fire of suffering will mature him."[196]
> 'Abdu'l-Bahá

> "Naturally there will be periods of distress and difficulty, and even severe tests; but if that person turns firmly towards the Divine Manifestation [Baha'u'llah], studies carefully His Spiritual teachings and receives the blessings of the Holy Spirit, he will find that in reality these tests and difficulties have been the gifts of God to enable him to grow and develop."[197] On behalf of Shoghi Effendi

Powerfully Taking on the Challenges

Often the way people respond to difficulties may not seem very enlightened. It can sometimes be easier to whine and complain or try to escape them than to handle them in a positive and mature way. Here is a description of this behavior and an alternative approach:

> "When faced with a problem, the spiritually immature person tries to escape. Instead of facing the problem, he hopes that someone else will resolve it, or that it will just go away. If he has committed an error, he blames another. If someone else commits an error, he attaches great importance to it and has a hard time forgiving. Instead of trying to find a solution to the problem, he concentrates on its cause, blaming persons or circumstances other than himself.
>
> "In contrast, the spiritually mature person faces whatever problems arise with relative calm and decision. He recognizes and acknowledges whatever faults he may have committed which have contributed to the problem and accepts and forgives the errors made by others. He doesn't get bogged down in talking about who caused the problem or waste energy defending himself. He concentrates on searching for a good solution, using prayer for divine guidance, meditation, and consultation with others. Then he willingly cooperates in carrying out the actions necessary to apply the solution."[198] Joan B. Hernández

There are many spiritual benefits to tests and how we respond to them, as they are designed to strengthen our ability to be better people. Consider these quotations:

> "Meditate profoundly...that you may acknowledge the truth that from time immemorial even unto eternity the

Almighty hath tried, and will continue to try, His servants, so that light may be distinguished from darkness, truth from falsehood, right from wrong, guidance from error, happiness from misery, and roses from thorns."[199] Bahá'u'lláh

"The more one is severed from the world, from desires, from human affairs, and conditions, the more impervious does one become to the tests of God. Tests are a means by which a soul is measured as to its fitness, and proven out by its own acts. God knows its fitness before-hand, and also its unpreparedness, but man, with an ego, would not believe himself unfit unless proof were given him. Consequently his susceptibility to evil is proven to him when he falls into the tests, and the tests are continued until the soul realizes its own unfitness, then remorse and regret tend to root out the weakness. The same test comes again in greater degree, until it is shown that a former weakness has become a strength, and the power to overcome evil has been established."[200] 'Abdu'l-Bahá

When problems happen or we make a mistake, it's an opportunity to learn and strengthen our wisdom and good judgment. However, wisdom also comes from studying and internalizing spiritual teachings, so sometimes we can prevent damaging results when we pay attention in advance:

"In exasperating situations, we must find the time to pause and reflect if we are not afterwards to regret our words and actions. The Golden Rule, 'Do unto others what you would have them do unto you' or 'Do not do to others that which you do not wish done to yourself' is a useful guideline for action."[201] Mehri Sefidvash

Part of our journey in life is determining who a test belongs to. Sometimes we may try to rescue or manage other people's tests for them, which often interferes in their learning and development. Of course, we can still compassionately offer to assist or accompany others, but it's good to be clear and wise in the process that we aren't doing for others what is vital they do for themselves. What can look initially like kindness to another person can result in handicapping them over time. If we focus on our own challenges and inner battles in learning to live by spiritual principles, we will achieve our own victories and growth. Here is some guidance:

> "Ultimately all the battle of life is within the individual. No amount of organization can solve the inner problems or produce or prevent, as the case may be, victory or failure at a crucial moment. In such times as these particularly, individuals are torn by great forces at large in the world, and we see some weak ones suddenly become miraculously strong, and strong ones fail—we can only try, through loving advice...to bring about the act on the part of the believer which will be for the highest good of the Cause. Because obviously something bad for the Cause cannot be the highest good of the individual Bahá'í."[202] On behalf of Shoghi Effendi

The Bahá'í teachings encourage us in these ways:

> "... [A]s we suffer these misfortunes we must remember that the Prophets of God Themselves were not immune from these things which men suffer. They knew sorrow, illness and pain too. They rose above these things through Their spirits, and that is what we must try and do too, when afflicted. The troubles of this world pass, and what we have left is what we have made of our souls; so it is to this we must look—to becoming more spiritual, drawing nearer to God, no matter what our human minds and bodies go through."[203] On behalf of Shoghi Effendi

"Life in this world is a succession of tests and achievements, of falling short and of making new spiritual advances. Sometimes the course may seem very hard, but one can witness, again and again, that the soul who steadfastly obeys the Law of Bahá'u'lláh, however hard it may seem, grows spiritually, while the one who compromises with the law for the sake of his own apparent happiness is seen to have been following a chimera: he does not attain the happiness he sought, he retards his spiritual advance and often brings new problems upon himself."[204] Universal House of Justice

As we go through difficulties, our self-confidence grows, and we gain a mental toughness that can push us through the next one that comes. We learn what we can do, and this spreads to all areas of our life.

Hormones Are a Benefit and Test in Marriage

Our bodies are affected by a complex array of hormones, and we require them to function. When they are in balance, all our body systems function more smoothly. We both have hormones that affect our reproductive systems and influence our ability to feel connected with each other. However, variations in hormone levels occur with biological changes, stress, sexual activity, and some foods. In addition, many hormones decline with aging and are affected by illnesses and other conditions.

We know from living with each other that fluctuations in hormone levels can cause mood swings and physical symptoms such as pain or the ability to function well. These variations in our well-being are continually an opportunity to practice qualities like flexibility, compassion, patience, acceptance, and wisdom.

As we communicate directly with each other prior to known shifts in hormone levels, we can mutually deal with difficult times. For example, monthly, younger women go through shifts along with menses, and variations occur as well through birth control methods, pregnancy, childbirth, and breastfeeding. In their 40s and 50s, women going through perimenopause and then menopause causes new changes. Men can experience variations in testosterone levels linked to physical activity or aging. Both women and men can experience changes in sexual responses over time. As people marry later in life, managing fertility issues often involves injecting hormones, which adds to the mix already present, and that can present additional challenges.

We can assist each other to respond well to how our bodies are functioning, offering comfort and accompaniment as appropriate, and seeking conventional and alternative medical treatments as indicated. Stress, including relationship distress, is often a factor in hormonal fluctuations, and so managing our response to events and keeping issues addressed through consultation and other assistance can be balancing. Raising children while going through hormonal shifts can also be challenging. Practices like prayer, meditation, and various energy-balancing modalities can be useful. We may be able to discover herbs or foods that are beneficial as well.

Note: Managing hormones is an area that requires consulting with medical and nutritional professionals for understanding, testing, and help with balancing.

Utilizing Learning in Action

The Universal House of Justice encourages the culture of the Bahá'í community to be one of studying guidance, consulting, acting, and then learning through reflection and consultation. This process makes it easier to relax and not try so hard to be perfect. We can step forward in courage to try something new with less worry about failure or criticism from others. It's also easier to accept a mistake if we gain learning from it. Here is guidance about "learning in action":

> "... [T]he friends participate in an ongoing process of action, reflection, study, and consultation in order to address obstacles and share successes, reexamine and revise strategies and methods, and systematize and improve efforts over time."[205] Universal House of Justice

This is someone's perspective:

"You need to understand with compassion that being alive is hard work. It's okay to have a cushion to sit down on instead of a hard rock though. You think better, think further. I believe in Maslow's hierarchy of needs, but I also believe in miracles. So, if a person lives without all the basics in life, do I believe their spirit is capable of having transcendental experiences? Of course I do. But do I think it's the best way, the efficient way to train a human? No, I don't. Hardships and tests and difficulties do wake us up, but is it the only way to wake up? Very few of us trust the route of love, understanding, and education, waking up by learning it, and getting it."

The following can be our attitude:

> "See difficulties as learning opportunities that will expand your talents and capacities. Remind yourself that you can positively influence much of what happens in life. See yourself as capable and as an active participant in your world. Even when a problem has aspects that cannot be changed, trust that if you are resourceful, you will be able to use the situation to learn new ways of responding to it. Welcome change and challenge. Have faith that greater life

meaning and satisfaction will emerge from each stressful situation."[206] Stephen Post

Even when we know the standards for how to best behave, both individually and with others, we are still likely to struggle to meet them at times. Our goal as human beings is always to strive for excellence, but perfection isn't possible. Here is some encouragement:

"He is very happy to see that you have put into practice one of the most encouraging precepts of 'Abdu'l-Bahá in which He said that we should try and make every stumbling-block a stepping-stone to progress. In the course of your past life you have all stumbled very gravely; but, far from being embittered or defeated by this experience, you are determined to make it a means of purifying your natures, improving your characters, and enabling you to become better citizens in the future. This is truly pleasing in the eyes of God."[207] On behalf of Shoghi Effendi

Failures, which happen to everyone, teach us humility and trust in the mercy and forgiveness of God. They provide opportunities to ask for help, make amends, and learn new ways of speaking and acting. Problems give us opportunities to strengthen our characters and make better choices the next time. Addressing issues rather than hiding from them increases the possibility of having a stronger, happier marriage.

Getting a Hand Up from Others

As has been mentioned throughout the book, we can ask others for help when we have challenges, or to prevent challenges. Here is some guidance:

"When a believer has a problem concerning which he must make a decision, he has several courses open to him. If it is a matter that affects the interests of the Faith he should consult with the appropriate Assembly or committee, but individuals have many problems which are purely personal and there is no obligation upon them to take such problems to the institutions of the Faith; indeed, when the needs of the teaching work are of such urgency it is better if the friends will not burden their Assemblies with personal problems that they can solve by themselves. A Bahá'í who has a problem may wish to make his own decision upon it after prayer and after weighing all the aspects of it in his own mind; he may prefer to seek the counsel of individual friends or of professional counselors such as his doctor or lawyer so that he can consider such advice when making his decision; or in a case where several people are involved, such as a family situation, he may want to gather together those who are affected so that they may arrive at a collective decision. There is also no objection whatever to a Bahá'í asking a group of people to consult together on a problem facing him. It should be borne in mind that all consultation is aimed at arriving at a solution to a problem and is quite different from the sort of group baring of the soul that is popular in some circles these days which borders on the kind of confession that is forbidden in the Faith."[208] Universal House of Justice

Individual Actions

1. Identify a problem from the past and assess the learning or skill-building that came from it. Identify a current problem that could benefit from the learning and apply it.

2. Assess how hormones affect my functioning and choose two actions to address or improve my health or reactions to them.

Couple Actions

1. Invite a small group of trusted and experienced people to hold a reflection session about our marriage or some aspect of the marriage experience that the group could relate to. The goal will be to identify challenges that we are tripping over, capture learning opportunities, and devise potential solutions. Carry out the solutions and re-assess the situation(s) through consultation.

2. Plan and carry out a trip, looking ahead for what difficulties might arise and preparing for them. When difficulties arise, consult and work together to face them. After the trip, reflect on our ability to function in unity and what we learned from the experience.

Individual Reflection

1. What have been the three most difficult experiences I have had in life?
2. What have I learned from difficulties?
3. What has assisted me with recovering from difficulties?
4. How has strengthening my character helped me respond better to difficulties? [See Chapter 12.]

5. How have changes or disruptions in my hormone levels affected me and my life? What actions do I need to take if they are causing me or others difficulty now?
6. When have I found it useful to turn to counseling or a Bahá'í institution to help me deal with a difficulty? What was the outcome?
7. Who else has helped me at times with going through and recovering from a difficulty? Who has helped me gain new perspectives and learn from difficulties? Do I need to turn to someone now? Who could help?

Couple Reflection and Consultation

1. How do we generally respond to tests and challenges that arise?
2. When do we rely on avoidance or turn to our electronic devices, alcohol, drugs, shopping, sex, or other means of trying to ignore what happened?
3. What would we like to transform about our responses to difficulties?
4. What have we learned from a difficulty in the past?
5. When have we successfully used learning from a difficult situation in new circumstances?
6. What specific character qualities have we strengthened from working through a difficulty? [See Chapter 12.]
7. When have we found it useful to turn to counseling or a Bahá'í institution to help us manage a difficulty? What was the outcome?
8. When have we successfully reached out and found other help or accepted offered help when a problem was happening?

Chapter 19: Cleaning Up Messes and Bouncing Back

Reconnecting with God Through Forgiveness

It's wise to keep our life as "cleaned up" as possible, no matter what the size of the issue. Resolving issues includes being effective at:

- Reflecting to understand what happened and why (part of doing a daily accounting of our positive and negative actions) [See Chapter 13.]
- Acknowledging our errors and where our words or actions caused problems
- Regretting what happened; repenting
- Seeking forgiveness from God
- Cleaning up whatever problems we have caused or are partially responsible for, including asking each other for forgiveness
- Learning from what occurred and from the clean-up process
- Applying the learning
- Respecting ourselves and acknowledging our efforts to grow
- Being resilient in picking up and going on to work with, relate to, and serve each other and others

The longer we stay stuck in whatever poor choice we made and its consequences, the deeper the hole we will dig. We become emotionally and mentally stuck in the past, and this influences our present and future, as well as often our involvement in family and community activities. Making efforts to resolve the past and resiliently go forward empowers us to have a better future. We are lighter and happier when not dragging unresolved issues along with us.

Consider this:

> "Wherefore, hearken ye unto My speech, and return ye to God and repent, that He, through His grace, may have mercy upon you, may wash away your sins, and forgive your trespasses. The greatness of His mercy surpasseth the fury of His wrath, and His grace encompasseth all who have been called into being and been clothed with the robe of life, be they of the past or of the future."[209] Bahá'u'lláh

Here is a someone's perspective about the concept of "repenting":

"... [R]epentance is about conduct—you realize you've done something wrong, you resolve to change it in the future. ...Inside each of us is some spark of God—the real us. ... Sin, evil, murder—all those things have the ability to cover up our true selves. [Repenting]...means turning back to the part of God that's gotten concealed. When you repent, usually, you feel sad—because of the regret that led you there. But when you talk about [repentance], about making that connection with God again—well, it makes you happy. ... Happier even than you were before, because your sins separated you from God...."[210] Jodi Picoult

Once we are clear that we regret our part in what happened, asking for forgiveness from God reconnects us with Him. We can define forgiveness in some of these ways:

- Accepting pardon from God
- Pardoning someone else for saying or doing something hurtful or harmful
- Giving up a desire for revenge
- Letting go of anger and resentment

Drawing on courage and seeking God's forgiveness, requesting forgiveness from another person, and offering forgiveness to each other all contribute to respect and unity.

Transformation is a blessing that can arise out of asking for and receiving God's forgiveness. Unity between us and with others can be part of this transformation. Consider this:

> "Thy generous Lord will assist thee to labor in His vineyard and will cause thee to be the means of spreading the spirit of unity.... He will make thine inner eye to see with the light of knowledge, He will forgive thy sins and transform them into goodly deeds. Verily He is the Forgiving, the Compassionate, the Lord of immeasurable grace."[211]
> 'Abdu'l-Bahá

Many people notice that their missteps become learning, which then becomes deeds that benefit others. It can be powerful to look back at something that has transformed since we failed or sinned. We also may find a measure of serenity in understanding that God can take what went wrong and transform it.

Doing Clean-Up Actions

At this stage, we might be clear that we have asked for and received forgiveness from God. However, if our words or actions harmed someone else or a group of others, that forgiveness may not really sink in until we clean up the issue with them. There are concrete actions for us to take to resolve issues that arose from our behavior. We then have to overcome our natural resistance to admitting an error, while also paying attention to not causing further harm with any remedial actions we take. Below are some guidelines for how to proceed and what to be careful about.

"Bahá'u'lláh prohibits confession to, and seeking absolution of one's sins from, a human being. Instead one should beg forgiveness from God. ... Shoghi Effendi sets the prohibition into context. His secretary has written on his behalf that we '...are forbidden to confess to any person, as do the Catholics to their priests, our sins and shortcomings, or to do so in public, as some religious sects do. However, if we spontaneously desire to acknowledge we have been wrong in something, or that we have some fault of character, and ask another person's forgiveness or pardon, we are quite free to do so.' The Universal House of Justice has also clarified that Bahá'u'lláh's prohibition concerning the confession of sins does not prevent an individual from admitting transgressions in the course of consultations held under the aegis of Bahá'í institutions. Likewise, it does not preclude the possibility of seeking advice from a close friend or of a professional counselor regarding such matters."[212] *The Kitáb-i-Aqdas* by Bahá'u'lláh

We and others may pray and consult to understand what was said and done and where there was failure to speak or act in ways that aligned with spiritual principles or laws.

We may find these ways of resolving issues useful, as suggested by the authors of *When Sorry Isn't Enough*:

1. Expressing Regret: "I am sorry."
2. Accepting Responsibility: "I was wrong."
3. Making Restitution: "What can I do to make it right?"
4. Genuinely Repenting: "I want to change."
5. Requesting Forgiveness: "Can you find it in your heart to forgive me?"

The authors suggest that these factors listed below may also be important to consider when offering an apology.

- Our tone of voice and body language must match our words for the receiver to believe that our apology is sincere.
- State specifically what the apology is for and to acknowledge the hurt caused.
- Avoid any language (such as "...but...") that communicates blame to the person to whom we are apologizing; attacks do not usually lead to forgiveness and reconciliation.
- Do not use apology to try to manipulate someone; for example, apologizing in the hope that the recipient will change some behavior.
- Depending on the circumstances and relationship, we may find it most effective to put our apology in writing.[213]

(Summarized from Gary Chapman and Jennifer Thomas)

The next step then, of course, is for us to be clear what behaviors we must work on improving and begin to address these.

Forgiving Others

Forgiveness frees us from holding against the person what they did. Drs. Les and Leslie Parrott say that forgiving is choosing to reject "vengeance, renounce bitterness, break the silence of estrangement, and actually wish the best" for the other person. They also say, "Forgiveness is not for the faint-hearted. Our sense of justice usually recoils at the thought of this unnatural act. Only the brave forgive."[214] Les Parrott III and Leslie Parrott) In other words, it takes courage. It also takes both our hearts and our heads to accomplish the task. This is Bahá'u'lláh's entreaty:

> "Turn your faces from the darkness of estrangement to the effulgent light of the daystar of unity."[215] Bahá'u'lláh

Marriage counselor and educator Michele Weiner-Davis is very direct with couples:

> "Don't pretend that you are putting effort into your marriage when you have a mental ledger book detailing your spouse's every wrongdoing. As long as you are holding on to resentments of the past, you can't be forgiving. As long as you are not forgiving, you can't be loving. As long as you aren't loving, you can't do what it takes to make your marriage work. So decide. Are you going to carry a grudge and stand by while you and your spouse become a divorce statistic or are you going to rid yourself of the shackles of the past which have held *you* prisoner? Forgive your spouse and start anew."[216] Michele Weiner-Davis

Forgiveness is not the same as ignoring the situation or saying that what happened was okay. The initial problem still needs to be addressed—just as we are responsible for our own actions, so are others for theirs. The balance is illuminated by this quotation:

> "The Kingdom of God is founded upon equity and justice, and also upon mercy, compassion, and kindness to every living soul. Strive ye then with all your heart to treat compassionately all humankind—except for those who have some selfish, private motive, or some disease of the soul. Kindness cannot be shown the tyrant, the deceiver, or the thief, because, far from awakening them to the error of their ways, it maketh them to continue in their perversity as before. No matter how much kindliness ye may expend upon the liar, he will but lie the more, for he believeth you to be deceived, while ye understand him but too well, and only remain silent out of your extreme compassion."[217] 'Abdu'l-Bahá

A commitment to unity and an aversion to disunity are part of what can prompt people to forgive faster and make efforts to restore harmony. Forgiveness is directly connected to a sensitivity to unity and when it's disrupted. The more committed people are to maintaining harmony, the more they will not be able to tolerate disunity for any length of time. Then prompt forgiveness becomes possible.

It's important to be aware that forgiveness needs to be sincere and honest. It's not wise to forgive someone automatically just because the situation is difficult, or because we feel unhappy that the other person is regretful. If we say we forgive someone while we are still holding onto considerable anger, sadness, or pain from the incident, the situation will not be resolved. Some inner healing likely needs to happen first. Consider this:

> "When you forgive, you need to do more than say the words and mean them. You also have to extend a forgiving, helping hand. To truly forgive, you need to be gracious to your partner. Being kind and generous as well as granting pardon will put you back on the same footing and keep your love strong."[218] Howard J. Markman, Scott M. Stanley, Susan L. Blumberg, Natalie H. Jenkins, and Carol Whiteley

Once a situation is resolved, then it's important for us to leave it in the past and not bring it up again. Reminding someone about the situation can indicate that we did not completely forgive the first time. Of course, this also includes both people engaging in the necessary behavior adjustments, so the same situations drop in frequency and then stop occurring. This will help with building trust.

There are many factors that affect trust between a couple. Some that are important to include are listed below.

- Consistently being truthful and delivering it with kindness, tactfulness, and compassion
- Keeping promises and carrying out agreed actions
- Demonstrating respect to each other
- Keeping private information that each other shared in confidence or agreeing who it can be shared with

Bouncing Back Afterward

Here is a perspective about resilient people. The author says they:

> "... have three distinguishing characteristics: an acceptance of reality, a strongly held belief that life is meaningful, and an ability to find creative solutions to seemingly insoluble problems."[219] Janet A. Khan

People practice Resilience effectively when they:

- Accept and adjust to change rather than resisting it
- Act calmly during crises and take positive steps to manage them
- Seek creative and appropriate solutions to problems
- Look for what they can learn from a current or previous challenge to prevent or more effectively respond to future ones
- Adapt to changing circumstances, staying detached enough from what is occurring to respond appropriately
- Stay reasonably optimistic when faced with unwanted events or experiences, but do not engage in serious denial or avoid responding to circumstances
- Withstand, grieve, or quickly recover from the impact of failures, disruptive events, loss, and disappointments; quickly and confidently re-focus on goals and resume action

People need to strengthen Resilience when they:

- Grumble, whine, and complain about unexpected or disruptive events
- Ignore, panic, or respond poorly to problems, often making them worse
- Take an excessive amount of time to recover from challenges and changes [Note: What can be excessive for one person can be short for another, so this is a difficult area to be specific about; if there are concerns, a professional may be able to help.]
- Become unable to function in the face of problems
- Talk pessimistically about all the bad things that are occurring and that might occur in the future

When we achieve a significant degree of resilience after a problem or tragedy, people look at our power of example, and they want to be more resilient themselves.

Individual/Couple Actions

1. Identify something we did that is an unaddressed problem. Determine the spiritual principles that were missing and the ones that will apply to remediation options. Generate a list of possible ways to address the issue. Consult with each other or others as needed to clarify choices. Ensure that anything we do will not cause further or greater harm. Carry out our "clean-up" actions. Reflect on the situation and outcome and determine what will prevent something like this from occurring again.

2. Find a messy and disorganized area of our life, such as our bedroom, vehicle, office, garage, basement, closet, or storage area. Clean and organize the area, preferably with a positive attitude. While doing it, reflect about keeping our own lives clean, orderly, and in a state of integrity. How

do we feel when we're finished, and the area is more organized than it was before? Are there ways this activity might relate to how we feel when we "clean up" part of our social or spiritual life?

3. Identify one aspect of our behavior we are unhappy with and ask God to forgive us for it. Choose one or two actions that will transform this behavior. Set specific goals that will have us improve. Include our assessment of our progress as part of our daily self-accounting. [See Chapter 13 for more about this daily practice.]

Individual/Couple Reflection and Consultation

1. What is our experience with asking for forgiveness from God? What would make it happen more easily? Is there still an effect on us from our choices even after we have asked for God's pardon?
2. What are our experiences with asking for forgiveness from another person? Are we able to ask and then give the person time to reflect and respond without expecting them to grant it? Is there still an effect on us from our choices even after we have asked for the person's pardon and received it?
3. What do we perceive are current problems, difficulties, and obstacles to our progress?
4. What steps can we take to resolve issues that are troubling us?
5. What will facilitate us learning from difficulties, recovering resiliently, and moving forward?
6. How can we use humor at times to assist us to handle the ways we are different from each other and difficult situations more lightly?

Track 3: Empowering Our Marriage to Go Forward

Chapter 20: Re-Committing to Our Marriage Partnership

Valuing Commitment

Our marriage commitment is vitally important. It's essential for us to believe investing time in and paying attention to the quality and happiness of our marriage is worthwhile. It's a way that we serve God and humanity, as our family is a building block for global unity. It's vital that we be willing to build or rebuild our relationship health and unity. Powerful re-vitalizing forces are released in the act of making a commitment:

> "Until one is committed there is hesitancy, the chance to draw back, always ineffectiveness. Concerning all acts of initiative (and creation), there is one elementary truth, the ignorance of which kills countless ideas and splendid plans: that the moment one definitely commits oneself, then Providence moves too. All sorts of things occur to help one that would never otherwise have occurred. A whole stream of events issues from the decision, raising in one's favor all manner of unforeseen incidents and meetings and material assistance, which no man could have dreamt would have come his way."[220] W. H. Murray

> "The moment you believe you can do something, power seems to stream into you; the moment you believe you cannot do it, you have lost more than half the battle, you seem to be drained of the force necessary to do it."[221] Rúhíyyih Rabbani

Consider this perspective about marriage:

> "Success in marriage today requires two ingredients that no previous generation has ever had to put together:

powerful commitment combined with an intentional focus on maintaining and growing one's marriage. Commitment without intentionality leads to stable but stale marriages. Intentionality without commitment leads to lively marriages that cannot endure bad weather."[222] William J. Doherty

Dr. Doherty emphasizes these important aspects for focus:

- Having a rock-solid commitment to our marriage and one another
- Engaging in marital practices or rituals that build connection and intimacy
- Building a supportive community around our marriage [See Chapter 2 for details about this topic.][223]

Staying Connected

It's important to remember that marriage is intended to be a place of well-being for us as a couple, and its unity provides a secure foundation for our children. When our marriage is healthy, our children are happier and achieve better outcomes.

Staying connected to one another is a vital contribution to our marriage well-being. Brené Brown defines connection this way: "the energy that exists between people when they feel seen, heard, and valued; when they can give and receive without judgment; and when they derive sustenance and strength from the relationship."[224] Brené Brown

Life is full of responsibilities, challenges, and devices that can pull our time and attention away from each other and our family. Some days it may seem as if we barely see one another. It can be even more difficult to have a conversation that strengthens our friendship and intimate connection. It can be easy to slide into thinking that everything else is higher priority, and that our marriage should not require a lot of time to maintain. In a world filled with distractions and responsibilities, losing track of key aspects of one another's life can easily happen.

Couples with young children, very demanding jobs, or both are at higher risk for this slide away from each other. Consider this:

> "The natural drift of contemporary married life, in our busy, distracted, individualistic, consumer-driven, media-saturated, and work-oriented world, is toward less spark, less connection, less intimacy, and less focus on the couple relationship. Add in the demands of child-sensitive parenting, and you have a pretty good picture of why our marriages decline over time."[225] William J. Doherty

As we become parents, it's wise to think about how we will maintain the quality of our connection. These are warnings:

> "Children are natural and eager consumers of whatever time, attention, and goods and services that parents will provide. It's the job of parents to discern how much is enough, how much is too much, and to enforce the difference."[226] William J. Doherty

> "Adjustments [to having a child] ... are natural and inevitable. But there is a difference between adjusting your marriage to meet your children's needs and losing your marriage to parenthood."[227] William J. Doherty

> "The greater danger for most of us is to lose our marriage to the demands of parenthood rather than losing our kids to the demands of our marriage (although this happens sometimes in stepfamilies). In a two-parent family, we either fight to create and keep a marriage-centered family, in which the couple relationship is the stable fulcrum of the family and the couple together care for their children, or

we become a child-centered family in which the marriage goes on the shelf."[228] William J. Doherty

Dr. Sue Johnson says we all need to be able to turn to a partner for emotional support, and this is a source of strength, not a weakness. When we have a secure connection with a loved one, we are:

- Better at seeking and giving support
- Able to roll with hurts and are less likely to hold onto anger and bitterness or be aggressively hostile with anger
- More open to new experiences and more flexible
- More confident about solving problems
- More likely to successfully achieve our goals[229]

An additional factor may affect us, which is assuming that we *should* know what to do to be successful in marriage. It's not universally recognized yet that learning and skill-building about marriage is possible and valuable. Many people do not learn good skills in this area from parents or formal education. However, it's not too late for you to learn now. [See Appendix E for more information about marriage and family education.]

Believing the Best of Each Other

Scientific study on the characteristics of highly happy couples indicates that they believe the best of their marriage partner and assume that they care deeply about each other. This belief facilitates personal and couple spiritual connection and growth. Here are examples from the study:

> "The internal assumption of the highly happy spouses was 'He must not have known how that would make me feel, or he wouldn't have done it.'"[230] Shaunti Feldhahn
>
> "When highly happy spouses are legitimately hurt, they refuse to believe that their mate *intended* to hurt them,

> and they look for the most generous explanation instead."[231] Shaunti Feldhahn

As we observe and assess our own feelings, we can shift into thoughts that take the approach of believing our partner did not intend harm.

Relationship author Susan Page identified the vital practice of couples demonstrating "goodwill partnership" as a consistent way of positively influencing their relationship. She writes:

> "I interviewed thirty-five couples who described themselves as 'thriving.' I thought I might find that they all came from happy, functional families, or that they had unusual degrees of compatibility, or that their problems were relatively minor compared with other couples—none of that was true. Some of them had rotten childhoods and enormous challenges. But there was a quality I found in all of these thriving couples that I find is usually missing in more troubled relationships. I now believe that quality is a deeper key to happiness than even good communication or mutual respect.
>
> "It's a quality I call a *spirit of goodwill.* Successful couples are on each other's side. They view themselves as allies, not adversaries. They *want* to be happy together, and together they make this happen. In a spirit of goodwill, they accept the traits in their partner that they wish were different. They have given up trying to change each other. When they argue, they understand that a different point of view may be valid. Because they want to experience their love all the time, they would rather work toward a solution than hang on stubbornly to their own 'right' point of view.
>
> "The most widespread belief about marriage is that it is hard work—that true happiness in marriage is a myth.... But what you *believe* has a great deal to do with what you

experience, because you view all of life through your beliefs! This pervasive negativity about love in our culture is extremely damaging.

"Happy couples simply don't buy it! They *believe* they can be happy together, and their happiness is a priority for them. They keep a sense of adventure and excitement in their lives."[232] Susan Page

Dr. John Gottman and Nan Silver talk about couples connecting and attuning to one another by turning toward each other, which builds mutual trust and goodwill. These couples make what they call minor and major "bids" for "each other's attention, affection, humor, or support." They say, "A tendency to turn toward your partner is the basis of trust, emotional connection, passion, and a satisfying sex life." Responding well to each other then strengthens connection.[233] While this request for attention and support is vital for marriage, it can also apply in extended families, friendships, and work environments.

A wife shares:

"I took an online course that included a section on 'Building Marital Unity'. I read through the first piece of advice about the need for partners to respond to each other's emotional calls. This explained what I had felt for years in our marriage—that I wasn't valued or recognized and was isolated and alone.

"I wasn't sure how to share this information with my husband. I started with sending a funny video from the class about how men and women communicate differently. I also sent a link to the information on emotional calls, hoping to spark a discussion around this concept. But, like all of us, he was busy and didn't get to the links. But, I really wanted him to read this material, as it finally put into words how I felt about his lack of emotional sharing in our relationship.

"After a few days, I asked if he had read any of it, and when he said 'no', I responded with anger and finger-pointing. While our initial conversation was very strained, the materials from the course did provide me with a vocabulary to understand that I needed emotional support, even though I had tried to convince myself to be independent and self-nurture.

"My husband read the material and made a conscious effort to engage with me differently. He offered words of appreciation every day. He also tried to listen for the feelings and emotions in the information I relayed to him, instead of just responding to the details. Now when I share about my work, he asks follow-up questions about how I am feeling or how my co-workers are feeling. Sometimes he also offers support and sympathy, like saying, 'Wow! That sounds tough.'

"Now that a few weeks have passed, we are at a different place in our relationship and feel more connected. Today I asked him how it felt to offer emotional support using words, as I knew it was an effort and was sometimes uncomfortable for him. He said it felt like he was using new muscles and that some attempts felt like a wobble, trip, and fall. For me, it has also been a new experience—mostly positive—but I struggle at times with his questions seeming intrusive. I need to remind myself to have patience, and that with continued practice, we will find a better balance in this phase of our marriage."

Practice and skill are required for us to tune into these requests for attention from each other and respond to them well. Perhaps we ask for a backrub, assistance with a family member, or simply some sharing and listening time. At times we have to take a deep breath and not react if the bid/call for attention from each other comes in the form of a complaint. Tuning into the need for connection that is often behind the complaint will empower a better outcome.

A husband shares:

"For years my wife Keri and I struggled. Looking back, I'm not exactly sure what initially drew us together, but our personalities didn't quite match up. And the longer we were married the more extreme the differences seemed. ... Our fighting became so constant that it was difficult to even imagine a peaceful relationship. We became perpetually defensive, building emotional fortresses around our hearts. We were on the edge of divorce and more than once we discussed it.

"Through time I've learned that our experience was an illustration of a much larger lesson about marriage. The question everyone in a committed relationship should ask their significant other is, "What can I do to make your life better?" That is love. ... Real love is not to desire a person, but to truly desire their happiness—sometimes, even, at the expense of our own happiness. Real love is not to make another person a carbon copy of one's self. It is to expand our own capabilities of tolerance and caring, to actively seek another's well-being. All else is simply a charade of self-interest."[234]

With practice and careful observation, thoughtfulness toward each other can grow. We become more proactive by responding to the anticipated needs of each other, such as by noticing when we are having a difficult day and sending an encouraging text message or making an offer of assistance. Sometimes we can also respond in ways that prompt us both to laugh. The goal is to increase our feelings of being connected and unified partners.

Couple Actions

1. *Turn Toward Each Other:* Consciously notice over the next few days when we turn away from each other and when we turn toward each other instead. Practice having the

receiving partner consciously accept and respond to the overture with attention and respect.

2. *Reconnect to Positive Memories and Behaviors:* Marriage researcher Dr. John Gottman and Nan Silver say:

   "In a happy marriage couples tend to look back on their early days fondly. Even if the wedding didn't go off perfectly, they tend to remember the highlights rather than the low points. The same goes for each other. They remember how positively they felt early on, how excited they were when they met, and how much admiration they had for each other. When they talk about the tough times they've had, they glorify the struggles they've been through, drawing strength from the adversity they've weathered together. But when a marriage is not going well, history gets rewritten—for the worse."[235]

   Materials needed: 2 sheets of paper and markers or pens

   Instructions: Each of us takes a piece of paper and draws a large heart on it. Write inside the heart at least one positive memory from our courting relationship or from earlier in our marriage. Share our positive memory or memories with each other. How do we respond?

   Someone shared, *"This activity started an intimate conversation between the two of us. That's not easy to do. We're that couple that served the kids, the house, and the community before we took care of our relationship. Now that the kids are grown, we still do that, but it's getting harder. We are now committed to some actions that will strengthen our relationship: He's going to call me at lunch time each day, I'm going to cook dinner for him more often, and we're going to have a date night once a month."*

3. Create a positive memory folder and keep notes, cards, photos, printed emails, and more that come from each other. Include notations of special dates, celebrations, and momentous events. When we are having a difficult time with each other, we can look in the folder for a good memory to uplift us and a related action to carry out that brings us closer.

Couple Reflection and Consultation

1. When have we seen the power of making a commitment?
2. Who and what keeps us in motion with re-vitalizing our marriage?
3. What seems to be interfering with our ability to spend time together and connect in a unified way as a couple? (Do our best to be in open exploration, without blaming or criticizing; we do not need to solve this issue now; simply identify key areas to address.)
4. What would show that our marriage is child-centered rather than our children being supported by our marriage?
5. What factors show the current state of our emotional connection? What do we want to improve?
6. What are some key areas where emotional support from each other would be encouraging and increase connection and intimacy?
7. What could we do to show a spirit of "goodwill" toward each other?
8. How can we re-create in the present or near future some of the positive experiences we shared in our past?
9. What did we promise in our wedding vows and ceremony? How are we fulfilling our promises in our marriage now?

Chapter 21: Completing Our Marriage Commitments

In Chapter 5, we began to collect our ideas for "Creating Our Marriage Commitments". We have gathered ideas from throughout the book, and we have generated additional ones through prayer, consultation, creative thought, and action. Now is the time to refine and complete a good working version of that list. These are our committed and specific action statements to re-vitalize and maintain our marriage to the best of our ability. We will use these as goals to strive for, and we will also give ourselves the mercy and grace to not be perfect with achieving them.

Below are some additional ideas and advice from married couples that we can consider, keep for ourselves, or set aside because they are not a fit for us. If the process of creating our commitments begins to feel a bit overwhelming, we can mercifully remind ourselves that we are re-creating our marriage over time with these items as our vision of where we want to be. Not everything can be accomplished at once. We will have regular reflection and consultation opportunities to assess our progress and refine our commitments and our actions.

Including Character Qualities

"We recently had our 10th anniversary, so we made a list of 10 virtues that we want to call on for the next 10 years. They are acceptance, compassion, creativity, discernment, grace, kindness, prayerfulness, sacrifice, trust, and trustworthiness."

"We wish to continue our marriage in a creative and manageable way, paying close attention to being courteous, kind, patient, and loving to each other."

"We use daily appreciations with each other and our children in the form of virtues acknowledgments."

Daily Practices

"We once got advice from an elderly couple who always looked as if they had just fallen in love with each other. Their secret was they never went to sleep at night upset with each other. They also asked the other if they had offended the other throughout the day (without knowing it). If they had, they would apologize. If this was practiced by all couples, it would probably result in more successful marriages and a guarantee of a good night's sleep!" [*Note:* There are times when exhaustion at night makes consulting and resolving issues unwise and this is best left for the next day, so use discernment and wisdom.]

Raising Children

"Have a family meeting or a couple meeting and negotiate who will do what chores so that there is fair distribution of work. Start children on chores very young by giving them a list of what needs to be done that they can do and having them pick. Our boys loved this and did it every Saturday before play or any outing. Our younger son at age 3 put a happy face beside his choices, and our older son printed his name. We had a process where they took turns picking, then spent a couple of hours doing the chores. In a family consultation they decided they would do the work on Saturdays instead of every day. We didn't think it would work, but it did!"

Personal and Couple Behavior

"We chose these commitments:

- Be friends with each other and be united in mind, body, heart, and soul.

- Treat others, and especially each other, family, and friends with love, honor, respect, courtesy, and integrity.
- Encourage and accompany one another's personal growth and transformation and the spiritual transformation of others.
- Regularly, lovingly, and tactfully share any hurts or annoyances we are feeling using 'I feel...' terms rather than 'You do...' language. Set up a regular time to share openly and honestly.
- Honor and respect our own and each other's spiritual, physical, mental, and emotional needs and assist each other to meet those needs as much as is possible.
- Pray together daily.
- Respond to issues that arise as quickly as possible, using consultation as a tool in all matters.
- Demonstrate and accept affection and intimacy from one another regularly.
- Be involved in regular service to each other, our families, friends, and communities.
- Be playful, have fun, and incorporate humor into daily life.
- Have regular family meetings, including children in the consultation process for problem-solving and planning.
- Regularly participate in Bahá'í or other religious activities, including 19-Day Feasts, Holy Days, conventions, and family schools, taking care to observe each other's energy level and adjust participation as is wise.
- Be patient, accepting, and nurturing, maintaining the constancy of our relationship through times of adversity and when we are not being our best selves."

Musician and vocalist Elika Mahony, who has a wonderful album on the theme of love and marriage titled "Birds of

Love", shared a blog posting about the significant items, in no particular order, that have contributed to the progress of her marriage to her husband Tarry. They are:

- "Learning about the needs of one another,
- Being thoughtful,
- Paying attention to and giving priority to our relationship,
- Spending quality time together,
- Serving and praying together,
- Learning how to communicate and consult more effectively,
- Reading and studying books together on varying subjects including the subjects of love and marriage,
- Learning about each other's love language (read a book called 'The 5 Love Languages'),
- Having a weekly lunch date to check in with one another and plan (this has been especially effective),
- Having a day date once in a while (setting aside time to go for an outing)"

She added: *"Of course there are more things on the list, but these are the ones that stood out for us."*[236]

Continuing Learning and Strengthening

"When we were in the early part of our marriage, we discovered we stayed actively engaged in carrying out our commitments when we reflected on our progress about every three months. After that we made reviewing our list of commitments an annual part of celebrating our wedding anniversary. We noticed that the same item was unfulfilled two years in a row. That prompted us to consult about whether we were really committed to it. When we agreed it would still be good to have as part of our marriage, we put more reminders and actions into place, and then we made better progress."

Honoring Our Marriage

"The final thing that we keep reminding each other is that this marriage is forever, and it is a sacred institution that must be honored and appreciated as a gift from God."

Couple Actions

1. Complete our "Creating Our Marriage Commitments" document.

2. Create a visible reminder for us of our commitments.

3. Set a regular interval to review our commitments, such as quarterly or annually. We could also provide greater support to ourselves for the next year through reflecting weekly or monthly. Then we could reflect at less frequent intervals after that.

Couple Reflection and Consultation

1. What do we think and how do we feel about the commitments that we have written down? Are they practical and realistic enough that we can see specific ways to accomplish them?
2. What is the effect on us and our marriage by setting these commitments in place? From striving to achieve them?
3. What have we been learning from our initial efforts to act on our commitments?
4. Which commitments will we focus on now?
5. What are we looking forward to from the process of acting on these commitments?

Chapter 22: How Will We Know We Are Re-Vitalizing Our Marriage?

Some possible indicators that we are successfully re-vitalizing our marriage are that we:

- Engage in consistent personal growth individually and are also growing together
- Regularly seek out and apply helpful knowledge
- Make marriage-strengthening tools our own
- Build new relationship skills as needed
- Share our learning with others
- Spend quality time with each other, keeping up with what is important to each other, and sharing thoughts, feelings, and perspectives
- Relax, laugh, and enjoy our time together, feeling more connected afterward
- Peacefully and happily serve each other and serve others together, or do moderate community service separately with mutual agreement
- Speak and interact with each other with loving kindness and respect most of the time
- Share home-related responsibilities in a fair way
- Interact and make decisions as equal partners
- Communicate and consult smoothly and skillfully; have minimal conflicts, arguments, or fights
- Consistently carry out our agreements with a positive attitude and excellence
- Accomplish the goals we mutually set
- Encourage each other to improve spiritually and prepare our souls for life in the next world
- Carry out agreed acts of physical and emotional intimacy

- Regularly deepen our relationship with God and faith and these sustain our well-being
- Act for what is best for our marriage and family
- Handle missteps with forgiveness, mercy, grace, and at times a sense of humor
- Hear from our children that they appreciate our improved interactions
- Hear from our friends that we appear to be happier and less stressed
- Mentor others in their relationship or marriage preparation or in their marriages
- Reach out for help as needed

Re-vitalizing our marriage is an ongoing journey, not a one-time event. Each day we can make choices that bring us closer together in unity and harmony. Where we notice that we have slipped backward, we can re-commit to positive words and actions going forward.

Couple Actions

1. Create a list of ways we will ongoingly celebrate our progress, no matter how small.

2. Celebrate our wedding anniversary annually. It can also be a prompt to do a regular date night if we do something once a month on the day of the month that matches our wedding day.

3. Honor other couples on their wedding anniversaries, such as friends, family members, or community members.

Couple Reflection and Consultation

1. What positive progress have we made in our marriage? In our family life?

2. What signs are there that we are increasing the vitality of our relationship?
3. How are we handling slips backward into poor behavior?
4. What new actions do we choose to commit to that keep us moving in a positive direction?

Note: Many more topics affect marriages than could be covered in this book. Please subscribe to the Marriage Transformation newsletter and watch for new publications, courses, and other marriage learning opportunities at www.marriagetransformation.com.

Appendices

Appendix A: The Bahá'í Faith

The Bahá'í Faith and Its Teachings

> "The beginning of religion is love for God and for His Chosen Ones, and its end is to manifest that love to His servants."[237]
> Bahá'u'lláh

The Bahá'í Faith is an independent religion, with around 6 million formally enrolled members in established communities in almost every country of the world and representing the greatest diversity of race, class, and ethnicity. At the heart of Bahá'í belief is the conviction that humanity is a single people with a common destiny. In the words of Bahá'u'lláh, the Founder of the Bahá'í Faith, "The earth is but one country, and mankind its citizens."[238]

Bahá'u'lláh taught that there is one God Who progressively reveals vital messages to humanity through Messengers of God. Some with whom we are likely familiar include Moses, Jesus, Muhammad, Krishna, and Buddha. Others, including from the indigenous peoples, likely existed but have been lost to recorded history. Each has contributed to the spiritual development of civilization, bringing humanity to spiritual and moral maturity. Bahá'u'lláh, the most recent Messenger, has brought teachings that address the challenges of the modern world—making possible the unification of the human family and the building of a unified and peaceful global society.

Among the teachings of the Bahá'í Faith are the importance of prayer and meditation, that each person has an eternal soul and virtues, and that everyone is responsible for searching for truth for themselves. The Faith is committed to the equality of women and men, universal education, the importance of achieving personal moral and spiritual excellence, service to others, the harmony of science and religion, the elimination of all forms of prejudice, and unity founded upon justice.

Bahá'ís believe that lasting social transformation starts at the local level, carried out by individuals, couples, and families. In neighborhoods across the world, Bahá'ís and their friends are engaged in a systematic community building process that cultivates love and translates it into social action, breaking down prejudice and promoting the model of a unified global society, beginning at the family and neighborhood level.

This brief introduction merely scratches the surface of this richly diverse, unique, and fascinating global Faith. You can learn more about the Bahá'í teachings and plans for action by visiting any of these websites: bahai.org; news.bahai.org; bahai.us.

Sources in the Bahá'í Teachings

This book contains quotations with sources written from the mid-1850's up to the present time. Many are translated from Persian or Arabic, so there is wide variation in language usage. For example, when various words are translated as "man" in English, the original terms almost always imply "humanity", or "man" and "woman", interchangeably. Additionally, you may see words capitalized that you are used to seeing in lowercase letters; this is often to demonstrate that something is significant or sacred. These quotations reflect the teachings of Bahá'u'lláh; they are considered divine in nature for members of the Bahá'í Faith.

You may already be familiar with the history of the Bahá'í Faith and the various people and entities that have contributed to the body of its teachings or offer guidance. However, if this is new for you, included below is a brief orientation and pronunciation guide. Throughout the book, you will see source names and notes connected to each quotation, and you can refer to the list below if you want to better understand the reference.

1. **The Báb** (pronounced like Bob), translates as "The Gate." He founded the Bábí Faith in 1844 in Iran and is sometimes referred to as a "Manifestation" of God. He prepared people for the coming of Bahá'u'lláh and the Bahá'í Faith.

2. **Bahá'u'lláh** (pronounced Bah-ha-oo-LAH), translates as the "Glory of God". He founded the Bahá'í Faith in what is now Iran and Iraq in 1863 and is sometimes referred to as a "Manifestation" of God. He taught that every human being has a unique purpose to help build a unified world, that justice enables each of us to fulfill this potential, and that the

inequalities between women and men and all races, as well as the extremes between rich and poor must be addressed and resolved. His teachings span over 100 volumes and are still being translated.

3. **'Abdu'l-Bahá** (pronounced Ab-dool-bah-HAH), was Bahá'u'lláh's eldest son. Upholding unity as the fundamental principle of His teachings, Bahá'u'lláh established the necessary safeguards to ensure that His religion would never suffer the same fate as others that split into sects after the deaths of their Founders. In His writings, He instructed all to turn to His eldest Son, 'Abdu'l-Bahá, not only as the authorized interpreter of the Bahá'í writings but also as the "perfect Exemplar" of the Faith's spirit and teachings. 'Abdu'l-Bahá wrote extensively and gave talks internationally.

4. **Shoghi Effendi** (pronounced SHOW-ghee, e-FEN-dee; Effendi means "sir") was appointed by 'Abdu'l-Bahá to be the Guardian of the Bahá'í Faith after 'Abdu'l-Bahá's death in 1921. He wrote many letters and books, developed the global administration of the Bahá'í Faith ordained by Bahá'u'lláh and 'Abdu'l-Bahá, and explained many facets of the Faith and its role in advancing civilization. After his passing in 1957, there could be no further individual leaders of the Bahá'í Faith.

5. **The Universal House of Justice** is the international governing council, first established in 1963 and elected every 5 years by Bahá'ís around the world. Its offices are in Haifa, Israel. There is no clergy in the Bahá'í Faith. Bahá'u'lláh conferred divine authority upon the Universal House of Justice. It uses a consultative approach to guide Bahá'ís about steps toward the advancement of the welfare of humankind, education, peace, unity, and global prosperity. It is charged with applying the Bahá'í teachings to the requirements of an ever-evolving society, and it is therefore empowered to legislate on matters not explicitly covered in the Faith's sacred texts.

6. **National and Local Spiritual Assemblies** are 9-member councils elected annually in their corresponding geographic locations. All

Bahá'í elections are free of nominations and campaigning. Local Spiritual Assemblies are charged with promoting the spiritual education of children and young people, strengthening the spiritual and social fabric of Bahá'í community life, assessing and utilizing the community's resources, and encouraging community members to devote their energies and talents to advance collective goals. They help inspire and coordinate efforts to contribute to the well-being of the areas where they serve. National Assemblies serve in a similar manner at the national level, coordinating efforts across a country.

7. **The Continental Boards of Counsellors and Auxiliary Board members** are appointed to assist the Bahá'í community to maintain unity and growth, providing moral leadership without the administrative authority vested in the elected institutions. They often consult with individuals about personal and relationship issues. They also have assigned geographic areas for their service. These appointees serve a set term and are not invested with individual authority.

Appendix B: Couple Prayers

Below are selected prayers from Bahá'í and other sources that a couple can use to support their marriage.

Prayers for Our Marriage

"O my God! O my God! Unite the hearts of Thy servants, and reveal to them Thy great purpose. May they follow Thy commandments and abide in Thy law. Help them, O God, in their endeavor, and grant them strength to serve Thee. O God! Leave them not to themselves, but guide their steps by the light of Thy knowledge, and cheer their hearts by Thy love. Verily, Thou art their Helper and their Lord."[239]
Bahá'u'lláh

"Glory be unto Thee, O my God! Verily, this Thy servant and this Thy maidservant have gathered under the shadow of Thy mercy and they are united through Thy favor and generosity. O Lord! Assist them in this Thy world and Thy kingdom and destine for them every good through Thy bounty and grace. O Lord! Confirm them in Thy servitude and assist them in Thy service. Suffer them to become the signs of Thy Name in Thy world and protect them through Thy bestowals which are inexhaustible in this world and the world to come. O Lord! They are supplicating the kingdom of Thy mercifulness and invoking the realm of Thy singleness. Verily, they are married in obedience to Thy command. Cause them to become the signs of harmony and unity until the end of time. Verily, Thou art the Omnipotent, the Omnipresent and the Almighty!"[240]
'Abdu'l-Bahá

"O my Lord, O my Lord! These two bright orbs are wedded in Thy love, conjoined in servitude to Thy Holy Threshold, united in ministering to Thy Cause. Make Thou this marriage to be as threading lights of Thine abounding grace, O my Lord, the All-Merciful, and luminous rays of Thy bestowals, O Thou the Beneficent, the Ever-Giving, that there may branch out from this great tree boughs that will grow green and flourishing through the gifts that rain down from Thy clouds of grace. Verily Thou art the

Generous, verily Thou art the Almighty, verily Thou art the Compassionate, the All-Merciful."[241] 'Abdu'l-Bahá

Prayer for Women/Wives

"Magnified be Thy name, O Lord my God! Behold Thou mine eye expectant to gaze on the wonders of Thy mercy, and mine ear longing to hearken unto Thy sweet melodies, and my heart yearning for the living waters of Thy knowledge. Thou seest Thy handmaiden, O my God, standing before the habitation of Thy mercy, and calling upon Thee by Thy name which Thou hast chosen above all other names and set up over all that are in heaven and on earth. Send down upon her the breaths of Thy mercy, that she may be carried away wholly from herself, and be drawn entirely towards the seat which, resplendent with the glory of Thy face, sheddeth afar the radiance of Thy sovereignty, and is established as Thy throne. Potent art Thou to do what Thou willest. No God is there beside Thee, the All-Glorious, the Most Bountiful."[242] Bahá'u'lláh

Prayer for Men/Husbands

"O God, my God! This Thy handmaid is calling upon Thee, trusting in Thee, turning her face unto Thee, imploring Thee to shed Thy heavenly bounties upon her, and to disclose unto her Thy spiritual mysteries, and to cast upon her the lights of Thy Godhead.

"O my Lord! Make the eyes of my husband to see. Rejoice Thou his heart with the light of the knowledge of Thee, draw Thou his mind unto Thy luminous beauty, cheer Thou his spirit by revealing unto him Thy manifest splendors.

"O my Lord! Lift Thou the veil from before his sight. Rain down Thy plenteous bounties upon him, intoxicate him with the wine of love for Thee, make him one of Thy angels whose feet walk upon this earth even as their souls are soaring through the high heavens. Cause him to become a brilliant lamp, shining out with the light of Thy wisdom in the midst of Thy people.

"Verily Thou art the Precious, the Ever-Bestowing, the Open of Hand."[243] 'Abdu'l-Bahá

Finances

"O Thou kind Lord! We are servants of Thy Threshold, taking shelter at Thy holy Door. We seek no refuge save only this strong pillar, turn nowhere for a haven but unto Thy safekeeping. Protect us, bless us, support us, make us such that we shall love but Thy good pleasure, utter only Thy praise, follow only the pathway of truth, that we may become rich enough to dispense with all save Thee, and receive our gifts from the sea of Thy beneficence, that we may ever strive to exalt Thy Cause and to spread Thy sweet savors far and wide, that we may become oblivious of self and occupied only with Thee, and disown all else and be caught up in Thee.

"O Thou Provider, O Thou Forgiver! Grant us Thy grace and loving-kindness, Thy gifts and Thy bestowals, and sustain us, that we may attain our goal. Thou art the Powerful, the Able, the Knower, the Seer; and verily Thou art the Generous...."[244] 'Abdu'l-Bahá

"Giver of all things, You have blessed us with far more than we need in our lives. You have given us shelter and food, clothing and transportation, employment and children. And yet we struggle and sometimes disagree about how we should spend our money. We can't always decide whose needs or wants should have priority. We can't always agree on how much we should spend on...gifts. We can't always be clear about which charities should receive our gifts. We can't always decide whether we should buy a new car or repair the old one.

"Forgive us, Lord, when we forget to thank You for Your abundance. Help us to distinguish between what is necessary and what is desired. Cleanse us from the sin of covetousness and direct our decisions about how to spend or save our money. Help us to remember to give to You first and to trust that You will provide the rest. Keep our hearts focused on what is most important—You, our faith, our family. Guard us against greed and the desire to accumulate earthly goods, which are only temporary. Keep our eyes trained on Your eternal treasures so that what we have here becomes less important. ... Then show us how to use Your gifts wisely and to Your glory. Amen."[245] Ruthanne Wangerin

Different Ways of Facing Life

"We often tend to forget that we are two unique individuals with two different personalities and two very different ways of coping with life. As a result, we sometimes get impatient with each other's method of doing things and stubbornly insist on handling things our own way. At times we are even tempted to believe that our way is the only right way. Help us, Lord, to be more tolerant of the way our partner chooses to cope with life. Teach us how to always be open-minded enough to consider alternate ways of doing things...honest enough to admit when our way is not best...fair enough to realize when it doesn't really matter which way things are done...and kind enough to occasionally give in to our partner's way of handling things. Let us learn, Lord, not only how to use the art of compromise wisely and efficiently but always to temper it with a generous dose of understanding and love."[246] Renee Bartkowski

Being One Together

"I add my breath to your breath that our days may be long on the Earth, that the days of our people may be long, that we shall be as one person, that we may finish our road together."[247] Pueblo Prayer

"O God of peace, unite our hearts by your bond of peace, that we may live with one another continually in gentleness and humility, in peace and unity. O God of patience in the time of trial, and steadfastness to endure to the end."[248] Berhard Albrecht

Appendix C: Grappling with Serious Issues

Due to the range and complexity of issues that affect people, it's not possible here to either include all the possible issues or provide in-depth solutions. The purpose of this section is simply to highlight some issues that may be arising and affecting your marriage and to encourage you to persevere in finding the resources and resource people necessary for healing and learning new patterns, whatever the issue is. Being a Bahá'í does not make someone immune from experiencing serious issues. Due to the sensitive nature of the issues addressed here, the language below in this Appendix is changed from "we" and "our" to being more general.

Note: The quotations included in this Appendix are a fraction of the available guidance available on these topics. For more information, please contact the appropriate Bahá'í institutions. Quotations from professionals in the marriage field are also brief, and many more sources are available. Please search for what you need.

Addressing Serious Issues

There are many serious issues that humans face in this world, including disruptions in physical, mental, emotional, and spiritual well-being. These of course affect marriages and families. There are also issues that specifically relate to marriage and reduce its vitality. When a serious issue occurs that impacts a marriage and family, it's wise to promptly address the matter with many sources of assistance, as applicable, such as:

- Prayer; meditation
- Consulting with and obtaining prayer and guidance from a Spiritual Assembly
- Medical intervention
- Civil authorities' intervention
- Community-based social services
- Psychological counseling
- Therapeutic tools
- Support groups

- Education
- Legal advice and measures

Consulting with a professional counselor is particularly vital when someone's behavior is linked to abuse (that may be multi-generational), mental or emotional illnesses, addictions, violence, or self-destructive tendencies.

Utilizing spiritual guidance along with professional help and services available in society can transform behavior and situations. In cases where general evolving social mores are not in alignment with the Bahá'í teachings, it may be advisable for those seeking professional counseling and mental health professionals to find someone who is a Bahá'í or who comes from other religious backgrounds that include strong moral values. Many Bahá'í professionals now work over the internet with people, which may help.

It can take courage and time to identify that there is an issue, overcome denial and resistance, carefully observe a situation to understand what is happening, seek resources, and take healing steps forward. Chapter 2 presented many of the ways people can build a support team. This Appendix, in addition, includes some more information about 12-Step support groups [see also Chapter 13].

Addictions

Some people can be involved in activities or be exposed to substances, and their bodies and minds do not become addicted. For other people, they can shop, take prescription drugs, play videogames, work, use a mobile phone, exercise, have sex, or eat certain foods in certain ways, and they develop obsessive behavior or an addiction illness. When this happens, they have a need for escalating involvement in the activity to the point it can interfere with their health, responsibilities, relationships, work, and community service.

If one or both individuals in a couple struggles with addiction, healing is needed. They may find help in 12-Step programs; for example, Alcoholics Anonymous, Narcotics Anonymous, Overeaters

Anonymous, Sexaholics Anonymous, and more, as well as obtain professional counseling. There are also 12-Step programs to help family members or friends of the person affected. Experienced members accompany participants and aid them in learning which behaviors are supportive and which enable the illness in the home to worsen. Examples of these types of groups include Al-Anon, Nar-Anon, S-Anon, and more.

Someone shares her experience being married to an alcoholic:

"It's my certain belief that finding the Al-Anon 12-Step program literally saved my life—physically, mentally, emotionally, and spiritually. The disease of alcoholism in our home had caused me to stop functioning in healthy ways, reject a God Who I believed was punishing me unfairly, and set up a distance between myself and Bahá'u'lláh. Until I received help with and guidance about the illness, I could not pray or find the means of connecting with the Bahá'í community—the gap was too wide, and I could not see any way across to the other side.

"Within my first few support group meetings, I began to make changes. I stopped reading romance novels all day for escape, started paying more attention to my child, got out of the middle of the relationship between our child and her father, and listened when my Al-Anon group told me I could not survive living with alcoholism without God. Since God for me was the Bahá'í Faith, I spiritually re-entered the community. I had not officially resigned—after all what would everyone think?! My parents were well known—this would be terrible! I started to really read the Bahá'í Writings at this point too. I had been in a Bahá'í home for most of my growing-up years, but I had absorbed the Bahá'í atmosphere more often than studied its teachings. So, I started to get spiritually on track.

"In addition to the needed help I received in recovering and staying connected to the Faith, a marvelous synergistic side benefit occurred. My involvement with a 12-Step Program and the Bahá'í Faith both together in many ways assisted me to be a better Bahá'í. In particular, I increased my understanding of relying on God's Will and developed the tools to increase my self-knowledge and self-responsibility. Both the Faith and support groups are strong

advocates of prayer and conscious contact with God (most 12-Step groups refer to Him as a Higher Power) and have strong commitments to unity as being vital for the health of the whole."[249]

Here is some guidance:

"The Bahá'í community should feel free to call upon such agencies as Alcoholics Anonymous for assistance and upon public agencies who work with the problem, but must realize that the greatest healing of this social and individual disease is God's Cause which in its fullness will eliminate the causes of alcoholism.... [T]here is no objection to Bahá'ís being members of Alcoholics Anonymous, which is an association that does a great deal of good in assisting alcoholics to overcome their lamentable condition."[250] On behalf of the Universal House of Justice)

Infidelity

Couples can prevent infidelity when they encourage the development of openness in the marriage that includes setting clear boundaries, not based on jealousy or mistrust, but a healthy loving bond. Most people do not set out to begin an affair or choose it. It's the mini choices along the way that are not initially perceived as betrayal that can lead to a bigger problem.

Couples who experience infidelity will benefit from professional counseling. Individuals being unfaithful to their marriage partner is a profound issue that cuts deep into the integrity of the marriage bond and results in the other partner feeling betrayed. Trust is strongly affected.

To deal with this issue and to honor the marriage requires a level of self-awareness and honesty, as well as a deep understanding about re-instating and maintaining healthy boundaries within the marriage. The virtues of discernment and self-accountability are needed spiritual capacities.

In addition to sexual infidelity, sometimes people engage in an emotional affair. This can be defined as non-sexual behavior that involves sharing intimate feelings and thoughts with an extramarital partner. It includes secrecy that violates the explicit or implicit expectations of the relationship (for example: secretly sending flowers to an extramarital partner and expressing feelings of romantic attraction; secretly spending a large amount of one-to-one time together in non-sexual encounters). Emotional affairs, which can often begin through encounters at work or through an internet or social media connection, can also lead to physical infidelity.

There are extensive books, websites, and specialized counselors that can assist couples who experience emotional or physical infidelity to understand, heal, and potentially rebuild their marriage. Divorce is not an automatic occurrence, if a couple is willing to:

- End the unfaithful actions
- Honestly assess what happened
- Explore and accept how they each may have contributed to the situation
- Make key positive changes in their behaviors
- Forgive
- Rebuild trust
- Establish the marriage on a stronger and healthier basis

Here are comments from counselors:

> "Most couples caught up in the tragedy of an affair tell us that they have never felt such intense emotions. They are overwhelmed by anger, depression, fear, guilt, loneliness, and shame.
>
> "A betrayed spouse will ask, How could my spouse do this to me—cheating on me, lying to me over and over again? I can never trust my spouse again. I have so much anger and resentment it scares me. My feelings go way beyond hurt—I can't even put into words the pain I am feeling.
>
> "A wayward spouse often says, I used to beg my spouse for more attention but I never beg anymore—my lover gives me all the attention I need. But I don't know if the attention I'm getting is worth the price. One moment I'm sure I've done the right thing. Then I look into the faces of my children and I'm not sure anymore. I don't want to give up my family but if I give up my

lover, I'll be losing the best thing that ever happened to me. What should I do? I'm an emotional wreck!

"When a couple feels such strong emotions, many question if marital reconciliation is possible. How can we ever recover from such pain? And even if we recover, can we live with the memory of betrayal? Can we ever trust each other again? Can we ever love each other again?

"As marriage counselors we have been asked these questions thousands of times and have been able to respond with a definite *yes*."[251] Willard F. Harley, Jr and Jennifer Harley Chalmers

The following story is from a couple about their response to infidelity.

"We use consultation in our marriage so much that it's a way of life. We use it for simple things, such as planning dinner, and for addressing the toughest problems. We get up every morning and say prayers and then go out for a two-mile walk. The joy and calm of the prayers follow us, and consultation is always best at this time. We are fresh and alone, and the presence of God abounds. We feel united in our love and intentions, and we consult about how we can help make our marriage partner's day smoother.

"One of the thorniest problems for us to consult through has been infidelity, and obviously our issues were charged and intense. A professional therapist assisted us as well; we couldn't have succeeded without that. During and after therapy, we had to face each other and figure out a way to utilize consultation to maintain unity in our marriage. We needed a big space for consulting, and so we did most of it on walks outside. This gave each of us the chance to say what we needed to say. We had the space and distance to process our feelings and consider our options and responses without having to immediately speak. We were surrounded by nature and by God, and it gave us privacy.

"As we walked, we were mindful about each other's emotional needs and state. Each of us had permission to say that we needed time to process our feelings and were not in a space to listen. Each of us had permission to say that we would not speak unless we knew

that the other person was present in the moment and receptive to utilizing whatever comments came forth to keep our marriage together. When we began sharing or listening, if our feelings changed, we let the other person know. When we knew the consultation might be hard and swampy, we often benefited from a warning. This gave us a few moments to prepare to listen for the truth and to listen for understanding from a state of compassion for each other and the situation.

"Once we made the decision to try to work through the infidelity and rebuild our marriage, each of us acted fully towards that end. It was hard at first to practice trust and have full reliance on God and our plan, but we knew this was the only way we could create sustained unity and a secure future together.

"Each person's needs were honored, including giving the time to process and understand what the other said. Sometimes this required time alone or bringing up the same point in a slightly different way several times to gain understanding. Sometimes it meant releasing resentment, fear, and sorrow, and we gave the space to be sad. We needed time and space for each of us to process our feelings, to grieve, and to forgive.

"While consultation in marriage is used to 'solve' something, it's also a vehicle to get to truth. We use it to discover our own personal truths by sharing our thoughts and feelings and remaining open to one another's insights. We build upon our understanding of each other's dreams and desires and learn whether we need to make or renegotiate our agreements. Consultation in our marriage has deepened our friendship, devotion, sense of purpose and peace. Whether or not problems exist we know we have a tool to navigate our lives, create unified action, use respectful words, and elevate our perspective in our marriage."

Helpful Resources (in no particular order):

- www.dearpeggy.com
- www.preventingaffairs.com
- www.marriagebuilders.com
- www.affairrecovery.com
- www.divorcebusting.com

- www.beyondaffairs.com
- *Healing from Infidelity,* Michele Weiner-Davis
- *The Divorce Remedy: The Proven 7-Step Program for Saving Your Marriage*, Michele Weiner-Davis
- *The Secrets of Surviving Infidelity*, Scott Haltzman, MD
- *Not "Just Friends": Rebuilding Trust and Recovering Your Sanity After Infidelity*, Shirley P. Glass, PhD, with Jean Coppock Staeheli
- *Surviving Infidelity: Making Decisions, Recovering from the Pain*, Rona B Subotnik, LMFT, Gloria Harris, PhD
- *After the Affair: Healing the Pain and Rebuilding Trust When a Partner Has Been Unfaithful*, Janis A. Spring, PhD, with Michael Spring
- *Staying Together When an Affair Pulls You Apart*, Stephen M. Judah, PhD
- *Surviving an Affair*, Dr. Willard F. Harley, Jr. and Dr. Jennifer Harley Chalmers
- *My Husband's Affair Became the Best Thing That Ever Happened to Me*, Anne Bercht
- *Unfaithful: Rebuilding Trust After Infidelity*, Gary & Mona Shriver
- *Torn Asunder: Recovering from Extramarital Affairs*, Dave Carder
- *You Can't Have Him—He's Mine*, Marie H. Browne, RN, PhD
- *Avoiding the Greener Grass Syndrome, How to Grow Affair-Proof Hedges Around Your Marriage*, Nancy C. Anderson
- *To Have and to Hold*, Peggy Vaughan

Pornography

Use of and dependence upon pornography can be a form of emotional and physical infidelity, and this is a growing issue strongly affecting individuals and marriages, both those that are challenged and those that are relatively healthy otherwise. Sometimes pornography use begins when a couple stops having sex for some reason, and then usage becomes ongoing. Couples may experience such outcomes as those listed below.

- Be unable to engage in sexual experiences together
- Have difficult encounters that mimic unhealthy or violent behaviors from pornographic images
- Make escalating demands for attention
- Be disappointed that their experiences don't live up to what is portrayed in pornography
- Experience emotional affairs with individuals online

Sometimes people can believe that having a religious marriage ceremony or being in a marriage that includes spiritual practices can cure or prevent pornography use or addiction. While spiritual practices can build the ability to be detached and to purify thoughts, they are not a magic formula that makes the problem go away.

Those with previous pornography usage who stopped before marriage may be at risk again during natural times in marriage of abstinence, such as during menstruation, childbirth, birth recovery, or the illness of a marriage partner. These may be times when additional support services are wise.

Professionals share some of the signs to watch for and responses:

> "If your partner seems like they want more and more and more over a period of time, that would be a sign of possible escalation. Or if it's not just a matter of frequency, they will constantly want a certain level of variety.
>
> "Another symptom—albeit somewhat counterintuitive—is if they seem to become bored with you or tired of you. If they are not as sexually demanding or initiating, it could be because they are going to other places in their mind (looking at pornography or Internet sites) or masturbating more frequently. In the worst-case scenario, they're actually having sexual encounters with other partners.
>
> "Sexuality will become dissatisfying to them in some extreme way. There may be too much absence of it, which we oftentimes refer to as sexual anorexia, or there's too much sexual demand in it. There's too much boredom, or there's too much anger and aggression.

"When you're engaged in an act of sexuality, intuitively most people can tell whether their partner is actually emotionally present in the room. If their mind is elsewhere, you know that's a good symptom that your partner is struggling with something.

"Trust your own intuition, which a lot of people have tried to turn off. They say, 'Oh, I love him, and I don't want to confront him.' If you are somewhat co-dependent to begin with, you know you will deny your own awareness and intuition. There is a level of denial that exists for some people that they simply have to get past."[252] Mark Laaser

"As with other addictions, the obsessive craving overrides everything the sufferer once valued, including family, friends, work, ethics, religion, community. The addict cannot conquer the temptation and salvage the primary relationship without first reversing the impaired thinking, compulsive behavior, and unmanageable urges."[253] John Gottman and Nan Silver

Helpful Resources (in no particular order):

- http://fightthenewdrug.org/
- https://brainheartworld.org/
- https://bahaiteachings.org/author/kelly-monjazeb-and-susanne-alexander/
- *Healing the Wounds of Sexual Addiction*, Dr. Mark R. Laaser; https://faithfulandtrue.com/
- Shattered Vows, Hope and Healing for Women Who Have been Sexually Betrayed, Debra Laaser

Sexual Abuse

When sex is manipulatively coerced, happens as a result of threats, or when there is rape, a marriage is in serious trouble and requires intervention and assistance. Here is one person's perspective:

"My husband was drinking alcohol excessively. The more he drank, the more difficult sex between us became. He was forcefully insistent at times. He would get angry at me for no good reason,

have sex with me that looked like we were making up, and then he would be just as angry afterward. One night he held me down and raped me. It was devastating to me and to our marriage. Thankfully, an Assembly responded to my outreach for help and prayed with me and for us. We found a marriage counselor, and we both got additional assistance from support groups. Our lives turned in a more positive direction."

The quotation below addresses abuse toward females as this is more common; however, the same principles apply if the abuse is toward a male:

> "If a Bahá'í woman suffers abuse or is subjected to rape by her husband, she has the right to turn to the Spiritual Assembly for assistance and counsel, or to seek legal protection. Such abuse would gravely jeopardize the continuation of the marriage, and could well lead to a condition of irreconcilable antipathy."[254] On behalf of the Universal House of Justice

Incest/Sexual Abuse of Children/Youth

Incest can arise in a marriage in two ways. One is if the abuse is occurring currently in the home. The other is when one or both partners experienced sexual abuse as children or teens, either from parents or from someone else. If either or both partners experienced sexual abuse from someone prior to the marriage with one another, hopefully they have already received counseling and are not putting themselves in positions where further abuse can occur. However, it's still likely that the effect of the abuse will arise and affect marital intimacy at times. Here is some information about this:

> "By sexual abuse, I mean any sexual activity—verbal or physical—which is forced upon another individual without his or her consent, which uses him or her as an object to meet another person's sexual desires. Such an act perpetrated upon a child sets in motion a whole series of emotional and physical reactions that have a detrimental effect upon a child's normal sexual maturation process.

> "This distortion of sexuality follows the child to adulthood and often causes problems in the marital relationship. These victims of sexual abuse will often find it extremely difficult to enjoy healthy sexual interaction with their spouses. Many are filled with shame, guilt, fear, anger, and often a revulsion toward sex. These deep-seated emotions are often accompanied by the inability to enjoy kissing, touching of breast or penis, and often an aversion to looking at a naked body, including one's own. The person does not desire to have these negative emotions related to sexual matters but finds it impossible to feel differently. Thus, we are dealing with an extremely serious roadblock to a physically intimate marriage."[255] Gary Chapman

Loving and supportive communication between the couple is vital, as is gentleness and sensitivity. Couples will need to learn what types of touch and communication can trigger the emotions and reactions from the past to arise, especially if post-traumatic stress is an issue. Couples can also experiment with what minimizes problems. For example, having a dim light on or a candle lit can make it easier to see and identify the current partner, which can prompt a feeling of safety and security. If there are ongoing challenges, the couple is wise to seek marital and/or individual counseling and potentially treatment for trauma.

Here is guidance for when the abuse is currently happening:

> "It is difficult to imagine a more reprehensible perversion of human conduct than the sexual abuse of children, which finds its most debased form in incest. At a time in the fortunes of humanity when, in the words of the Guardian, 'The perversion of human nature, the degradation of human conduct, the corruption and dissolution of human institutions, reveal themselves...in their worst and most revolting aspects,' and when 'the voice of human conscience is stilled,' when 'the sense of decency and shame is obscured,' the Bahá'í institutions must be uncompromising and vigilant in their commitment to the protection of the children entrusted to their care, and must not allow either threats or appeals to expediency to divert them from their duty. A parent who is aware that the marriage partner

is subjecting a child to such sexual abuse should not remain silent, but must take all necessary measures, with the assistance of the Spiritual Assembly or civil authorities if necessary, to bring about an immediate cessation of such grossly immoral behavior, and to promote healing and therapy."[256] On behalf of the Universal House of Justice)

Violence

Here is a definition of domestic violence that may be useful to you:

"Domestic violence is a pattern of behaviors used among family members or within a home by one or more persons to oppress, dominate, and control another person or persons. Abuse occurs among people from every socioeconomic, racial, educational, cultural, and religious background. It may occur between partners in a relationship, married or not married, living together, separated or dating. It may also occur between siblings, between a parent and child(ren), between an adult child and an elderly parent, or between other relatives. Sociological research indicates that in the absence of remedial action, abusive behaviors that do not directly incorporate physical violence may lead to it and that such behaviors usually worsen over time."[257] National Spiritual Assembly of the Bahá'ís of the United States

Most Bahá'í quotations address violence toward females as this is more common; however, the same principles apply if the violence is toward a male. Here is guidance:

"The National Spiritual Assembly wishes to convey to the Bahá'í community a clear message that acts of domestic violence are at complete variance with the teachings of Bahá'u'lláh and that violence in the family is a practice to be condemned. In addition, domestic violence is a criminal act in the United States. Such behaviors, on the part of either men or women, are rooted in longstanding social practices connected with an inability or unwillingness to apply the fundamental spiritual principle of the equality of women and men, and to recognize the fundamental right of every human being to be treated with consideration and respect."[258] National Spiritual Assembly of the Bahá'ís of the United States

Most incidents of violence will involve turning to civil authorities or crisis agencies as needed and/or legally required, as the safety of the adult and any children is paramount. The healthier partner must take the lead in securing this protection. Many national Bahá'í institutions have also developed guidelines for handling violent situations that include their country's legal guidelines.

Here is guidance:

> "The use of force by the physically strong against the weak, as a means of imposing one's will and fulfilling one's desires, is a flagrant transgression of the Bahá'í Teachings. There can be no justification for anyone compelling another, through the use of force or through the threat of violence, to do that to which the other person is not inclined. 'Abdu'l-Bahá has written, 'O ye lovers of God! In this, the cycle of Almighty God, violence and force, constraint and oppression, are one and all condemned.' Let those who, driven by their passions or by their inability to exercise discipline in the control of their anger, might be tempted to inflict violence on another human being, be mindful of the condemnation of such disgraceful behavior by the Revelation of Bahá'u'lláh.
>
> "Among the signs of moral downfall in the declining social order are the high incidence of violence within the family, the increase in degrading and cruel treatment of spouses and children, and the spread of sexual abuse. It is essential that the members of the community of the Greatest Name take the utmost care not to be drawn into acceptance of such practices because of their prevalence. They must be ever mindful of their obligation to exemplify a new way of life distinguished by its respect for the dignity and rights of all people, by its exalted moral tone, and by its freedom from oppression and from all forms of abuse."[259] On behalf of the Universal House of Justice

"The stress laid in the statements of Bahá'u'lláh and 'Abdu'l-Bahá on love and harmony as the hallmark of marriage, and in view of 'Abdu'l-Bahá's exhortation that each member of the family must uphold the rights of the others, makes it clear that violence in the family is contrary to the spirit of the Faith and a practice to be condemned. It is clear that no husband should subject his wife to abuse of any kind, whether emotional, mental or physical. Such a reprehensible action would be the very antithesis of the relationship of mutual respect and equality enjoined by the Bahá'í writings—a relationship governed by the principles of consultation and devoid of the use of any form of abuse, including force, to compel obedience to one's will."[260] On behalf of the Universal House of Justice

"When a Bahá'í wife finds herself in such a situation [of emotional, mental, or physical abuse] and feels it cannot be resolved through consultation with her husband, she could well turn to the Local Spiritual Assembly for advice and guidance...."[261] On behalf of the Universal House of Justice

"... [H]e feels that you should turn to your Local Assembly, in the strictest confidence, and seek their aid and advice. These bodies have the sacred obligation to help, advise, protect, and guide the believers in every way within their power when appealed to—indeed they were established just for the purpose of keeping order and unity and obedience to the law of God amongst the believers. You should go to them as a child would to its parents...."[262] On behalf of Shoghi Effendi

"If the broad structure of society is to remain intact, resolute efforts, including medical ones, as necessary, should be made to curb acts of aggression within families particularly their extreme forms of wife beating and child abuse by parents."[263] On behalf of the Universal House of Justice

Warning Signs of Abuse

It can be common for people to not recognize that they are interacting with an abuser until after they are deeply involved. Then sometimes their response is to try to be kind and loving, which can instead prompt the abuse to continue rather than to stop.

The items below can be indicators to observe early on. Abuse can be physical, mental, emotional, or spiritual. The abuser is often male, but not always. Watch out and seek help when someone acts in these ways listed below, especially when multiple indicators are present. The person:

1. "Shows unhealthy perfectionism with unreasonable and inflexible high standards, and a strong negative reaction when they feel disappointed in another person's actions
2. Criticizes and puts-down self and others
3. Displays emotional instability with extreme reactions
4. Manipulates with guilt, scorn, and shame
5. Refuses to accept responsibility for their actions or life
6. Behaves in an overly jealous way and attempts to restrict contact with other people
7. Focuses only on themselves and are unable to compassionately see others' perspectives
8. Contacts someone constantly and through multiple ways
9. Disrespects boundaries or personal space; engages in stalking behavior
10. Threatens to hurt themselves or others if some specific action is or is not taken
11. Insists on co-mingling and managing money on behalf of someone else
12. Appears to be putting on an act or behaves initially according to all the "proper relationships rules" but can't sustain the behavior
13. Exerts strong pressure to move a relationship forward too fast
14. Behaves with cruelty toward animals and children
15. Displays rigidity about gender roles
16. 'Accidentally' hurts others during intimate moments"[264]

(Joyce B. Lakewood)

When someone is receiving abuse, others can observe behaviors and initiate assistance. Indicators that someone is being abused can be that the person is:

- Seen less often at social or community events
- Very self-critical, including around others
- Reluctant to share an opinion or point of view, when formerly would have
- Stressed or worried all the time
- Unusually quiet
- Showing loss of appetite or weight
- Hypervigilant about possible dangers
- Jumpy, nervously responding to small things
- Wearing inappropriate clothing for the season or temperature to cover bruised or injured body parts
- Frequently checking-in with their partner
- Afraid of their partner or always very anxious to please them
- Wary about holding or continuing conversations when their partner is nearby
- Losing self-confidence and self-respect due to their partner often criticizing or humiliating them in front of other people
- Suffering from poorly explained physical injuries, such as bruises, broken bones, sprains, or cuts

The abused person may become defensive and be reluctant to talk about any or all of the above for obvious reasons, but in general terms, if several of the above behaviors are being displayed, it would be completely natural for someone to ask them if there is anything wrong out of general concern. It often takes someone trained or alert to the signs to spot a person experiencing abuse. This then can open the door for the person to obtain help.

Separation and Divorce

The Bahá'í Faith discourages divorce, and its teachings encourage all possible efforts to be made to save a marriage. However, it does allow for divorce in some serious circumstances.

Here is guidance:

"Truly, the Lord loveth union and harmony and abhorreth separation and divorce."[265] Bahá'u'lláh

"Regarding divorce, the Guardian stated that it is discouraged, deprecated and against the good pleasure of God. ... Divorce is conditional upon the approval and permission of the Spiritual Assembly. The members of the Assembly must in such matters independently and carefully study and investigate each case. If there should be valid grounds for divorce and it is found that reconciliation is utterly impossible, that antipathy is intense and its removal is not possible, then the Assembly may approve the divorce."[266] On behalf of Shoghi Effendi

Couples in difficulty can obtain guidance from a Spiritual Assembly and may find assistance through compilations called "Preserving Bahá'í Marriages" (rev. ed. 2009) and "Divorce". [See also Chapter 2 and Appendices D and E]

Other Topics

Complex topics such as homosexuality and gender identity are not included here. However, the Bahá'í institutions have current guidance on these topics to guide people who need assistance, so please obtain it from them. Other issues not covered in this chapter may also be challenging your marriage; guidance is available from the institutions about most topics.

Individual/Couple Actions

1. Spend time in nature deeply reflecting on and praying about the health of our marriage and family. Identify areas where there are issues to address. Make a plan to address them and begin to carry out the remedial actions.

2. Research the topic affecting our marriage or family and consult about it with a professional or support group. Seek guidance on the topic from Bahá'í sources and institutions.

Individual/Couple Reflection and Consultation

1. What signs indicate our experiences individually or together may be unhealthy or unwise?
2. What indicators are there that a serious situation exists? How could we recognize abuse or an addiction?
3. What positive improvements are we able and willing to make in our personal behavior? What will make it more likely these are consistent and long-term?
4. What help do we need from others? Who would be good choices? How will we proceed to obtain this help?
5. What will assist our healing process?

Appendix D: For Counselors Who Are Not Bahá'ís When Counseling Bahá'ís and Partners About Marriage, Separation, Reconciliation, or Divorce

[Note: Copies can be made of Appendix D to give to a counselor. Downloadable copies are also on www.bahaimarriage.net.]

The following information is provided as an aid to understanding the relevant religious beliefs of your clients who are members of the Bahá'í Faith, and in support of your approach to assisting them in addressing and remedying their difficulties.

Overview of the Bahá'í Faith

The Bahá'í Faith was founded in Persia (now Iran) in the mid-1800's by its Prophet, Bahá'u'lláh, and is now established in more than 100,000 localities around the world. The United Nations and a majority of the governments of the world recognize the Bahá'í Faith as an independent worldwide religion.

The Bahá'í teachings provide a renewal and strengthening of the messages in previous religions that encourage people to make positive, spiritual, and moral choices in their lives. In addition, the religion provides guidance to establish a worldwide global family of humanity living in peace that embraces the diversity of its peoples, cultures, and languages.

The essential message of the Bahá'í Faith is that of unity. Bahá'ís believe that there is only one God, that there is only one human race, and that all the world's major religions represent stages in the revelation of God's will and purpose for humanity. Bahá'ís also believe that the family is the basic unit of society and that monogamous marriage between a man and a woman is the foundation of family life and civilization.

There is no clergy in the Bahá'í Faith. Administrative and spiritual matters affecting the members of the Bahá'í Faith are handled by local, regional, national, and international councils. Among the responsibilities of the local Spiritual Assemblies (local councils) is ensuring that couples know about and follow Bahá'í laws and guidance related to marriage and divorce. It also ensures that the civil legalities for both are completed. Local Spiritual Assemblies are involved even if only one member of the couple is a Bahá'í.

Bahá'í Views of Marriage

Bahá'u'lláh teaches that marriage is an historic and continuing Divine institution. Marriage should be of benefit to both partners, establish a strong foundation for the rearing and education of children, provide stability for the community, and aid the progress of humanity. In His Writings, Bahá'u'lláh states that God "established the law of marriage" and "made it as a fortress for well-being and salvation...." Marriage requires that the couple choose each other without parental interference and then the marriage happening is dependent upon consent from the couple's parents. Bahá'í marriage is:

> ... [T]he commitment of the two parties one to the other, and their mutual attachment of mind and heart. Each must, however, exercise the utmost care to become thoroughly acquainted with the character of the other, that the binding covenant between them may be a tie that will endure forever. Their purpose must be this: to become loving companions and comrades and at one with each other for time and eternity....
> 'Abdu'l-Bahá, *Selections from the Writings of 'Abdu'l-Bahá*, #86

As an indication of the couple's relationship to God, the Bahá'í wedding ceremony includes the vow, "We will all, verily, abide by the Will of God."

Bahá'í Principles That Guide Healthy Marriages

The Bahá'í Writings encourage individuals to be involved in **personal and spiritual growth** throughout their lives, and married couples are asked to "ever improve the spiritual life of each other" ('Abdu'l-Bahá, *Selections from the Writings of 'Abdu'l-Bahá*, #86). The more that marriage partners develop and practice spiritual character qualities within the marriage such as compassion, courtesy, encouragement, faithfulness, flexibility, forgiveness, gentleness, helpfulness, love, moderation, patience, respect, responsibility, trustworthiness, and truthfulness, the more benefit this brings to the marriage and family.

Personal spiritual practices include **daily prayer and meditation**. Bahá'ís believe that praying together as a couple can also strengthen marriages, although there is no requirement that couples do this.

In a materialistic society, people tend to think that their value lies in their ability to exercise power over one another. The Bahá'í teachings specifically warn against such a concept, because it leads to competition, domination, and power plays. Therefore, couples facing marital challenges may need assistance in recognizing spiritual qualities in one another and in demonstrating to one another that these qualities are more meaningful than material standards.

Bahá'í beliefs include individuals and couples **practicing gender equality** within their relationships to the best of their abilities. The Bahá'í Writings state, "Divine Justice demands that the rights of both sexes should be equally respected since neither is superior to the other...." ('Abdu'l-Bahá, *Paris Talks*, p. 162) Equality does not mean that the roles and responsibilities of the man and the woman are identical. Rather, they are to function within their marriage as equal partners, noting that there are numerous ways to meet their collective responsibilities.

This principle of equality is especially applicable when the couple discusses issues, builds understanding, and makes decisions, a process Bahá'ís call **consultation**. The following is applicable guidance from the Universal House of Justice, the international Bahá'í governing body:

> "... [I]n a marriage relationship, neither husband nor wife should ever unjustly dominate the other, and...there are times when the husband and the wife should defer to the wishes of the other, if agreement cannot be reached through consultation; each couple should determine exactly under what circumstances such deference is to take place." (On behalf of the Universal House of Justice, 1992, "Violence and Sexual Abuse of Women and Children")

The ability to consult effectively is a practice that the Bahá'í teachings strongly encourage. Therefore, Bahá'í couples will readily understand the importance of learning to listen, to be detached and non-reactive, and to remove self-interest from their spoken communications. Consultation includes the following principles:

- Maintaining harmony, love, and unity
- Engaging in full and truthful expression
- Encouraging and listening
- Holding pure motives
- Detaching from strong emotions and personal opinions
- Using difference of opinion to create unique solutions
- Taking a timeout, pausing as needed for reactions to calm down
- Avoiding disruptive behaviors and maintaining respectful boundaries
- Agreeing at times to defer to one another
- Supporting unified decisions

Love and consideration are vital within marriage, and abuse is forbidden. This is clear from the following quotation:

> "The stress laid in the statements of Bahá'u'lláh and 'Abdu'l-Bahá on love and harmony as the hallmark of marriage, and in view of 'Abdu'l-Bahá's exhortation that each member of the family must uphold the rights of the others, makes it clear that violence in the family is contrary to the spirit of the Faith and a practice to be condemned. It is clear that no husband should subject his wife to abuse of any kind, whether emotional, mental or physical. Such a reprehensible action would be the very antithesis of the relationship of mutual respect and equality enjoined by the Bahá'í writings—a relationship governed by the principles of consultation and devoid of the use of any form of abuse, including force, to compel obedience to one's will." (On behalf of the Universal House of Justice to a National Spiritual Assembly, April 12, 1990)

Of course, **abuse of children is also forbidden**. Some National Spiritual Assemblies provide guidance in alignment with their country's laws for Spiritual Assemblies on handling domestic violence and abuse. With the couple's permission, you may be able to obtain more detailed information from a Spiritual Assembly in your area through contact information supplied to you by the couple you are counseling.

The Bahá'í Faith holds a **balanced view of sex and sexual relations**. Sexual expression between a monogamous, heterosexual married couple is considered a natural right and part of the purpose of marriage. However, chastity applies, which includes abstinence from arousing touch and sex before marriage, and faithfulness and purity of thought and action after marriage. This precludes the use of pornography. Sexual relations between unmarried individuals or between people not married to one another is not permissible in the Bahá'í teachings.

Children

The creation and rearing of children is a primary purpose of marriage. The Bahá'í Writings emphasize the mother's role in the early education of children, but both parents are responsible for the health, education, and well-being of their children.

If a married couple is struggling to get along with each other, the well-being of the children must be a consideration:

> "It is always a source of sorrow in life when married people cannot get on well together, but...you and your husband, in contemplating divorce, should think of the future of your children and how this major step on your part will influence their lives and happiness." (On behalf of Shoghi Effendi, *Compilation of Compilations, Vol. II*, #2324)

Help for Challenged Couples

Bahá'í couples experiencing marital difficulties are encouraged to consult with a Spiritual Assembly, preferably before the problems become entrenched. In areas where there is not a Local Spiritual Assembly, or where the couple is unwilling to approach them for some reason, the couple is free to contact any Assembly in a neighboring Bahá'í community or ask their National Spiritual Assembly for assistance. The Spiritual Assembly generally provides the parties with spiritual guidance and resources and encourages them to seek professional assistance as well. The Universal House of Justice provides this guidance:

> "The House of Justice is distressed to learn that you and your husband are continuing to experience marital difficulties. It has frequently advised believers in such situations to turn to the Spiritual Assemblies for advice and counsel, and to follow this advice in their efforts to preserve the unity of their marital relationship. It has been found useful in many instances to also seek the assistance of competent professional marriage counselors, who can provide useful insights and guidance in the use of constructive measures to bring about a greater degree of unity." (On behalf of the Universal House of Justice, *Compilation of Compilations, Vol. II*, #2346)

Discussion of Actions and Occurrences in a Challenged Marriage

Bahá'ís believe that it's inappropriate to confess sins to anyone other than God for the purpose of absolution of the sins and that it's harmful to backbite and gossip about others. However, in a therapeutic setting, effective treatment requires that the problems counseling is designed to address are clearly communicated. So strong is the admonition against backbiting that some Bahá'ís are reticent to be open about the problems they have with their marriage partner and, for some, time may need to be taken in therapy to discuss the differences between backbiting and consulting to seek understanding and to resolve problems.

Bahá'ís may also confuse confession of sins with actions of apology and forgiveness that can be vital in healing or reconciling a marital relationship. Guidance on this topic includes:

> "... [I]f we spontaneously desire to acknowledge we have been wrong in something, or that we have some fault of character, and ask another person's forgiveness or pardon, we are quite free to do so. ...[W]e are not obliged to do so. It rests entirely

with the individual." (On behalf of Shoghi Effendi, *Lights of Guidance*, #589)

Some Bahá'ís may also be reticent to turn for guidance to a Spiritual Assembly, often from embarrassment and reluctance to air such personal issues before the members serving on the institution, who they may regard as personal friends. If this is the case with the couple you are counseling, their concerns should be explored in therapy. The couple should be encouraged to gain this help from a different local Spiritual Assembly, or they can do outreach to their National Assembly for assistance or to some other Bahá'í institution. Some Assemblies have counseling teams or committees that can assist this process, and spiritual guidance and religious conviction are often powerful motivators for new behaviors and growth. All matters brought to a Spiritual Assembly are held in the strictest confidence by its members.

Separation, Reconciliation, and Divorce

Separation and divorce generally go against unity as the foundational principle of the Bahá'í Faith, although there are times when they are appropriate and allowed. "The Bahá'í attitude is that marriage is a very serious and sacred relationship and divorce a last resort to be avoided if humanly possible." (On behalf of Shoghi Effendi, *Compilation of Compilations, Vol. II*, #2323)

An individual or a couple wishing to have a marital separation for the purpose of divorcing approaches a Spiritual Assembly and makes the request. The Assembly works with both individuals and the couple to ensure they understand the relevant Bahá'í teachings and facilitates them with attempting reconciliation, ensuring first that any issues of safety have been addressed. If reconciliation is not possible, and the couple is intent upon divorcing, they are then required to enter a year of waiting (sometimes referred to as a "year of patience"). Living apart allows the couple to calm their thoughts and emotions, make further attempts at reconciliation as safe and appropriate, obtain counseling, and hopefully resume their marriage. If the couple resumes having sexual relations or living together, the separation is considered ended. If the couple wishes to separate following this, the divorce application and the year of waiting must both start anew.

Dating other people in the spirit of courtship is contrary to the spirit of the Bahá'í teachings during separation or the year of waiting, as the focus during that time is to be on reconciliation between the marriage partners. Applying for civil divorce should generally wait until after the year of waiting is completed, but there are exceptions in some cases. If a couple completes the year of waiting without reconciliation and obtains a civil divorce, the Bahá'í divorce is granted, and the parties are free to marry others.

The quotations below may guide you in working with a couple that is discussing separation or divorce:

> "Should resentment or antipathy arise between husband and wife, he [or she] is not to divorce her [or him] but to bide in patience throughout the course of one whole year, that perchance the fragrance of affection may be renewed between them. If, upon the completion of this period, their love hath not returned, it is permissible for divorce to take place." (Bahá'u'lláh, *Kitáb-i-Aqdas*, #K68)

> "Irreconcilable antipathy arising between the parties to a marriage is not merely a lack of love for one's spouse but an antipathy which cannot be resolved." (On behalf of the Universal House of Justice, "Preserving Bahá'í Marriages" (2009), #37)

> "In the strict legal sense there are no 'grounds' for a Bahá'í divorce. No question of misbehavior of either party is involved and the only condition under which a Bahá'í divorce may be considered is the irreconcilable antipathy of the parties." (Universal House of Justice, letter dated May 24, 1972, to a National Spiritual Assembly)

> "Bahá'ís should be profoundly aware of the sanctity of marriage and should strive to make their marriages an eternal bond of unity and harmony. This requires effort and sacrifice and wisdom and self-abnegation. A Bahá'í should consider the possibility of divorce only if the situation is intolerable and he or

she has a strong aversion to being married to the other partner. This is the standard held up to the individual. It is not a law, but an exhortation. It is a goal to which we should strive." (On behalf of the Universal House of Justice, *Lights of Guidance*, #1303)

"... '[A]version' is not a specific legal term that needs to be defined. Indeed a number of other terms are used in describing the situation that can lead to divorce in Bahá'í law, such as 'antipathy', 'resentment', 'estrangement', 'impossibility of establishing harmony', and 'irreconcilability'. The texts, however, point out that divorce is strongly condemned, should be viewed as 'a last resort' when 'rare and urgent circumstances' exist, and that the partner who is the 'cause of divorce' will 'unquestionably' become the 'victim of formidable calamities.' (On behalf of the Universal House of Justice, *Lights of Guidance*, #1305)

Further Information

If you require further information about the Bahá'í Faith and its approach to marriage and to counseling, with consent from the couple you are working with, you can contact the Spiritual Assembly closest to you or the offices of a National Spiritual Assembly. You may also find helpful information and specific country contact information at this website: www.bahai.org.

Appendix E:
Relationship, Marriage, and Family Education in the Bahá'í Faith Community

Potential Ideas to Consider from Marriage Transformation®

[Note: Copies can be made of Appendix E for community use. Downloadable copies are also on www.bahaimarriage.net.]

This document invites Bahá'ís and Bahá'í communities to engage as appropriate, needed, and timely in relationship, marriage, and family education for building happy, unified, and lasting character-based marriages and families.

This document reflects the current understanding of Susanne M. Alexander. She draws on her experience in the Bahá'í community and as a relationship and marriage educator both with her company Marriage Transformation and also as online course faculty and Chair of the Department of Relationships, Marriage, and Family with the Wilmette Institute, an agency of the National Spiritual Assembly of the Bahá'ís of the United States. This is not an official administrative document; it's simply offered as an educational resource for Bahá'ís to consider as they strive to strengthen the institution of marriage and unify families in their lives and communities.

Any questions about the application of marriage laws in the community should be directed to the Bahá'í institutions:

> "... [T]he provision of guidance on administrative matters such as the laws of engagement, marriage, and divorce falls under the purview of Local and National Spiritual Assemblies...." (On behalf of the Universal House of Justice to an individual, September 24, 2014)

Marriages and families are complex and socially vital entities that form the foundation of society. The Bahá'í community and its institutions have a strong interest in forming healthy and unified marriages and families. The Bahá'í Covenant from Bahá'u'lláh draws into unity all people and entities in the community. As individuals, married couples, and families stay connected to and faithful to this Covenant, they increase their opportunity to be unified.

The Universal House of Justice provides this guidance:

> "...[Y]oung women and men become acutely conscious of the exhortations of the Supreme Pen to 'enter into wedlock' that they may 'bring forth one who will make mention of Me amid My servants'.... ...This generation of youth will form families that secure the foundations of flourishing communities. Through their growing love for Bahá'u'lláh and their personal commitment to the standard to which He summons them will their children imbibe the love of God, 'commingled with their mother's milk', and always seek the shelter of His divine law." (Universal House of Justice, *Framework for Action*, #35)

DEFINING RELATIONSHIP and MARRIAGE EDUCATION

Systematic Relationship and Marriage Education Based on the Bahá'í Writings

It's important to note that there is no one system for Bahá'í relationship, marriage, and family education that exists. The methods and focus for any of these types of educational efforts will vary significantly across the planet depending on the needs of the population, available resources, and venues. How scientific findings are included will vary as well. Here are quotations about the organic evolution underway:

> "As you know, courtship practices differ greatly from one culture to another, and it is not yet known what pattern of courtship will emerge in the future when society has been more influenced by Bahá'í Teachings. However, there is no indication that it will resemble the practices extant in existing cultures.... In this interim period, the friends are encouraged to make great efforts to live in conformity with the Teachings and to gradually forge a new pattern of behavior, more in keeping with the spirit of Bahá'u'lláh's Revelation." (Universal House of Justice, August 28, 1994, to an individual, published in *Marriage Can Be Forever—Preparation Counts!*, 3rd ed., p. 141)

> "Besides assisting couples through their professional expertise, counselors can draw upon their insights into the Bahá'í Teachings to provide further assistance, such as by encouraging them to develop the skill of consultation and by helping them to distinguish concepts and practices current in society from those found in the Teachings. The views of professionals and of the wider society that are contrary to the Teachings will naturally have an impact on the friends in this age of transition. As the community grows in strength and as the Teachings become more fully understood and practiced by Bahá'ís, the distinctive characteristics of Bahá'í family life will become increasingly apparent." (On behalf of the Universal House of Justice to an individual, September 24, 2014)

Communities will make decisions about whether to use materials already developed by a variety of people, organizations, and institutions or those that develop locally as needed. The people involved will utilize study of the guidance, consultation, learning-in-action, and reflection to discern what works. As materials evolve as part of the Ruhi Institute offerings, family life will also likely be part of the institute process of community building and service.

A Description of Relationship, Marriage, and Family Education

The field of relationship, marriage, and family education focuses on strengthening knowledge and skills in individuals, couples, and families as well as on preventing future problems. It's aimed at empowering people to create marriages that provide healthy and happy stability and unity for families and communities. It includes results from scientific research as well as the experience of professionals working with clients, participants, and groups. This education can include such activities as reading books, studying in groups, taking courses in-person and online, participating in workshops, mentoring, and counseling. This education provides important knowledge, skills, and attitudes about relationships, marriage, re-marriage to someone new, parenting, and family functioning to foster a gradual and organic transformation process.

When the fruits of this field are paired with and influenced by the Bahá'í teachings, there is a powerful harmony of resources.

This type of education builds capacity and understanding and increases competencies. Ideally, it equips people to be healthy individuals with many character strengths who can then be successful partners in a relationship and then marriage. It includes preparation for relationships and marriage for individuals and couples of all ages and experience levels. It provides marriage-strengthening tools for healthy married couples who want to continue learning, growing, and developing. It pairs well with spiritual and professional counseling for challenged marriages. It includes skill-building for those who are parenting, and it provides assistance for those forming and maintaining families. Ideally, this type of education continues across the life span of couples and families.

Relationship, marriage, parenting, and family education serves:

- Unmarried individuals interested in learning about relationships and how to prepare for them
- Couples considering and involved in friendship, dating, courtship, and marriage
- Unmarried individuals and couples considering marrying again after divorce or death of a partner
- Parents of individuals considering dating, courtship, consent, engagement, and marriage
- Newly married couples
- Couples experiencing the usual ups and downs of married life
- Couples experiencing external tests that are affecting their relationship
- Couples in life-stage transitions; such as, becoming parents, guiding those in teen-age years, their children leaving home, or retirement
- Parents who want to raise children according to Bahá'í principles
- Couples with strong marriages who enjoy enriching their marriage further

- Challenged married couples who need knowledge and skill-building

What Relationship, Marriage, and Family Education is Not

Relationship, marriage, and family education is not counseling or therapy; although counselors can use it along with their services. It's not generally for couples and families in active crisis who are dealing with major issues most suited to be addressed with a counselor. Although marriage education can provide skill building and assistance for challenged couples considering separation or divorce, these couples usually need additional help from a trained couples' counselor and consultation with a Spiritual Assembly.

The *timing* of education sometimes may not be appropriate when there is an active crisis or sudden decline. Symptoms of crisis may include:

- Ongoing signs of estrangement or aversion
- Daily conflict
- Any type of coercive, abusive, violent, or addictive behavior
- Infidelity (including pornography use)

Seriously challenged couples and families may find education in groups or workshops to be discouraging or difficult where others are having a much healthier experience in their relationships. Troubled individuals may also disrupt the experience for or discourage others who are not in crisis.

SOME FOUNDATION STATEMENTS AND PRINCIPLES

The following statements and quotations outline the role of Assemblies, describe marriage as the foundational element of society, underscore the significance of Bahá'í marriage and family unity as a model, and emphasize the essential art of consultation (and other knowledge and skills).

Assemblies may wish to reflect on these statements and share them periodically with those they serve. This may expand everyone's awareness of the importance of working conscientiously to build strong marriages and families, both for their own sakes and for the ultimate sake of the Bahá'í Faith and humanity.

Some purposes of marriage and family

"And when He [God] desired to manifest grace and beneficence to men, and to set the world in order, He revealed observances and created laws; among them He established the law of marriage, made it as a fortress for well-being and salvation, and enjoined it upon us in that which was sent down out of the heaven of sanctity in His Most Holy Book [*The Kitáb-i-Aqdas*]. He saith, great is His glory: 'Enter into wedlock, O people, that ye may bring forth one who will make mention of Me amid My servants. This is My bidding unto you; hold fast to it as an assistance to yourselves.'" (Bahá'u'lláh, *Bahá'í Prayers* (US 2002), p. 118)

"The creation and rearing of children is a primary purpose of marriage. The Bahá'í Writings emphasize the mother's role in the early education of a child, but both parents are held accountable for the health, education, and well-being of the child." (On behalf of Shoghi Effendi, *Compilation of Compilations, Vol. II*, #2324)

"Marriage is a very sacred institution. Bahá'u'lláh said its purpose is to promote unity. [We] are trying to create a high moral standard, and reinstate the sanctity of marriage." (On behalf of Shoghi Effendi, *Compilation of Compilations, Vol. I*, #903)

"The Bahá'í teachings on sexual morality center on marriage and the family as the bedrock of the whole structure of human society and are designed to protect and strengthen that divine institution. Bahá'í law thus restricts permissible sexual intercourse to that between a man and the woman to whom he is married." (*The Kitáb-i-Aqdas* by Bahá'u'lláh, Note #134)

Assemblies have a responsibility to educate the community about marriage and to respond to requests for help

"The Spiritual Assembly should always be concerned that the believers in its community are being deepened in their understanding of the Bahá'í concept of marriage, especially the young people, so that the very thought of divorce will be abhorrent to them." (On behalf of the Universal House of Justice, *Lights of Guidance*, #1304)

"The House of Justice is distressed to learn that you and your husband are continuing to experience marital difficulties. It has frequently advised believers in such situations to turn to the Spiritual Assemblies for advice and counsel, and to follow this advice in their efforts to preserve the unity of their marital relationship. It has been found useful in many instances to also seek the assistance of competent professional marriage counselors, who can provide useful insights and guidance in the use of constructive measures to bring about a greater degree of unity." (On behalf of the Universal House of Justice, "Preserving Bahá'í Marriages" (2009), #45)

Fostering obedience to the Bahá'í marriage laws is an important duty of Spiritual Assemblies

"The carrying out of the Bahá'í marriage laws, as given to the friends throughout the world, is a vital obligation of every believer who wishes to marry, and it is an important duty of every Local Spiritual Assembly to ensure that these laws are known to, and obeyed by, the believers within their jurisdiction, whether or not the Bahá'í marriage ceremony is recognized by civil law. Each Assembly, therefore, must conscientiously carry out its responsibilities in connection with the holding of Bahá'í marriage ceremonies, the recording of Bahá'í marriages in a register kept for this purpose, and the issuing of Bahá'í marriage certificates." (Universal House of Justice, *Messages 1963 to 1986*, pp. 488-489)

Marital and family unity among the Bahá'ís builds credibility for their message to the world about unity; seriously courting a partner and maintaining marriages are part of an individual's and couple's service to God

"...[I]f the friends are not able to maintain harmony within their families, on what other basis do they hope to demonstrate to a skeptical world the efficacy of the pre-eminent character of the Revelation of Bahá'u'lláh? What possible influence could they hope to exert on the development of nations and the establishment of world peace?" (On behalf of the Universal House of Justice, *Lights of Guidance*, #740)

"... [E]very aspect of a person's life is an element of his or her service to Bahá'u'lláh: the love and respect one has for one's parents; the pursuit of one's education; the nurturing of good health; the acquiring of a trade or profession; one's behavior towards others and the upholding of a high moral standard; one's marriage and the bringing up of one's children; one's activities in teaching the Faith and the building up the strength of the Bahá'í community, whether this be in such simple matters as attending the Nineteen Day Feast or the observance of Bahá'í Holy Days, or in more demanding tasks required by service in the administration of the Faith; and, not least, to take time each day to read the Writings and say the Obligatory Prayer, which are the source of growing spiritual strength, understanding, and attachment to God." (Universal House of Justice, December 7, 1992, European Bahá'í Youth Council; www.bahairesearch.com)

Relationship and marriage preparation are key elements in establishing healthy marriages

"... [T]here is nothing in the Bahá'í Writings which relates specifically to the so-called dating practices prevalent in some parts of the world, where two unmarried people of the opposite sex participate together in a social activity. In general, Bahá'ís who are planning to involve themselves in this form of behavior should become well aware of the Bahá'í Teachings on chastity and, with these in mind, should scrupulously avoid any actions which would arouse passions which might well tempt them to violate these Teachings. In deciding which acts are permissible in the light of these considerations, the youth should use their own judgment, giving due consideration to the advice of their parents, taking account of the prevailing customs of the society in which they live, and prayerfully following the guidance of their conscience. It is the sacred duty of parents to instill in their children the exalted Bahá'í standard of moral conduct, and the importance of adherence to this standard cannot be overemphasized as a basis for true happiness and for successful marriage." (On behalf of the Universal House of Justice to an individual, February 5, 1992)

"Careful preparation for marriage is an essential first step in the preservation of Bahá'í marriage." (Research Department of the Universal House of Justice, "Preserving Bahá'í Marriages" Memorandum (1990), #3)

Building knowledge and skills with character/virtues supports relationships and marriages as well as all aspects of the Core Activities [devotional gatherings, study circles, children's classes, and junior youth spiritual empowerment groups], each of which can include a focus on character; parents have a vital role in building strong characters in their children

"Bahá'í marriage is the commitment of the two parties one to the other, and their mutual attachment of mind and heart. Each must, however, exercise the utmost care to become thoroughly acquainted with the character of the other, that the binding covenant between them may be a tie that will endure forever." ('Abdu'l-Bahá, *Selections from the Writings of 'Abdu'l-Bahá*, #86)

"No less pertinent [than rectitude of conduct] to the success of the Bahá'í enterprise today are the Guardian's forthright comments on the importance of a chaste and holy life, 'with its implications of modesty, purity, temperance, decency, and clean-mindedness'. He was unequivocal in his language, summoning the friends to a life unsullied 'by the indecencies, the vices, the false standards, which an inherently deficient moral code tolerates, perpetuates, and fosters'. ... The forces at work on the hearts and minds of the young, to whom the Guardian directed his appeal most fervently, are pernicious indeed. Exhortations to remain pure and chaste will only succeed to a limited degree in helping them to resist these forces. What needs to be appreciated in this respect is the extent to which young minds are affected by the choices parents make for their own lives, when, no matter how unintentionally, no matter how innocently, such choices condone the passions of the world—its admiration for power, its adoration of status, its love of luxuries, its attachment to frivolous pursuits, its glorification of violence, and its obsession with self-gratification. ... May every one of them [the youth] come to know the bounties of a life adorned with purity and learn to draw on the powers that flow through pure channels." (Universal House of Justice, *Framework for Action*, #16.33)

Consultation is a fundamental skill in marriages and families for maintaining harmony and unity and as a tool to seek help from others

[When asked about specific rules of conduct to govern the relationship between husbands and wives] "...for example, the principle that the rights of each and all in the family unit must be upheld, and the advice that loving consultation should be the keynote, that all matters must be settled in harmony and love, and that there are times when the husband and the wife should defer to the wishes of the other. Exactly under what circumstances such deference should take place is a matter for each couple to determine. If, God forbid, they fail to agree, and their disagreement leads to estrangement, they should seek counsel from those they trust and in whose sincerity and sound judgment they have confidence, in order to preserve and strengthen their ties as a united family." (On behalf of the Universal House of Justice, "Preserving Bahá'í Marriages" (2009), #40)

"Family consultation employing full and frank discussion, and animated by awareness of the need for moderation and balance, can be the panacea for domestic conflict. Wives should not attempt to dominate their husbands, nor husbands their wives...." (On behalf of the Universal House of Justice, *Compilation of Compilations, Vol. II*, #2160)

POTENTIAL ACTIONS TO PROMOTE UNIFIED, HAPPY, AND HEALTHY MARRIAGES AND FAMILIES

Ideas to Consider from Marriage Transformation®

Below are potential actions that can contribute to creating strong marriages and families. They are categorized by how Bahá'ís can conduct themselves individually and in couple relationships and marriages. They include educating the community about having healthy relationships, marriages, and families. They also address how to become models and advocates who promote the importance of good relationships, marriages, and families in the Bahá'í community and beyond.

When individuals, couples, Spiritual Assemblies, and their communities begin the process of transforming the quality of their marriages and families, it will likely be important to examine when ongoing education efforts can be beneficial. Each Assembly and community will choose its own gradual and organic process and set its own goals. Ongoing education will accompany individuals in developing knowledge and skills. Further development of the art of reflection, consultation, and learning-in-action in a community will also be useful in this unfolding and organic process.

Involvement in the Core Activities of community life generally enhances people's ability to be in relationships of all types. Building character/virtues, making moral choices, and carrying out spiritual behavior are part of the materials and practices for children's classes, junior youth spiritual empowerment groups, and study circles. Devotional gatherings can have themes that include relationship, marriage, and family topics as well as provide opportunities for courting and married couples and families to worship together. As participants engage in service as part of these activities, friendships and relationships can strengthen. Service to each other and others becomes a way of life that benefits couples and families. Families whose members serve each other well and who also have an outward-looking service orientation can become strong examples and foundational elements for transforming neighborhoods and communities.

FOR INDIVIDUALS AND COUPLES

Enhancing Personal Conduct

- Engage in ongoing character development
- Be involved in service activities
- Regularly use prayer, reflection, and consultation for character discernment of potential partners; within couple relationships that are moving toward marriage; and within marriages to maintain awareness of strengths and growth areas, set goals, and take necessary actions to achieve improvement
- Seek help early from skilled and trustworthy sources for any needed courting-couple relationship strengthening and premarital education, or for addressing marital couple difficulties
- Maintain marital faithfulness and sustain family love and unity to the best of our ability
- Regard marriage as a sacred commitment
- Practice forgiveness, seeking healing, reconciliation, and unity-building to the best of our ability as promptly as possible in any upset or difficulty; and be willing to seek confidential consultative assistance with this process as needed from skilled and trustworthy sources
- Eliminate gossip and backbiting about relationships, marriages, and families of our own or others
- Pray on my/our own for relationships and marriages generally and my/our own in particular
- Be accepting of the choice some make not to be married

Participating in Study/Education

- Encourage children, youth, and adults to study, understand, and live their lives according to the Bahá'í teachings, guidance, and laws about character, relationships, marriage, parenting, and family
- Participate in relationship, marriage, and family education opportunities provided by Spiritual Assemblies or other institutions, agencies, Bahá'í schools (weekly, seasonal, and

permanent), companies, or organizations; seek further education and skill building opportunities as needed
- Engage in the process of character education and transformation to empower practicing rectitude of conduct in relationships, marriages, and families
- Periodically include prayers and readings focused on the strengthening of the well-being of marriages and families as part of community occasions such as the Nineteen-Day Feast or family and neighborhood activities such as devotional gatherings

Becoming Examples for Others

- Demonstrate through our words and actions respect and love for the sacred institution of marriage as the foundation for family, neighborhood, community, and global unity and prosperity and as a "fortress for well-being and salvation" (Bahá'u'lláh)
- Share encouragement and hope, as well as a vision and model of marital and family success with others
- Share laughter, humor, and hospitality together and with others
- Model purity and chastity for our families, neighbors, friends, and coworkers; these complex concepts include maintaining uplifting and chaste thoughts, positive words, honest motivations, a loving heart, and a spiritually focused soul and keeping sexual intimacy as a God-given gift to occur only within marriage for building unity between marriage partners and as a sacred act that brings children into the marriage to create a family
- Regard the health and happiness of marriages as a major contributor to the well-being of children
- Be sensitive, moderate, wise, and consultative related to requests for service or volunteering for service beyond the family to avoid being involved in activities that significantly interfere in marriage partner or family relationships

FOR A SPIRITUAL ASSEMBLY

This section contains some possible actions for an Assembly to consult about and consider implementing as appropriate for the conditions and demographics of their community.

Gaining Skills and Knowledge

- Use prayer, consultation, and reflection to gain understanding about the general health of the relationships, marriages, parents, and families in the community
- Track statistical data and trends for marriages and divorces in their jurisdiction to be able to set clear goals for improving trends, such as reducing the divorce rate or increasing pre-marriage preparation
- Strengthen the knowledge and ability of the Spiritual Assembly and its representatives to skillfully meet with individuals and couples before marriage, those who are troubled about their relationships or marriages, and those who are applying for divorce or attempting to reconcile; building knowledge includes being aware of the signs of abusive or violent relationships and guidance for how to respond to ensure the safety of all involved
- Strengthen the ability of the Spiritual Assembly and its representatives to skillfully guide couples who are in challenged marriages or who apply for divorce to achieve reconciliation before or after the granting of a year of waiting (alt: year of patience); provided the Assembly has first ensured the safety of all involved
- Be aware that some individuals may feel that they must accept and carry out service requests others make of them, even though saying "yes" may cause negative repercussions within their marriage or family. They may need consultative assistance with evaluating their choices.

Providing Education

- Provide regular, proactive opportunities for spiritually based relationship education, both knowledge and skill building, to unmarried individuals such that they have excellent characters and character discernment and are well prepared for being in a friendship, relationship, courtship, and marriage and positioned to prevent divorce; provide referrals for stepfamily education prior to marriage where applicable

- Provide parenting education to those raising children of all ages
- Provide spiritual guidance to parents on how to assist their children to practice chastity, when they should not interfere in an unmarried relationship, how they can help a couple make the free choice to marry, and about their role in considering parental consent for marriage
- Discourage cohabitation and adultery with a balance of love, forbearance, and understanding along with firmness on laws and principles
- Provide regular, proactive opportunities for spiritually based marriage education, both knowledge and skill building, to married members such that they are maintaining strong, happy, and faithful marriages that are of service to their families and community as well as examples to their children and others
- Provide education about Bahá'í marriage laws and the teachings about divorce and its harm
- Provide information about Bahá'í-based relationships and marriage as needed to seekers and those collaborating with their community

CONSIDERING POSSIBLE LINES OF ACTION

Potential Ideas to Consider from Marriage Transformation®

Through the processes of consultation, learning-in-action, and reflection over time, Spiritual Assemblies, other institutions, and community members may begin to develop their own purposes and lines of action that are unique to the experience and developing knowledge of the community. These will reflect the creative and diverse ideas of individuals, institutions, communities, and others as the transformation process takes shape and evolves.

Some possible actions to consider are to:

- Track and celebrate wedding anniversaries as part of honoring the institution of marriage and the perseverance of couples in their marriages
- Consider and provide opportunities for single Bahá'ís, both youth and adults, to meet and spend time with each other in a safe, supportive atmosphere, including service opportunities whenever possible; Behavior to avoid could be embarrassing comments, teasing, and gossip that could prompt a couple to hide a developing relationship
- Provide opportunities for pre-youth and youth and those working with them to learn about character choices and relationship skills
- Provide thorough marriage preparation for each seriously courting or engaged couple over a period of months, preferably along with some time with a skilled or trained married mentor couple
- Set-up follow-up meetings (at least two) between a mentor couple and a married couple during the first year of marriage for support and to answer questions
- Provide ongoing facilitated relationship and marriage strengthening groups with trained individuals or couples leading them at the community level or as part of sessions at seasonal or permanent schools*
- Offer relationship and marriage education and skill building study sessions or workshops periodically

* The concept of ongoing groups guided by non-professional individuals and couples who have gone through facilitator training and are also participants willing to gain ongoing growth in their own relationship or marriage (similar principle to the Ruhi study circle tutoring process) is a possibility to help the relationships and marriages of Bahá'ís. Challenges to address include the identification within a community of those appropriate and willing to be trained and carry out this service, as well as a practical method and funds to accomplish the facilitator training. This model of marriage enrichment has been successful for over 40 years through Better Marriages (formerly Association for Couples in Marriage Enrichment; www.bettermarriages.org). Collaborating with experienced organizations such as this could benefit the Bahá'í community as appropriate over time.

Appendix F: Forming a Book Study Group

After looking through this book, we may decide we will be most successful at studying its content and carrying out its activities if we involve a few friends, other couples, or institutional representatives to study and complete parts of it—or all of it—with us. Informal study groups can assist participants to progress through the material and allow each to gain new insights from the group discussions without overly sharing personal details about our situations.

Groups can also support friends keeping each other accountable for actions they decide to take as a result of exercises and reflection questions.

Those in the group may be at different stages of literacy and understanding of English. The group can encourage participants to increase their ability to read, write, and articulate their thoughts. Group members may need to accompany each other in the process.

Consult About Ground Rules

At the beginning, before diving into the content, it will be wise for us to discuss and agree on a few ground rules. It may be useful to write these on a whiteboard or easel pad, so everyone can see them throughout the discussion. This practice allows each participant to feel a sense of ownership for the group and its guidelines. The group can refer to them as needed, or they can add or revise an agreement.

Here are some ground rules we may wish to consider, if they don't come up naturally in our initial discussion:

1. Uphold confidentiality, through a firm agreement that "what's said in the group stays in the group," and is not mentioned outside the group.
2. Scrupulously avoid the tendency in society to engage in gossip and backbiting—either within or outside of group sessions.
3. Do not use personal devices (mobile phones, tablets...) during group discussions and social time, so as to give full support and attention to the group, out of respect for its purpose and intentions. Exceptions can be agreed upon, such as using a

smartphone in a way that advances the efforts of the group, using a tablet to take notes, or arranging breaks where people can check their electronic devices before they put them away again.

4. Allocate time for prayer, meditation, or other spiritual enrichment activities.
5. Allocate time for social connection and fellowship.
6. Integrate the arts into the group's activities. Expressing ideas artistically often brings vitality to the learning process and enables us to understand a concept in a new, refreshing way.
7. Be respectful and considerate of others. Give everyone time to share, and guard against individuals dominating the conversation.
8. Avoid terminology, jargon, and acronyms—religious or otherwise—that some group members might not understand.
9. Agree on what everyone will read—and do—between sessions. At the same time, if life circumstances and events prevent a participant from fulfilling their commitment, they can still attend sessions, and strive to catch up with the reading and activities, perhaps with another group member accompanying and supporting them.
10. Participants can invite and bring friends to the group, and new people can join the group at any time. (Or, alternatively, once the group begins, no one new should join.)

A Simple Version

1. Opportunity for equal speaking time
2. Right to pass and not speak about a topic
3. Non-judgmental atmosphere
4. Respect self and others
5. Everyone responsible for their own learning
6. Confidentiality
7. Enjoy!

Consider the Logistics

Groups are more successful and function more smoothly when they agree on some of the logistics and other basic considerations. These questions may serve as useful prompts for our group:

1. How often, when, for how long, and where will we meet? (Meeting at least every week or two usually helps participants stay motivated and purposeful. Being clear about whether to start on time will be wise.)
2. Who, if anyone, will be responsible for sending the meeting details to the group members? What method of communication will work for all members?
3. Will there be food? If so, who will provide it?
4. Will anyone facilitate the sessions? If so, will it be the same person each time or rotate among the members?
5. How will we start and end each session?
6. Would it be beneficial, for any reason, to take notes of the discussion? If so, who will record the notes and what types of information will they capture from the conversation? Will it be the same person each time, or will it happen on a rotating basis?
7. Do we need or want a group name? How will we talk about the group with others?
8. Will the group share what they learn with others? What are the boundaries, so no one shares confidential information? What opportunities exist for outreach and sharing? Perhaps we could share our learning at a community meeting? With family members? With courting couples? How and when will we carry this out?

Additional Resources

If additional resource materials or assistance are needed, please contact Susanne M. Alexander at Marriage Transformation, susanne@marriagetransformation.com.

Quotation References

A Brief Bahá'í Context for Strengthening Marriages

[1] Bahá'u'lláh, *Kitáb-i-Aqdas*, Question #3
[2] Bahá'u'lláh, *Bahá'í Prayers*, US 2002, p. 118
[3] Bahá'u'lláh, *Gleanings from the Writings of Bahá'u'lláh*, #V, p. 9
[4] Research Department of the Universal House of Justice, with inserted quotations on behalf of Shoghi Effendi; "Preserving Bahá'í Marriages" (1990), Memorandum #3.1
[5] On behalf of Shoghi Effendi, "Preserving Bahá'í Marriages" (1990), Memorandum #3.1
[6] Research Department of the Universal House of Justice, "Preserving Bahá'í Marriages" (1990), Memorandum #1
[7] Research Department of the Universal House of Justice, "Preserving Bahá'í Marriages" (1990), Memorandum #1
[8] On behalf of Shoghi Effendi, "Preserving Bahá'í Marriages" (1990), Memorandum #3.4

Chapter 1: Hope for a New Beginning

[9] Michele Weiner-Davis, *Divorce Remedy*, p. 95
[10] A.C.M.E/Better Marriages, "Building a Better Marriage", p. 3

Chapter 2: Building a Support System

[11] Richard Carlson and Joseph Bailey, S*lowing Down to the Speed of Life*, p. 94
[12] William J. Doherty, PhD, *Take Back Your Marriage*, pp. 86-87
[13] William J. Doherty, PhD, *Take Back Your Marriage*, pp. 167-168
[14] William J. Doherty, PhD, *Take Back Your Marriage*, p. 171
[15] On behalf of the Universal House of Justice, *Compilation of Compilations, Vol. II*, #2339
[16] Universal House of Justice, *Compilation of Compilations, Vol. II*, #1346
[17] Universal House of Justice to a National Spiritual Assembly, dated May 24, 1972
[18] On behalf of the Universal House of Justice, *Lights of Guidance*, #1303
[19] On behalf of the Universal House of Justice, *Lights of Guidance*, #1304
[20] On behalf of Shoghi Effendi, *Lights of Guidance*, #321
[21] On behalf of Shoghi Effendi, *Compilation of Compilations, Vol. II*, #1289

[22] On behalf of the Universal House of Justice quoted in the "Understanding Tests" letter from the Research Department to the Universal House of Justice, July 17, 1989
[23] On behalf of the Universal House of Justice, "Preserving Bahá'í Marriages" (2009), #3.6
[24] On behalf of the Universal House of Justice, *Compilation of Compilations, Vol. II*, #2345
[25] On behalf of the Universal House of Justice to an individual, September 24, 2014
[26] Research Department of the Universal House of Justice, "Preserving Bahá'í Marriages" 1990, Memorandum conclusion, with quotations on behalf of the Universal House of Justice to an individual believer, August 6, 1989
[27] 'Abdu'l-Bahá, https://www.bahai.org/library/authoritative-texts/compilations/prayer-devotional-life/, #6
[28] Universal House of Justice, *Compilation of Compilations, Vol. II*, #2339
[29] Justice St Rain, *Love, Lust, and the Longing for God,* pp. 261-263

Chapter 3: Declaring a Cease-Fire
[30] Bahá'u'lláh, *Epistle to the Son of the Wolf*, p. 15
[31] Bahá'u'lláh, *Hidden Words*, Persian #44
[32] On behalf of the Universal House of Justice to an individual, September 24, 2014
[33] 'Abdu'l-Bahá, *Selections from the Writings of 'Abdu'l-Bahá*, #221
[34] Mehri Sefidvash, *Coral and Pearls*, p. 10
[35] 'Abdu'l-Bahá, quoted in Shoghi Effendi, *Advent of Divine Justice*, p. 26
[36] Joan B. Hernández, *Love, Courtship, and Marriage*, p. 100
[37] Sandra Gray Bender, *Recreating Marriage with the Same Old Spouse*, 11-12; 15
[38] 'Abdu'l-Bahá, *Selections from the Writings of 'Abdu'l-Bahá*, #86
[39] Bahá'u'lláh, Gleanings from the Writings of Bahá'u'lláh, CXLVI, p. 315
[40] Shaunti Feldhahn, *Kindness Challenge*, p. 14

Chapter 4: Achieving Early Positive Results
[41] Mehri Sefidvash, *Coral and Pearls*, pp. 11-12

Chapter 5: Envisioning a Re-Created Marriage
[42] Judith S. Wallerstein and Sandra Blakeslee, *Good Marriage*, pp. 68-69
[43] 'Abdu'l-Bahá, *Selections from the Writings of 'Abdu'l-Bahá*, #225
[44] On behalf of Shoghi Effendi, "Preserving Bahá'í Marriages" (2009), #33

[45] On behalf of Shoghi Effendi, *Afire with the Vision*, #122
[46] On behalf of the Universal House of Justice, *Compilation of Compilations, Vol. II*, #2161

Chapter 6: Considering Aspects of Marriage and Family
[47] 'Abdu'l-Bahá, *Selections from the Writings of 'Abdu'l-Bahá*, #87
[48] H. B. Danesh, "Marriage and Sexuality", April 13, 1991, https://bahai-library.com/danesh_marriage_sexuality
[49] On behalf of Shoghi Effendi, *Compilation of Compilations, Vol. I*, #903
[50] On behalf of the Universal House of Justice, *Lights of Guidance*, #1303
[51] 'Abdu'l-Bahá, *Selections from the Writings of 'Abdu'l-Bahá*, #84
[52] 'Abdu'l-Bahá, *Selections from the Writings of 'Abdu'l-Bahá*, #86
[53] 'Abdu'l-Bahá, *Selections from the Writings of 'Abdu'l-Bahá*, #92
[54] On behalf of Shoghi Effendi, *Lights of Guidance*, #689
[55] John M. Gottman, Ph.D., and Nan Silver, *Seven Principles for Making Marriage Work*, 2nd ed., pp. 21-22; 28
[56] Paul Coleman, Psy.D., *30 Secrets of Happily Married Couples*, 2nd Ed., pp. 26-27
[57] Shaunti Feldhahn, *Surprising Secrets of Highly Happy Marriages*, pp. 145-147
[58] Harville Hendrix, *Getting the Love You Want*, p. 116

Chapter 7: Preserving Our Marriage
[59] Research Department of the Universal House of Justice, "Preserving Bahá'í Marriages" (1990) Memorandum preamble
[60] The Báb, *Selections from the Writings of the Báb*, p. 172
[61] Bahá'u'lláh, *Bahá'í Prayers*, US 2002, p. 118
[62] David Bowers, quoted in *Marriage Can Be Forever—Preparation Counts!*, 3rd ed., pp. 578-579
[63] Universal House of Justice, *Framework for Action*, #35.39
[64] 'Abdu'l-Bahá, *Selections from the Writings of 'Abdu'l-Bahá*, #88
[65] On behalf of the Universal House of Justice, *Compilation of Compilations, Vol. II*, #2160
[66] Universal House of Justice, December 7, 1992, European Bahá'í Youth Council, www.bahairesearch.com
[67] On behalf of Shoghi Effendi, *Lights of Guidance*, #1948
[68] Research Department of the Universal House of Justice, "Preserving Bahá'í Marriages" (1990), Memorandum #3.8

Chapter 8: Communicating with One Another

[69] 'Abdu'l-Bahá, "Give Me Thy Grace to Serve thy Loved Ones", compilation for the 2018 Counsellors' Conference

[70] Richard Carlson and Joseph Bailey, *Slowing Down to the Speed of Life*, p. 121

[71] Summarized from Patricia Love and Steven Stosny, *How to Improve Your Marriage Without Talking About It*, pp. 67-69

[72] Summarized from John Gottman, PhD, and Nan Silver, *Seven Principles for Making Marriage Work*, Ch. 3; 2nd ed.)

[73] Raymond and Furugh Switzer, *Mindful Matrimony*, pp. 126-129

[74] Universal House of Justice, "Individual Rights and Freedoms", p. 16

[75] Bahá'u'lláh, *Tablets of Bahá'u'lláh*, p. 88

[76] Linda Kavelin Popov, quoted in Susanne M. Alexander, *Pure Gold*, p. 52

[77] 'Abdu'l-Bahá, *Paris Talks*, p. 162

[78] Howard Colby Ives, *Portals to Freedom*, pp. 194-195)

[79] Summarized from Kathlyn Hendricks and Gay Hendricks, *Conscious Heart*, pp. 267-272

[80] On behalf of Shoghi Effendi, *Lights of Guidance*, #291

[81] This activity draws on the work of Susanne M. Alexander and Johanna Merritt Wu in *Marriage Can Be Forever—Preparation Counts!* 3rd ed.

Chapter 9: Understanding, Managing, and Expressing Feelings

[82] John M. Gottman, Ph.D., and Nan Silver, *Seven Principles for Making Marriage Work,* 2nd ed., p. 54

[83] Patty Howell, Ed.M., A.G.C., https://www.yourtango.com/experts/patty-howell/nurturing-yourself-widowhood-3

[84] 'Abdu'l-Bahá, *Promulgation of Universal Peace*, p. 60, #12

[85] Research Department of the Universal House of Justice, "Issues Concerning Community Functioning", section 2, p. 6

[86] Marshall B. Rosenberg, PhD, *Nonviolent Communication, A Language of Compassion*, 2nd ed., pp. 41-46

[87] Bahá'u'lláh, *Compilation of Compilations, Vol. I*, #1020

[88] 'Abdu'l-Bahá, *Promulgation of Universal Peace*, pp. 92-93)

[89] On behalf of the Universal House of Justice, "Preserving Bahá'í Marriages" (2009), #38

[90] A.C.M.E./Better Marriages, "Creative Use of Conflict", pp. 5-7

[91] 'Abdu'l-Bahá, *Some Answered Questions*, 2014 ed., #57.10

[92] 'Abdu'l-Bahá, *Selections from the Writings of 'Abdu'l-Bahá*, #130

[93] Quoted in Annamarie Honnold, *Vignettes from the Life of 'Abdu'l-Bahá*, p. 155
[94] 'Abdu'l-Bahá, *Promulgation of Universal Peace*, p. 218
[95] 'Abdu'l-Bahá, *Tablets of 'Abdu'l-Bahá, Vol. 1*, p. 45; On behalf of the Universal House of Justice to an individual, quoted in a Memorandum from the Research Department of the Universal House of Justice, January 12, 1997, "The Humorist"
[96] On behalf of the Universal House of Justice, *Compilations of Compilations, Vol. I*, #138
[97] Susan Sparks, *Laugh Your Way to Grace—Reclaiming the Spiritual Power of Humor*, pp. 9-10
[98] Stephen Post, *Why Good Things Happen to Good People*, p. 144
[99] Howard Colby Ives, recalling the words of 'Abdu'l-Bahá, *Portals to Freedom*, p. 120, when 'Abdu'l-Bahá was imprisoned with many others in the Holy Land

Chapter 10: Utilizing Consultation As a Couple
[100] Khalil A. Khavari and Sue Williston Khavari, *Creating a Successful Family*, p. 68
[101] 'Abdu'l-Bahá, *Promulgation of Universal Peace*, p. 72
[102] Office of Social and Economic Development at the Bahá'í World Centre, *Framework for Action*, #59.50
[103] Bahá'u'lláh, *Lights of Guidance*, #577
[104] Bahá'u'lláh, *Compilation of Compilations, Vol. I*, #168
[105] 'Abdu'l-Bahá, *Compilation of Compilations, Vol. I*, #168
[106] 'Abdu'l-Bahá, *Compilation of Compilations, Vol. I*, #180
[107] Susan Heitler, PhD, *Power of Two, Secrets to a Strong & Loving Marriage*, p. 11
[108] Summarized from Susan Heitler and Abigail Hirsch, *Power of Two Workbook*, pp. 74-75
[109] 'Abdu'l-Bahá, *Selections from the Writings of 'Abdu'l-Bahá*, #43
[110] 'Abdu'l-Bahá, *Compilation of Compilations, Vol. I*, #187
[111] 'Abdu'l-Bahá, *Selections from the Writings of 'Abdu'l-Bahá*, #45; revised translation
[112] Universal House of Justice, *Lights of Guidance,* #590
[113] Universal House of Justice, May 19, 2009, to the Bahá'ís of Iran
[114] Universal House of Justice, *Messages 1963 to 1986*, p. 95
[115] Universal House of Justice, January 24, 1993

[116] On behalf of the Universal House of Justice, quoted in the "Understanding Tests" memorandum from the Research Department of the Universal House of Justice, July 17, 1989
[117] Shoghi Effendi, *Lights of Guidance*, #751
[118] On behalf of the Universal House of Justice, *Compilations of Compilations, Vol. II*, #2341
[119] Draws from Susanne M. Alexander, *Deciding in Unity*, Chapter 10, and Susanne M. Alexander with Johanna Merritt Wu and Jeremy Lambshead, *Starting with Me*, Appendix C

Chapter 11: Honoring Our True Selves
[120] 'Abdu'l-Bahá, *Secret of Divine Civilization*, p. 19
[121] Daniel C. Jordan, "Becoming Your True Self", p. 5
[122] Bahá'u'lláh, *Gleanings from the Writings of Bahá'u'lláh*, #XXVII, p. 65
[123] 'Abdu'l-Bahá, *Paris Talks*, p. 60
[124] On behalf of Shoghi Effendi, *Lights of Guidance*, #386
[125] On behalf of Shoghi Effendi, *Compilation of Compilations, Vol. II*, #1295
[126] On behalf of Shoghi Effendi, *Compilations of Compilations, Vol. II*, #1272
[127] Bahá'u'lláh *Gleanings from the Writings of Bahá'u'lláh*, #CXXII, p. 260
[128] On behalf of the Universal House of Justice to an individual, July 2, 1996

Chapter 12: Seeing and Polishing Our Character Gems
[129] On behalf of the Universal House of Justice to an individual, July 2, 1996
[130] Bahá'u'lláh, *Gleanings from the Writings of Bahá'u'lláh*, #XC, p. 177
[131] 'Abdu'l-Bahá, *Selections from the Writings of 'Abdu'l-Bahá*, #2
[132] 'Abdu'l-Baha, *Some Answered Questions* (2014 ed.), p. 247, #57.8
[133] On behalf of Shoghi Effendi, *Compilation of Compilations, Vol. II*, #1271
[134] Universal House of Justice, *Framework for Action*, #16.35
[135] 'Abdu'l-Bahá, *Secret of Divine Civilization*, p. 60

Chapter 13: Transforming Ourselves Each Day
[136] Bahá'u'lláh, *Tablets of Bahá'u'lláh*, p. 35
[137] Bahá'u'lláh, *Hidden Words*, Arabic #31
[138] Bahá'u'lláh, *Hidden Words*, Arabic #22
[139] 'Abdu'l-Bahá, *Lights of Guidance*, #1485

[140] On behalf of Shoghi Effendi, *Compilation of Compilations, Vol. II*, #1777
[141] Sharon Hatcher Kennedy and Andrew Kennedy, "Bahá'í Youth and Sexuality A Personal/Professional View", Association for Bahá'í Studies, Vol. 1, #1
[142] Excerpt from the 12 Steps of Alcoholics Anonymous; www.alcoholics-anonymous.org
[143] Bahá'u'lláh, *Tablets of Bahá'u'lláh*, p. 156
[144] National Spiritual Assembly of the Bahá'ís of the United States, Office of the Secretary, to an individual believer, December 17, 1981
[145] On behalf of Shoghi Effendi, *Light of Divine Guidance*, pp. 69-70
[146] Hooper Dunbar, *Forces of Our Time*, p. 78
[147] On behalf of Shoghi Effendi, *Lights of Guidance*, #394
[148] On behalf of Shoghi Effendi, "Prayer and Devotional Life", 2019, #10
[149] Dan Popov, quoted in Susanne M. Alexander, *Creating Excellent Relationships*, p. 40
[150] Sandra Gray Bender, PhD, *Recreating Marriage with the Same Old Spouse*, pp. 150-51
[151] Stephen M. R. Covey, *Speed of Trust*, pp. 62-63
[152] Paul Coleman, *30 Secrets of Happily Married Couples*, p. 161

Chapter 14: Being Kind to Ourselves

[153] On behalf of Shoghi Effendi, *Lights of Guidance*, #389
[154] Bahá'u'lláh, *Hidden Words*, Arabic #5
[155] Universal House of Justice, *Framework for Action*, #23.14
[156] Linda Kavelin Popov, *A Pace of Grace*, p. 93
[157] David Seamands, *Healing for Damaged Emotions*, pp. 84-85
[158] Universal House of Justice, *Messages 1986-2001*, #200.12
[159] On behalf of the Universal House of Justice to individual believers, April 19, 2013

Chapter 15: Directing Our Thoughts in Positive Ways

[160] Bahá'u'lláh, *Days of Remembrance*, #3.7
[161] 'Abdu'l-Bahá, *Paris Talks*, pp. 109-110
[162] Raymond and Furugh Switzer, *Mindful Matrimony*, p. 11
[163] 'Abdu'l-Bahá, *Promulgation of Universal Peace*, p. 63
[164] 'Abdu'l-Bahá, *Bahá'í Prayers*, p. 71
[165] 'Abdu'l-Bahá, *Paris Talks*, p. 17
[166] 'Abdu'l-Bahá, *Paris Talks*, pp. 30-31
[167] Bahá'u'lláh, *Prayers and Meditations by Bahá'u'lláh*, #CLXXXIII, p. 323

[168] George Pransky, *Relationship Handbook*, pp. 27-28
[169] Richard Carlson and Joseph Bailey, *Slowing Down to the Speed of Life*, p. 94
[170] Howard Colby Ives, *Portals to Freedom*, p. 13

Chapter 16: Easing Up on Controlling
[171] Susan M. Campbell, PhD, *Beyond the Power Struggle*, p. 75
[172] H. B. Danesh, "Violence-Free Family: Building Block of Peaceful Civilization", https://www.bic.org/statements/violence-free-family-building-block-peaceful-civilization
[173] Bahá'u'lláh, *Prayers and Meditations by Bahá'u'lláh*, p. 240
[174] Shoghi Effendi, *Bahá'í Administration*, p. 2
[175] Universal House of Justice, "Individual Rights and Freedoms", p. 13
[176] On behalf of the Universal House of Justice, *Compilation of Compilations, Vol. II*, #2160

Chapter 17: Developing Spiritual Habits
[177] 'Abdu'l-Bahá, *Paris Talks*, #31
[178] Bahá'u'lláh, *Tablets of Bahá'u'lláh*, p. 156
[179] Universal House of Justice, *Messages 1963 to 1986*, #375.5
[180] Universal House of Justice, *A Wider Horizon, Selected Letters 1983-1992*, p. 64
[181] 'Abdu'l-Bahá, *Selections from the Writings of 'Abdu'l-Bahá*, #35
[182] 'Abdu'l-Bahá, *Importance of Obligatory Prayer and Fasting*, Section 2, #VII
[183] Bahá'u'lláh, "Prayer and Devotional Life", 2019, #56
[184] Bahá'u'lláh, "Prayer and Devotional Life", 2019, #56
[185] On behalf of Shoghi Effendi, "Prayer and Devotional Life", 2019, #52
[186] Universal House of Justice, "Prayer and Devotional Life", 2019, #14)
[187] On behalf of the Universal House of Justice, *Lights of Guidance*, #1836
[188] Bahá'u'lláh, *Gleanings from the Writings of Bahá'u'lláh*, #LXXIV, p. 141
[189] 'Abdu'l-Bahá, *Will and Testament*, Part 1, p. 5, www.bahai.org
[190] Shoghi Effendi, *Advent of Divine Justice*, pp. 26-27, www.bahai.org
[191] Bahá'u'lláh, *Bahá'í Prayers*, p. 4
[192] Bahá'u'lláh, *The Kitáb-i-Aqdas*, #K18
[193] On behalf of Shoghi Effendi, "Prayer and Devotional Life", 2019, #13
[194] On behalf of Shoghi Effendi, "Prayer and Devotional Life", 2019, #45

Chapter 18: Learning and Growing from Difficulties
[195] 'Abdu'l-Bahá, *Paris Talks*, #14

[196] 'Abdu'l-Bahá, *Paris Talks*, #57
[197] On behalf of Shoghi Effendi, *Lights of Guidance*, #247
[198] Joan B. Hernández, *Love, Courtship, and Marriage*, p. 28
[199] Bahá'u'lláh, *Kitáb-i-Íqán*, p. 8
[200] 'Abdu'l-Bahá, quoted in the "Understanding Tests" Memorandum from the Research Department of the Universal House of Justice, July 17, 1989
[201] Mehri Sefidvash, *Coral and Pearls*, pp. 27-28
[202] On behalf of Shoghi Effendi, *Compilation of Compilations, Vol. II*, #1297
[203] On behalf of Shoghi Effendi, *Compilation of Compilations, Vol. II*, #1322
[204] Universal House of Justice, *Lights of Guidance*, #1209
[205] Universal House of Justice, *Framework for Action*, #54.5
[206] Stephen Post, *Why Good Things Happen to Good People*, p. 114
[207] On behalf of Shoghi Effendi to the Bahá'ís of Kitalya Farm Prison, *Compilation of Compilations, Vol. II*, #1337
[208] Universal House of Justice, *Lights of Guidance*, #589

Chapter 19: Cleaning Up Messes and Bouncing Back
[209] Bahá'u'lláh, *Gleanings from the Writings of Bahá'u'lláh*, #LXVI, p. 130
[210] Jodi Picoult, *Change of Heart*, p. 162
[211] 'Abdu'l-Bahá, *Selections from the Writings of 'Abdu'l-Bahá*, #141
[212] *The Kitáb-i-Aqdas* by Bahá'u'lláh, Note #58
[213] Summarized from Gary Chapman, PhD, and Jennifer Thomas, PhD, *When Sorry Isn't Enough*
[214] Dr. Les Parrott III; Leslie Parrott, *When Bad Things Happen to Good Marriages*, p. 142
[215] Bahá'u'lláh, *Tabernacle of Unity*, #1.10
[216] Michele Weiner-Davis, *Divorce Busting*, pp. 232-233
[217] 'Abdu'l-Bahá, *Selections from the Writings of 'Abdu'l-Bahá*, #138
[218] Howard J. Markman, Scott M. Stanley, Susan L. Blumberg, Natalie H. Jenkins, and Carol Whiteley, *12 Hours to a Great Marriage*, p. 207
[219] Janet A. Khan, *Prophet's Daughter*, p. 245

Chapter 20: Re-Committing to Our Marriage Partnership
[220] W. H. Murray, *Scottish Himalayan Expedition*, pp. 6-7
[221] Rúhíyyih Rabbani, *Prescription for Living*, 1950 ed., p. 39
[222] William J. Doherty, *Take Back Your Marriage*, p. 8
[223] William J. Doherty, *Take Back Your Marriage*, p. 18

[224] Brené Brown, *Gifts of Imperfection*, p. 19
[225] William J. Doherty, PhD, *Take Back Your Marriage*, p. 12
[226] William J. Doherty, PhD, *Take Back Your Marriage*, p. 50
[227] William J. Doherty, PhD, *Take Back Your Marriage*, p. 48
[228] William J. Doherty, PhD, *Take Back Your Marriage*, p. 59
[229] Sue Johnson, *Hold Me Tight* pp. 21-24
[230] Shaunti Feldhahn, *Surprising Secrets of Highly Happy Marriages*, p. 45
[231] Shaunti Feldhahn, *Surprising Secrets of Highly Happy Marriages*, p. 46
[232] Susan Page, quoted from an essay in Susanne M. Alexander, *All-in-One Marriage Prep*, pp. 284-285
[233] John Gottman and Nan Silver, *Seven Principles for Making Marriage Work*, 2nd ed., pp. 88-89
[234] Richard Paul Evans, https://www.huffpost.com/entry/how-i-saved-my-marriage_b_6958222?_guc_consent_skip=1561119484
[235] John Gottman and Nan Silver, *Seven Principles for Making Marriage Work*, 2nd ed., p. 47

Chapter 21: Completing Our Marriage Commitments
[236] https://www.elikamahony.com; January 8, 2019

Appendix A: The Bahá'í Faith
[237] Bahá'u'lláh, *Call of the Divine Beloved*, #3.8
[238] Bahá'u'lláh, *Gleanings from the Writings of Bahá'u'lláh*, #CXVII, p. 250

Appendix B: Couple Prayers
[239] Bahá'u'lláh, *Bahá'í Prayers* (US 2002), p. 238
[240] 'Abdu'l-Bahá, *Bahá'í Prayers* (US 2002), p. 120
[241] 'Abdu'l-Bahá, *Bahá'í Prayers* (US 2002), p. 121
[242] Bahá'u'lláh, *Prayers and Meditations*, pp. 147-148
[243] 'Abdu'l-Bahá, *Selections from the Writings of 'Abdu'l-Bahá*, #90
[244] 'Abdu'l-Bahá, *Selections from the Writings of 'Abdu'l-Bahá*, #193
[245] Ruthanne Wangerin, *A Prayerbook for Husbands and Wives*, p. 4
[246] Renee Bartkowski, *Prayers for Married Couples*, p. 30
[247] Pueblo Prayer, *Oneworld Book of Prayer*, p. 187
[248] Berhard Albrecht, quoted in *To Be Married* compiled by Wendi Momen, p. 180

Appendix C: Grappling with Serious Issues
[249] Joyce B. Lakewood, *Living with an Alcoholic*, pp. 21-22

[250] On behalf of the Universal House of Justice to an individual, November 5, 1987
[251] Willard F. Harley, Jr, PhD, and Jennifer Harley Chalmers, PhD, *Surviving an Affair*, pp. 9-10
[252] Mark Laaser, PhD, "The Challenges of Sexual Addiction on Relationships", quoted in Susanne M. Alexander, *All-in-One Marriage Prep*, pp. 202-204
[253] John Gottman, PhD, and Nan Silver, *What Makes Love Last?*, p. 62
[254] On behalf of the Universal House of Justice, *Messages 1986-2001*, #149.13
[255] Gary Chapman, *Desperate Marriages*, pp. 152-153
[256] On behalf of the Universal House of Justice, *Messages 1986-2001*, #149.16
[257] National Spiritual Assembly of the Bahá'ís of the United States, "Guidelines for Local Spiritual Assemblies, Supplement on Domestic Violence", 2011, pp. 13-14
[258] National Spiritual Assembly of the Bahá'ís of the United States, "Guidelines for Local Spiritual Assemblies, Supplement on Domestic Violence", 2011, p. 12
[259] On behalf of the Universal House of Justice, *Messages 1986-2001*, #149.4-5
[260] On behalf of the Universal House of Justice to a National Spiritual Assembly, April 12, 1990
[261] On behalf of the Universal House of Justice, *Compilation of Compilations, Vol. II*, #2347
[262] On behalf of Shoghi Effendi, *Compilation of Compilations, Vol. II*, # 1375
[263] On behalf of the Universal House of Justice, *Lights of Guidance*, #7
[264] Joyce B. Lakewood, *Living with an Alcoholic*, Appendix 3
[265] Bahá'u'lláh *The Kitáb-i-Aqdas,* #K70
[266] On behalf of Shoghi Effendi, "Preserving Bahá'í Marriages" (2009), #12

Acknowledgements

I so appreciate those who sacrificed time and energy to read and use drafts of this book and provide feedback and editing suggestions: my husband, my consulting partners on the Wilmette Institute faculty team, other colleagues, clients, and online course participants. All of you have contributed to this book, and I'm very grateful. Due to confidentiality, many of you I cannot thank publicly by name, but please know that I so appreciate your time and input.

Thank you in addition to the following people:

Leslie Asplund, Arzan Bharucha, Raven Deerwater, Janna Denton-Howes, Phil Donihe, Sara Ferdowsi, Gayle Gonzalez-Johnson, Johanna Merritt Wu, Maxcia Lizarraga, Leila Khazra, Nazanin Heydarian, Fiona McDonald, Keith McDonald, Wendi Momen, Jackie Najafian, Kathryn Hogenson Jewett, Lisa Kelly, Riaz Mostaghim, Ley Schleich, Fariba Vahdat, and Cecile Wabnitz.

Author Biography and Contact Information

Susanne M. Alexander is a Relationship and Marriage Educator, book author and publisher, and coach with Marriage Transformation®. She is certified to offer couple's assessments through Prepare-Enrich® and for individuals with the Character Foundations Assessment™. Susanne is passionate about facilitating individuals and couples making good relationship and marriage choices through knowledge and skill-building and thereby having happy, healthy marriages and preventing divorces. She meets with clients globally via the internet for relationship and marriage preparation and marriage strengthening.

Susanne, a former journalist, writes articles about relationships and marriage for www.bahaiteachings.org and www.bahaiblog.net. She serves as the Department Chair and also as a course developer and faculty member for the Wilmette Institute relationships, marriage, and family online courses (www.wilmetteinstitute.org).

The Wilmette Institute is an agency of the National Spiritual Assembly of the Bahá'ís of the United States.

Susanne shares: "I have had an adventurous time with relationships and marriages. My first marriage gave me a daughter—and now son-in-law and two granddaughters. However, it was very difficult, as he had many illnesses. The marriage ended in divorce when our daughter was 18. I married again, a very happy marriage, with three young adult stepchildren. We did marriage preparation and marriage enrichment efforts together. This second husband died from brain cancer just before our 10th wedding anniversary, after two years of caregiving. Matching websites, dating experiences, and moving led me to find a third husband with two adult stepchildren, and we are in a happy marriage.

"With all these adventures, as well as professional education, I've had many opportunities to experience, observe, and learn from the world of connecting and finding someone to marry and then building a good marriage. It has not been easy, but when I've learned marriage skills and when marriage works well with love, friendship, and consultation, it's absolutely the best place to be."

Susanne is originally from Canada and now lives with her husband Phil Donihe in Tennessee, in the United States. They often collaborate in working with couples. He is a coach and also certified with the Character Foundations Assessment™.

Susanne's books can be purchased through her website www.marriagetransformation.com, many global Bahá'í sources, and many online bookstores. Anyone wishing a discount on bulk purchases for group use or for re-selling should contact her directly.

Some Marriage Transformation Books that May Benefit You:

- Be Brave and Arise: My Life Quest As a Bahá'í Man
- Creating Well-Being for Couples and Families: Increasing Health, Spirituality, and Happiness
- Deciding in Unity: A Practical Process for Married Couples to Agree on Practically Everything

- Happy at Home, Happy at Work: The Powerful Rewards of Building Character
- Pure Gold: Encouraging Character Qualities in Marriage (English; Spanish: Oro Puro)

Contact:

- Susanne@marriagetransformation.com
- +1 423-599-0153 (US Eastern time zone)
- www.marriagetransformation.com
- www.bahaimarriage.net
- www.transformationlearningcenter.com

Social Media:

- https://www.facebook.com/MarriageTransformation
- https://www.facebook.com/transformationlearningcenter
- https://www.linkedin.com/company/marriage-transformation/
- Twitter: @bahaimarriage or marriage4ever

Purpose Statement:

Marriage Transformation® dynamically empowers individuals and couples to engage in skillful, character-based communications and actions that contribute to excellent relationships and happy, unified marriages and families that serve others. Couples are like two wings of a bird–both must be strong partners with equal voices for them to soar!

Please contact us, so we can be of service to you!

CPSIA information can be obtained
at www.ICGtesting.com
Printed in the USA
LVHW050850271120
672645LV00003B/174

9 781940 062136